MTEL History
06 Teacher Certification Exam

Sharon A. Wynne, M.S.

XAMonline, INC.
Boston

W9-AVB-707

To obtain permission(s) to use the material from this work for any purpose including workshops or seminars, please submit a written request to:

XAMonline, Inc.
21 Orient Avenue
Melrose, MA 02176
Toll Free 1-800-509-4128
Email: info@xamonline.com
Web www.xamonline.com
Fax: 1-617-583-5552

Library of Congress Cataloging-in-Publication Data
Wynne, Sharon A.

MTEL History 06: Teacher Certification / Sharon A. Wynne. -3rd ed.
ISBN 978-1-60787-469-0

1. History   2. Study Guides   3. MTEL
4. Teachers' Certification & Licensure.   5. Careers

Managing Editor   Jessica Egan, MS
Copy Editor   James Given

Disclaimer:
The opinions expressed in this publication are the sole works of XAMonline and were created independently from the National Education Association, Educational Testing Service, or any State Department of Education, National Evaluation Systems or other testing affiliates. Between the time of publication and printing, state specific standards as well as testing formats and website information may change that is not included in part or in whole within this product. Sample test questions are developed by XAMonline and reflect similar content as on real tests; however, they are not former tests. XAMonline assembles content that aligns with state standards but makes no claims nor guarantees teacher candidates a passing score. Numerical scores are determined by testing companies such as NES or ETS and then are compared with individual state standards. A passing score varies from state to state.

Printed in the United States of America   œ-1
MTEL History 06
ISBN: 978-1-60787-469-0

Table of Contents

Great Study and Testing Tips!

What to study in order to prepare for the subject assessments is the focus of this study guide but equally important is *how* you study.

You can increase your chances of truly mastering the information by taking some simple, but effective steps.

Study Tips:

1. <u>Some foods aid the learning process</u>. Foods such as milk, nuts, seeds, rice, and oats help your study efforts by releasing natural memory enhancers called CCKs (*cholecystokinin*) composed of *tryptophan*, *choline*, and *phenylalanine*. All of these chemicals enhance the neurotransmitters associated with memory. Before studying, try a light, protein-rich meal of eggs, turkey, and fish. All of these foods release the memory enhancing chemicals. The better the connections, the more you comprehend.

Likewise, before you take a test, stick to a light snack of energy boosting and relaxing foods. A glass of milk, a piece of fruit, or some peanuts all release various memory-boosting chemicals and help you to relax and focus on the subject at hand.

2. <u>Learn to take great notes</u>. A by-product of our modern culture is that we have grown accustomed to getting our information in short doses (i.e., TV news sound bites or *USA Today*-style newspaper articles.)

Consequently, we've subconsciously trained ourselves to assimilate information better in *neat little packages*. If your notes are scrawled all over the paper, it fragments the flow of the information. Strive for clarity. Newspapers use a standard format to achieve clarity. Your notes can be much clearer through use of proper formatting. A very effective format is called the *"Cornell Method."*

> Take a sheet of loose-leaf lined notebook paper and draw a line all the way down the paper about 1–2" from the left-hand edge.
>
> Draw another line across the width of the paper about 1–2" up from the bottom. Repeat this process on the reverse side of the page.

Now look at the result. You have ample room for notes, a left margin for special emphasis items or inserting supplementary data from the textbook, a large area at the bottom for a brief summary, and a little rectangular space for just about anything you want. This should make your note-taking much more effective.

3. <u>Get the concept then the details</u>. Too often we focus on the details and don't gather an understanding of the concept. However, if you simply memorize only dates, places, or names, you may well miss the whole point of the subject.

A key way to understand things is to put them in your own words. If you are working from a textbook, automatically summarize each paragraph in your mind. If you are outlining text, don't simply copy the author's words.

Rephrase them in your own words. You'll remember your own thoughts and words much better than someone else's, and subconsciously tend to associate the important details to the core concepts.

4. Ask Why? Pull apart written material paragraph by paragraph and don't forget the captions under the illustrations.

Example: If the heading is "Stream Erosion," flip it around to read "Why do streams erode?" Then answer the questions.

If you train your mind to think in a series of questions and answers, not only will you learn more, but it also helps to lessen the test anxiety because you are used to answering questions.

5. Read for reinforcement and future needs. Even if you only have 10 minutes, put your notes or a book in your hand. Your mind is similar to a computer; you have to input data in order to have it processed. *By reading, you are creating the neural connections for future retrieval.* The more times you read something, the more you reinforce the learning of ideas.

Even if you don't fully understand something on the first pass, *your mind stores much of the material for later recall.*

6. Relax to learn so go into exile. Our bodies respond to an inner clock called biorhythms. Burning the midnight oil works well for some people, but not everyone.

If possible, set aside a particular place to study that is free of distractions. Shut off the television, cell phone, and pager, and exile your friends and family during your study period.

If silence bothers you, try background music. Light classical music at a low volume has been shown to aid in concentration over other types of music. Music that evokes pleasant emotions without lyrics is highly suggested. Try just about anything by Mozart. It relaxes you.

7. <u>**Use arrows not highlighters.**</u> At best, it's difficult to read a page full of yellow, pink, blue, and green streaks. Try staring at a neon sign for a while and you'll soon see that the horde of colors obscure the message.

A quick note, a brief dash of color, an underline, and/or an arrow pointing to a particular passage is much clearer than a horde of highlighted words.

8. <u>**Budget your study time.**</u> Although you shouldn't ignore any of the material, *allocate your available study time in the same ratio that topics may appear on the test.*

Testing Tips:

1. **Get smart, play dumb. Don't read anything into the question.** Don't make an assumption that the test writer is looking for something else than what is asked. Stick to the question as written and don't read extra things into it.

2. **Read the question and all the choices *twice* before answering the question.** You may miss something by not carefully reading, and then re-reading both the question and the answers.

If you really don't have a clue as to the right answer, leave it blank on the first time through. Go on to the other questions, as they may provide a clue as to how to answer the skipped questions. If later on, you still can't answer the skipped ones . . . *Guess.* The only penalty for guessing is that you *might* get it wrong. Only one thing is certain; if you don't put anything down, you will get it wrong!

3. **Turn the question into a statement.** Look at the way the questions are worded. The syntax of the question usually provides a clue. Does it seem more familiar as a statement rather than as a question? Does it sound strange?

By turning a question into a statement, you may be able to spot if an answer sounds right, and it may also trigger memories of material you have read.

4. **Look for hidden clues.** It's actually very difficult to compose multiple-foil (choice) questions without giving away part of the answer in the options presented. In most multiple-choice questions, you can often readily eliminate one or two of the potential answers. This leaves you with only two real possibilities and automatically your odds go to fifty-fifty for very little work.

5. **Trust your instincts.** For every fact that you have read, you subconsciously retain something of that knowledge. On questions that you aren't really certain about, go with your instincts. **Your first impression on how to answer a question is usually correct.**

6. **Mark your answers directly on the test booklet.** Don't bother trying to fill in the optical scan sheet on the first pass through the test.

Just be very careful not to miss-mark your answers when you eventually transcribe them to the scan sheet.

7. **Watch the clock!** You have a set amount of time to answer the questions. Don't get bogged down trying to answer a single question at the expense of 10 questions you can more readily answer.

Current Teaching Trends

Digital pedagogy and the use of 21st century teaching methods have shifted the landscape of teaching to create a bigger focus on student engagement. Student-centered classrooms now utilize technology to create efficiencies and increase digital literacy. Classrooms that once relied on memorization and the regurgitation of facts now push students to *create* and *analyze* material. The Bloom's Taxonomy chart below gives a great visual of the higher order thinking skills that current teachers are implementing in their learning objectives. There are also examples of the verbs that you might use when creating learning objectives at the assignment, course, or program level.

21st Century Bloom's Taxonomy

Lower- order			Higher- order		
Remember	Understand	Apply	Analyze	Evaluate	Create
• Define • Describe • Recall	• Classify • Explain • Summarize	• Determine • Organize • Use	• Deduct • Estimate • Outline	• Argue • Justify • Support	• Construct • Adapt • Modify

Most importantly, you'll notice that each of these verbs will allow teachers to align a specific assessment to assess the mastery of the skill that's being taught. Instead of saying "Students will learn about parts of speech," teachers will insert a measurable verb into the learning objective. The 21st century model uses S.M.A.R.T. (Specific, Measurable, Attainable, Realistic, Time-bound) assessment methods to ensure teachers can track progress and zero in on areas that students need to revisit before they have fully grasped the concept.

When reading the first objective below, you might ask yourself the following questions:

> Students will:
>   1. Learn about parts of speech

How will they learn? How will you assess their learning? What does "learn" mean to different teachers? What does "learn" look like to different learning styles?

In this second example, the 21st century model shows specific ways students will use parts of speech.

> Students will be able to:
>   1. Define parts of speech (lower)
>   2. Classify parts of speech (lower)
>   3. Construct a visual representation of each part of speech (higher)

Technology in the 21st Century Classroom

Student-centered classrooms now also rely heavily on technology for content delivery (PowerPoint, LMS) assessment (online quizzes) and collaborative learning (GoogleDrive). Particular to ESL classrooms, teachers can now record themselves speaking using lecture capture software. Students can then watch the video multiple times to ensure they've understood concepts. They have the ability to pause/rewind/replay any sections they are confused about, and they can focus on taking better notes while having the ability to watch the video a second or third time.

Online assessments also give students and teachers a better idea for comprehension level. These quick, often self-grading assessments give teachers more time to spend with students instead of grading. They eliminate human error and give teachers data needed to zero in on concepts that need to be revisited. For example, if 12 of 15 students got number 5 wrong, the teacher will know to discuss this concept in class. Online assessments may include listening, speaking, reading, and/or writing practice. This reinforces the content that was taught in the classroom and gives opportunity for practice at students' leisure. In addition, adaptable learning will help teachers by tracking user data to demonstrate learning gains. This can be completed in pre-posttest form, with conditionals within an assessment, or through small, formative assessments.

SMART Technologies, Inc. is a very popular company that creates software and hardware for educational environments. You may have heard of a "SmartBoard" before. These are promethean boards (interactive whiteboards) and are most commonly gained using grant money. They can be used as a projector for PowerPoints, their speakers can be used for audio practice, and their video options can allow you to "bring" a guest speaker into your classroom using videoconferencing, such as Skype. They record notes made on the whiteboard and record audio from lectures, which can then be saved and sent to students that were absent, or used to review for tests on varying concepts.

Google has created ample opportunity for secondary teachers in creating efficiencies for document sharing, assessment tools, and collaborative learning environments. Their drive feature can allow for easy transfer of assignment instructions, essays, and group projects. Slides can be used to create and post PowerPoints for students to have ongoing access. Forms is a great way to create quizzes, and the data can be sorted and manipulated in a number of ways. They can also be used for self-assessment, peer evaluation, and for pre-post analyses.

As technology continues to evolve, it's critical for teachers to continue to implement tools that make their classrooms more effective and efficient while also preparing students to successfully function in a technology-driven society. Through simple lessons and technology demonstrations, students will have a great start at applying technology skills in the outside world. The classroom is a great starting place for ESL students to learn how to use technology and how to practice their own reading, writing, listening, and speaking.

COMPETENCY 1.0   **INDIGENOUS SOCIETIES OF NORTH AMERICA, EUROPEAN EXPLORATION, AND COLONIAL SOCIETIES TO 1760**

Skill 1.1   Understand key political, economic, and cultural features of Native American societies

In North America, the landscape was much more hospitable to settlement and exploration. The North American continent, especially in what is now the United States, had a few mountain ranges and a handful of wide rivers but nothing near the dense jungles and staggeringly high mountains that South America did. The area that is now Canada was cold but otherwise conducive to settlement. As a result, the Native Americans in North American were more spread out and their cultures more diverse than their South American counterparts.

Native American tribes lived throughout what we now call the United States in varying degrees of togetherness. They adopted different customs, pursued different avenues of agriculture and food gathering, and made slightly different weapons. They fought among themselves and with other peoples. To varying degrees, they had established cultures long before Columbus or any other European explorer arrived on the scene.

Perhaps the most famous of the Native American tribes is the **Algonquian**. We know so much about this tribe because it was one of the first to interact with the newly arrived English settlers in Plymouth, Massachusetts, and elsewhere. The Algonquian lived in wigwams and wore clothing made from animal skins. They were proficient hunters, gatherers, and trappers who also knew quite a bit about farming. Beginning with a brave man named Squanto, they shared this agricultural knowledge with the English settlers, including how to plant and cultivate corn, pumpkins, and squash. Other famous Algonquians included Pocahontas and her father, Powhatan, both of whom are immortalized in English literature, and Tecumseh and Black Hawk, known foremost for their fierce fighting ability. To the overall Native American culture, they contributed wampum and dream catchers.

Another group of tribes who lived in the Northeast were the **Iroquois**, who were fierce fighters, but also forward thinkers. They lived in long houses and wore clothes made of buckskin. They, too, were expert farmers, growing the "Three Sisters" (corn, squash, and beans). Five of the Iroquois tribes formed a Confederacy that was a shared form of government. The Iroquois also formed the False Face Society, a group of medicine men who shared their medical knowledge with others but kept their identities secret while doing so. These masks are one of the enduring symbols of the Native American era.

Living in the Southeast were the **Seminole** and **Creek**, a huge collection of people who lived in chickees (open, bark-covered houses) and wore clothes made from plant fibers. They were expert planters and hunters and were proficient at paddling dugout canoes, which they made. The bead necklaces they created were some of the most beautiful on the continent. They are best known, however, for their struggle against Spanish and English settlers, especially led by the great Osceola.

The **Cherokee** also lived in the Southeast. They were one of the most advanced tribes, living in domed houses and wearing deerskin and rabbit fur. Accomplished hunters, farmers, and fishermen, the Cherokee were known around the continent for their intricate and beautiful basketry and clay pottery. They also played a game called lacrosse, which survives to this day in countries around the world.

In the middle of the continent lived the Plains tribes, such as the **Sioux, Cheyenne, Blackfeet, Comanche, and Pawnee**. These peoples lived in teepees and wore buffalo skins and feather headdresses. (It is this image of the Native American that has made its way into most American movies depicting the period.) They hunted wild animals on the Plains, especially the buffalo. They were well known for their many ceremonies, including the Sun Dance, and for the peace pipes that they smoked. Famous Plains people include Crazy Horse and Sitting Bull, authors of the Custer Disaster; Sacagawea, leader of the Lewis and Clark expedition; and Chief Joseph, the famous Nez Perce leader.

Dotting the deserts of the Southwest were a handful of tribes, including the famous **Pueblo**, who lived in houses that bear their tribe's name, wore clothes made of wool and woven cotton, farmed crops in the middle of desert land, created exquisite pottery and Kachina dolls, and had one of the most complex religions of all the tribes. They are perhaps best known for the challenging vista-based villages that they constructed from the sheer faces of cliffs and rocks and for their *adobes*, mud-brick buildings that housed their living and meeting quarters. The Pueblos chose their own chiefs. This was perhaps one of the oldest representative governments in the world.

Another well-known southwestern tribe was the **Apache**, with their famous leader **Geronimo**. The Apache lived in homes called wickiups, which were made of bark, grass, and branches. They wore cotton clothing and were excellent hunters and gatherers. Adept at basketry, the Apache believed that everything in Nature had special powers and that they were honored just to be part of it all.

The **Navajo**, also residents of the Southwest, lived in hogans (round homes built with forked sticks) and wore clothes made of rabbit skins. Their major contribution to the overall culture of the continent was in sand painting, weapon-making, silversmithing, and weaving. Some of the most beautiful woven rugs ever were crafted by Navajo hands.

Living in the Northwest were the **Inuit**, who lived in tents made from animal skins or, in some cases, igloos. They wore clothes made of animal skins, usually seals or caribou. They were excellent fishermen and hunters and crafted efficient kayaks and umiaks to take them through waterways. They used harpoons to hunt animals. The Inuit are perhaps best known for the great carvings that they left behind. Among these are ivory figures and tall totem poles.

For the Native Americans, life was all about finding and growing food. The people were great farmers and hunters. They grew such famous crops as **maize**, or corn, potatoes, squash, pumpkins, and beans; and they hunted all manner of animals for food, including deer, bears, and buffalo. Despite the preponderance of crop-growing areas, many Native Americans, however, did not domesticate animals except for dogs. They might have killed pigs and chickens for food, but they certainly made it easy on themselves by growing them in pens right outside their houses.

Religion was a personal affair for nearly all of these tribes, with beliefs in higher powers extending to Spirits in the sky and elsewhere in Nature. Native Americans had none of the one-god-only mentality that developed in Europe and the Middle East, nor did they have the wars associated with the conflicts that those monotheistic religions had with one another.

Those people who lived in North America had large concentrations of people and houses, but they didn't have the kind of large civilization centers like the cities of elsewhere in the world. These people didn't have an exact system of writing, either. These were two technological advances that were found in many other places in the world including, to varying degrees, South America.

Though not greatly differing from each other in degree of civilization, the native peoples north of Mexico varied widely in customs, housing, dress, and religion. Among the native peoples of North America there were at least 200 languages and 1500 dialects. Each of the hundreds of tribes was somewhat influenced by its neighbors. Communication between tribes that spoke different languages was conducted primarily through a very elaborate system of sign language. Several groups of tribes can be distinguished:

The Woods Peoples occupied the area from the Atlantic to the Western plains and prairies. They cultivated corn and tobacco, fished, and hunted.

The Plains Peoples, who populated the area from the Mississippi River to the Rocky Mountains, were largely wandering and warlike, hunting buffalo and other game for food. After the arrival of Europeans and the re-introduction of the horse they became great horsemen.

The Southwestern Tribes of New Mexico and Arizona included Pueblos, who lived in villages constructed of *adobe* (sun-dried brick), cliff dwellers, and nomadic tribes. These tribes had the most advanced civilizations.

The California Tribes were separated from the influence of other tribes by the mountains. They lived primarily on acorns, seeds and fish, and were probably the least advanced civilizations.

The Northwest Coast Peoples of Washington, British Columbia, and Southern Alaska were not acquainted with farming but built large wooden houses and traveled in huge cedar canoes.

The Plateau Peoples who lived between the plains and the Pacific Coast lived in underground houses or brush huts and subsisted primarily on fish.

The native peoples of America, like other peoples of the same stage of development, believed that all objects, both animate and inanimate, were endowed with certain spiritual powers. They were intensely religious and lived every aspect of their lives as their religion prescribed. They believed a soul inhabited every living thing. Certain birds and animals were considered more powerful and intelligent than humans and capable of influence for good or evil.

Most of the tribes were divided into clans of close blood relations, whose **totem** was a particular animal from which they were often believed to have descended. The sun and the four principal directions were often objects of worship. The **shaman**, a sort of priest, was often the medicine-man of a tribe. Sickness was often supposed to be the result of displeasing some spirit and was treated with incantations and prayer. Many of the traditional stories resemble those of other peoples in providing answers to primordial questions and guidance for life. The highest virtue was self-control, which included hiding emotions and unflinchingly enduring pain or torture. Honesty was also a primary virtue, and promises were always honored no matter what the personal cost.

The communities did not have any formal government. Each individual was responsible for governing himself or herself, particularly with regard to the rights of other members of the community. The chiefs generally carried out the will of the tribe. Each tribe was a discrete unit with its own lands. Boundaries of tribal territories were determined by treaties with neighbors. There was an organized confederation among certain tribes, often called a nation. The Iroquois confederation was often referred to as The Five Nations (later The Six Nations).

Customs varied from tribe to tribe. One consistent cultural element was the smoking of the calumet, a stone pipe, at the beginning and end of a war. In Native American communities, no individual owned land. The plots of land that were cultivated were, however, respected. Wealth was sometimes an honor, but generosity was more highly valued. Agriculture was quite advanced and irrigation was practiced in some locations. Most tribes practiced unique styles of basket work, pottery, and weaving, either in terms of shape or decoration.

Skill 1.2   Be able European exploration, immigration and settlement of North America

Columbus's first trans-Atlantic voyage was an attempt to prove the idea that Asia could be reached by sailing west. And, to a certain extent, this idea was true. It could be done but only after figuring out how to go around or across or through the landmass in between. Long after Spain dispatched explorers and her famed conquistadors to gather the wealth for the Spanish monarchs and their coffers, the British were still searching valiantly for the **Northwest Passage**, an open-water route across North America, from the Atlantic to the Pacific, to the wealth of Asia. Not until after the Lewis and Clark Expedition, when Captains Meriwether Lewis and William Clark proved, conclusively, that there simply was no Northwest Passage, did this idea cease to hold sway.

However, lack of an open-water passage did not deter exploration and settlement. **Spain, France,** and **England**—along with some participation by the **Dutch**—led the way in expanding Western European civilization in the New World. These three nations had strong monarchial governments and were struggling for dominance and power in Europe. With the defeat of Spain's mighty Armada in 1588, England became undisputed ruler of the seas. Spain lost its power and influence in Europe and it was left to France and England to carry on the rivalry, leading to eventual British control in Asia as well.

Spain's influence extended across Florida, along the Gulf Coast of Texas all the way west to California, and south to the tip of South America. French control centered from New Orleans north to what is now northern Canada including the entire Mississippi Valley, the St. Lawrence Valley, the Great Lakes, and the land that was part of the Louisiana Territory. England settled the eastern seaboard of North America, including parts of Canada and the U.S. from Maine to Georgia. Each of the three nations controlled various islands of the West Indies. The Dutch had New Amsterdam for a period but later ceded it into British hands.

One interesting aspect of all of this was that each of these nations, especially England, laid claim to land that extended partly or all the way across the continent, regardless of the fact that the others claimed the same land. The wars for dominance and control of power and influence in Europe would undoubtedly and eventually extend to the Americas, especially North America.

The importance of the Age of Exploration was not only the discovery and colonization of the New World, but, also, a new hemisphere as a refuge from poverty, persecution, and a place to start a new and better life. It led to the development of better maps and charts and new, more accurate, navigational instruments. It led to increased knowledge, great wealth, and new and different foods and items not previously known in Europe. It was also proof that Asia could be reached by sea and that the earth was round. Ships and sailors would not sail off the edge of a flat earth and disappear forever into nothingness.

The part of North America claimed by **France** was called New France and consisted of the land west of the Appalachian Mountains. This area of claims and settlement included the St. Lawrence Valley, the Great Lakes, the Mississippi Valley, and the entire region of land westward to the Rockies. They established the permanent settlements of Montreal and New Orleans, thus giving them control of the two major gateways into the heart of North America, and its vast and rich interior. The St. Lawrence River, the Great Lakes, and the Mississippi River, along with its tributaries, made it possible for the French explorers and traders to roam at will, virtually unhindered in exploring, trapping, trading, and furthering the interests of France.

Most of the French settlements were in Canada along the St. Lawrence River. Only scattered forts and trading posts were found in the upper Mississippi Valley and Great Lakes region. The rulers of France originally intended New France to have vast estates owned by nobles and worked by peasants with the peasants living on the estates in compact farming villages—the New World version of the Old World's medieval system of feudalism. However, it didn't work out that way. Each of the nobles wanted his estate to be on the river for ease of transportation. The peasants working the estates wanted the prime waterfront location, also. The result of all this real estate squabbling was that New France's settled areas wound up mostly as a string of farmhouses stretching from Quebec to Montreal along the St. Lawrence and Richelieu Rivers.

In the non-settled areas in the interior were the **French fur traders.** They made friends with the friendly tribes of Indians, spending the winters with them, getting the furs needed for trade. In the spring, they would return to Montreal in time to take advantage of trading their furs for the products brought by the cargo ships from France, which usually arrived at about the same time. Most of the wealth for New France and its "Mother Country" was from the fur trade, which provided a livelihood for many, many people. Manufacturers and workmen back in France— ship-owners and merchants, as well as the fur traders and their Indian allies—all benefited. However, the freedom of roaming and trapping in the interior was a strong enticement for the younger, stronger men and resulted in the French not strengthening the areas settled along the St. Lawrence.

Into the eighteenth century, French rivalry with the **British** grew stronger. New France was united under a single government and enjoyed the support of many Indian allies. The French traders were very diligent in not destroying the forests and driving away game upon which the Indians depended for life. It was difficult for the French to defend all of their settlements as they were scattered over half of the continent. However, by the early 1750s, in Western Europe, France was the most powerful nation. Its armies were superior to all others and its navy was giving the British stiff competition for control of the seas. The stage was set for confrontation in both Europe and America.

Spanish settlement had its beginnings in the Caribbean with the establishment of colonies on Hispaniola at Santo Domingo which became the capital of the West Indies, Puerto Rico, and Cuba. There were a number of reasons for Spanish involvement in the Americas, among them:

- the spirit of adventure
- the desire for land
- expansion of Spanish power, influence, and empire
- the desire for great wealth
- expansion of Roman Catholic influence and conversion of native peoples

The first permanent settlement in what is now the United States was founded in 1565 at **St. Augustine**, Florida. A later permanent settlement in the southwestern United States was in 1609 at Santa Fe, New Mexico. At the peak of Spanish power, the area in the United States claimed, settled, and controlled by Spain included Florida and all land west of the Mississippi River.

Of course, France and England also laid claim to the same areas. Nonetheless, ranches and missions were built and the Indians who came in contact with the Spaniards were introduced to animals, plants, and seeds from the Old World that they had never seen before. Animals brought in included horses, cattle, donkeys, pigs, sheep, goats, and poultry.

Barrels were cut in half and filled with earth to transport and transplant trees bearing apples, oranges, limes, cherries, pears, walnuts, olives, lemons, figs, apricots, and almonds. Even sugar cane and flowers made it to America along with bags bringing seeds of wheat, barley, rye, flax, lentils, rice, and peas.

All Spanish colonies belonged to the King of Spain. He was considered **an absolute monarch** with complete or absolute power who claimed rule by divine right, the belief being that God had given him the right to rule and he answered only to God for his actions. His word was final and was the law. The people had no voice in government. The land, the people, the wealth all belonged to him to use as he pleased. He appointed personal representatives, or **viceroys**, to rule for him in his colonies. They ruled in his name with complete authority. Since the majority of them were friends and advisers, they were richly rewarded with land grants, gold and silver, privileges of trading, and the right to operate the gold and silver mines.

For the needed labor in the mines and on the plantations, Indians were used first as slaves. However, they either rapidly died out due to a lack of immunity from European diseases or escaped into nearby jungles or mountains. As a result, African slaves were brought in, especially to the islands of the West Indies. Some historians state that Latin American slavery was less harsh than in the later English colonies in North America.

Three reasons for that statement are given:

1. The following of a slave code based on ancient Roman laws.
2. The efforts of the Roman Catholic Church to protect and defend slaves because of efforts to convert them.
3. The lack of prejudice due to racial mixtures in Spain, which was once controlled by dark-skinned Moors from North Africa.

Regardless, slavery was still slavery and was very harsh—cruelly denying dignity and human worth.

Spain's control over its New World colonies lasted more than 300 years, longer than England's or France's. To this day, Spanish influence remains in the names of places, art, architecture, music, literature, law, and cuisine. The Spanish settlements in North America were not commercial enterprises but were for protection and defense of the trading and wealth from their colonies in Mexico and South America. The treasure and wealth found in Spanish New World colonies went back to Spain to be used to buy whatever goods and products were needed instead of setting up industries to make what was needed. As the amount of gold and silver was depleted, Spain could not pay for the goods needed and was unable to produce goods for themselves.

Also, at the same time, Spanish treasure ships at sea were being seized by English and Dutch "pirates" taking the wealth to fill the coffers of their own countries. On land, Russian seal-hunters came down the Pacific coast; the English moved into Florida and west into and beyond the Appalachians while French traders and trappers made their way from Louisiana and other parts of New France into Spanish territory. Facing encroachment on all sides, and without self-sustaining economic development and colonial trade, the Spanish settlements in the U.S. never really prospered.

The **English** colonies were divided generally into the three regions: New England, Middle Atlantic, and Southern. The culture of each was distinct and affected attitudes, ideas toward politics, religion, and economic activities. The geography of each region also contributed to the colonies' unique characteristics.

The **New England colonies** consisted of Massachusetts, Rhode Island, Connecticut, and New Hampshire. Life in these colonies was centered on the towns. Farming was done by each family on its own plot of land, but a short summer growing season and limited amount of good soil gave rise to other economic activities such as manufacturing, fishing, shipbuilding, and trade. The vast majority of the settlers shared similar origins, coming from England and Scotland. Towns were carefully planned and laid out the same way. The form of government was the town meeting where all adult males met to make the laws. The legislative body, the General Court, consisted of an upper and lower house.

The **Middle or Middle Atlantic colonies** included New York, New Jersey, Pennsylvania, and Delaware. New York and New Jersey were at one time the Dutch colony of New Netherland, and Delaware at one time was New Sweden. From their beginnings, these five colonies were considered "melting pots" with settlers from many different nations and backgrounds. The main economic activity was farming, with the settlers scattered over the countryside, cultivating rather large farms. The Indians were not as much of a threat as in New England so there was less need to settle in small farming villages. The soil was very fertile, the land was gently rolling, and a milder climate provided a longer growing season.

These farms produced a large surplus of food, not only for the colonists themselves but also for sale. This colonial region became known as the "breadbasket" of the New World. The New York and Philadelphia seaports were constantly filled with ships being loaded with meat, flour, and other foodstuffs for the West Indies and England.

There were other economic activities such as shipbuilding, iron mines, and factories producing paper, glass, and textiles. The legislative body in Pennsylvania was unicameral and, therefore, consisted of only one house. In the other four colonies, the legislative body had two houses. Also, units of local government were in counties and towns.

The **Southern colonies** were Maryland, Virginia, North and South Carolina, and Georgia. Virginia was the first permanent successful English colony and Georgia was the last. The year 1619 was a very important year in the history of Virginia and the United States with three very significant events. First, sixty women were sent to Virginia to marry and establish families; second, twenty Africans, the first of thousands, arrived; and third, most importantly, the Virginia colonists were granted the right to self-government and they began by electing their own representatives to the House of Burgesses, their own legislative body.

The major economic activity in this region was farming. Here, too, the soil was very fertile and the climate was very mild with an even longer growing season. The large plantations eventually requiring large numbers of slaves were found in the coastal or tidewater areas. Although the wealthy slave-owning planters set the pattern of life in this region, most of the people lived inland away from coastal areas. They were small farmers and very few, if any, owned slaves. Products from farms and plantations included rice, tobacco, indigo, cotton, some corn, and wheat. Other economic activities included lumber and naval stores (tar, pitch, rosin, and turpentine) from the pine forests and fur trade on the frontier.

The settlers in these four colonies came from diverse backgrounds and cultures. Virginia was colonized mostly by people from England while Georgia was started as a haven for debtors from English prisons. Pioneers from Virginia settled in North Carolina while South Carolina welcomed people from England and Scotland, French Protestants, Germans, and emigrants from islands in the West Indies. Cities such as Savannah and Charleston were important seaports and trading centers.

In the colonies, the daily life of the colonists differed greatly between the coastal settlements and the inland or interior. The Southern planters and the people living in the coastal cities and towns had a way of life similar to that of towns in England. That influence was seen and heard in the way people dressed and spoke, the architectural styles of houses and public buildings, and the social divisions or levels of society. Both the planters and city dwellers enjoyed an active social life and had strong emotional ties to England.

On the other hand, life inland, on the frontier, had marked differences. All facets of daily living—clothing, food, housing, and economic and social activities—were all connected to what was needed to sustain life and survive in the wilderness. Everything was produced practically by the settlers themselves. They were self-sufficient and extremely individualistic and independent. There were few, if any, levels of society or class distinctions as they considered themselves to be equal to all others, regardless of station in life. The roots of equality, independence, individual rights, and freedoms were extremely strong and well developed. People were not judged by their fancy dress, expensive house, eloquent language, or titles following their names.

The colonies had, from 1607 to 1763, to develop, refine, practice, experiment, and experience life in a rugged, uncivilized land. The Mother Country had virtually left them on their own to take care of themselves. So, when in 1763 Britain decided she needed to regulate and "mother" the "little ones;" to her surprise, she had a losing fight on her hands.

Skill 1.3   Describe the characteristics of and regional divisions among England's North American colonies

The thirteen British colonies that would become the first independent, American states were divided into three primary regions: New England, including the colonies of New Hampshire, Massachusetts, Rhode Island, and Connecticut; the middle colonies of New York, Pennsylvania, New Jersey, and Delaware; and the southern colonies of Maryland, Virginia, North Carolina, South Carolina, and Georgia.

These three regions developed different economic resources that were closely connected to the differing geography among the colonies. The relatively difficult growing conditions in the New England led to a reliance on fishing and shipbuilding, supplemented by subsistence farming. The large rivers and excellent harbors of the Middle Colonies allowed them to flourish as market centers, while agriculture took hold in the interior. In the South, rich soil provided a basis for large, self-sufficient farm plantations.

Before setting foot on land in 1620, the **Pilgrims,** aboard the Mayflower, agreed to a form of self-government by signing the Mayflower Compact. The Compact served as the basis for governing the Plymouth colony for many years, and set an example of small, town-based government that would proliferate throughout New England. The present-day New England town meeting is an extension of this tradition. This republican ideal was later to clash with the policies of British colonial government.

Slavery was present in the New World from the beginning, with the first slaves arriving in Virginia in 1619. Beginning in about 1700, the "**triangular trade**" began. Cotton, sugar, and tobacco were shipped to Britain, which then distilled rum and created textiles for export to Africa. In Africa, these goods were traded for slaves, which were then carried back to the Americas and traded for more raw materials. The slave trade, which was engaged in by both northern and southern colonies, contributed directly to the success of the new colonies, providing labor and trade opportunities.

As the American colonies moved toward independence, regional differences came into focus. In a democracy that awarded wealthy landowners more access, the southern plantation owners were at an advantage while the political and economic centers were in the north. The U.S. Constitution and Bill of Rights attempted to balance some of these tensions. Even the placement of the new U.S. Capitol between Maryland and Virginia can be seen as a symbolic compromise between the regions.

Skill 1.4   Understand the political and economic relations between the colonies and Europe

The New England colonies were primarily settled by English colonists, but other nations had a presence in the New World as well. Although one colony was founded as strictly a philanthropic enterprise, and three others were founded primarily for religious reasons, the other nine were started for economic reasons. Settlers who came to these colonies came for different reasons, but primarily they sought religious or political freedom, economic prosperity, or the opportunity to own land. Despite sentiments about freedom or economic independence, the colonies remained connected to the political and economic developments in Europe.

The Dutch West India Company founded a colony in what is now New York, establishing it as New Holland. It was eventually captured by English settlers and named New York, but many of the Dutch families that had been granted large segments of land by the Dutch government were allowed to keep their estates. As hostility built between England and the colonies over the taxation of tea, colonists turned to the Dutch to supply them with this important import.

To the north of the Anglo-American colonies, the French were establishing a significant presence in what is now eastern Canada. Spain was advancing in its colonization of parts of the Caribbean, where much of the early slave trade originated. Consequently, the American colonies found themselves swept into international political affairs whenever the homeland, Britain, found itself in conflicts in Europe.

The case of Britain's rivalry with France is an example. England and France were historic rivals who found themselves with a new common border in the New World. Disputes over control of the Ohio River between French and British colonies were one of the primary causes leading into the Seven Years' War among many of the European powers. Anglo-American colonists, still considering themselves British subjects, fought against the French and their Indian allies. George Washington emerged as an effective military leader during this conflict.

Later, the animosity between the English and French would work to the advantage of the revolutionary colonists, who received aid from France in their struggle against England. Holland, with its long connection to the American colonies, was the second nation, after France, to recognize their independence. Spain, while not officially recognizing the independence of the colonies, joined the Revolutionary War on the side of the colonists due to a disagreement with Britain over the possession of Gibraltar. Thus, from the earliest times, the fortunes of the colonists were caught up in international affairs, and even relied on their political and economic connections with Europe to advance and gain eventual independence.

The war for independence occurred due to a number of changes, the two most important ones being economic and political. By the end of the French and Indian War in 1763, Britain's American colonies were thirteen out of a total of thirty-three scattered around the earth. Like all other countries, Britain strove for having a strong economy and a favorable balance of trade. That combination required wealth, self-sufficiency, and a powerful army and navy. This is why Britain established overseas colonies.

The English colonies, with only a few exceptions, were considered commercial ventures founded to make a profit for the crown, or the company, or whoever financed its beginnings. The colonies would provide raw materials for the industries in the Mother Country, be a market for finished products by buying them and assist the Mother Country in becoming powerful and strong. In the case of Great Britain, a strong merchant fleet would provide training for the Royal Navy as well as provide places as bases of operation.

Trade explains the major reason for British encouragement and support of colonization, especially in North America. Between 1607 and 1763, at various times for various reasons, the British Parliament enacted different laws to assist the government in getting and keeping this trade balance. One series of laws required that most of the manufacturing be done only in England. There was a prohibition on exporting any wool or woolen cloth from the colonies, and no manufacture of beaver hats or iron products was permitted in the colonies. These regulations didn't concern the colonists as they had no money and no highly skilled labor to set up any industries, anyway. Other acts had greater impact.

The **Navigation Acts of 1651** put restrictions on shipping and trade within the British Empire by requiring that it was allowed only on British ships. This increased the strength of the British merchant fleet and greatly benefited the American colonists. Since they were British citizens, they could have their own vessels, and could build and operate them as well. By the end of the war in 1763, the shipyards in the colonies were building one-third of the merchant ships under the British flag. There were quite a number of wealthy, American, colonial merchants.

The **Navigation Act of 1660** restricted the shipment and sale of colonial products to England only. In 1663, another Navigation Act stipulated that the colonies had to buy manufactured products only from England and that any European goods going to the colonies had to go to England first. These acts were a protection from enemy ships and pirates and from competition from European rivals.

The New England and Middle Atlantic colonies at first felt threatened by these laws as they had started producing many of the same products being produced in Britain. But they soon found new markets for their goods and began their own **"triangular trade."** Colonial vessels started the first part of the triangle by sailing for Africa loaded with kegs of rum from colonial distilleries. On Africa's West Coast, the rum was traded for either gold or slaves. The second part of the triangle was from Africa to the West Indies where slaves were traded for molasses, sugar, or money. The third part of the triangle was home, bringing sugar or molasses (to make more rum), gold, and silver.

The major concern of the British government was that the trade violated the 1733 **Molasses Act**. Planters had wanted the colonists to buy all of their molasses in the British West Indies, but these islands could give the traders only about one-eighth of the amount of molasses needed for distilling the rum. The colonists were forced to buy the rest of what they needed from the French, Dutch, and Spanish islands, thus evading the law by not paying the high duty on the molasses bought from these islands. If Britain had enforced the Molasses Act, economic and financial chaos and ruin would have occurred. So, for this act and all the other mercantile laws, the government followed the policy of "salutary neglect," deliberately failing to enforce the laws.

In 1763, after the war, money was needed to pay the British war debt, for the defense of the empire, and to pay for the governing of thirty-three colonies scattered around the earth. It was decided to adopt a new colonial policy and pass laws to raise revenue. It was reasoned that the colonists were subjects of the king, and, since the king and his ministers had spent a great deal of money defending and protecting them (this especially for the American colonists), it was only right and fair that the colonists should help pay the costs of defense, especially theirs. The earlier laws passed had been for the purposes of regulating production and trade which generally put money into colonial pockets. These new laws would take some of that rather hard-earned money out of their pockets and it would be done, in colonial eyes, unjustly and illegally.

Skill 1.5   Make comparisons of the ethnic and religious diversity of American colonists and intellectual heritage of Anglo-American colonials

The thirteen English colonies were successful and, by the time they had gained their independence from Britain, were more than able to govern themselves. They had a rich historical heritage of law, tradition, and documents leading the way to constitutional government conducted according to laws and customs. The settlers in the British colonies highly valued individual freedom, democratic government, and getting ahead through hard work.

While some eighty percent of the American colonists were of European descent, the proportion of these who were of English descent decreased during the 1700s as more and more settlers from other countries settled in the colonies. Settlers from Germany, Scotland, and Ireland made up nearly a third of colonials from Europe, often settling in separate communities. By 1775, approximately one-fifth of the colonial population was of African ancestry, primarily living in slavery in the southern colonies. Some free black people did live and work in the northern colonies, however.

The colonists were a diverse group in terms of religion as well. Of those who were members of a church—and many colonists did not belong to a church—the vast majority were Protestant Christians. In Maryland and Delaware there were significant groups of Roman Catholics, and a small number of Jews lived in the northern colonies.

Within Protestantism, there were several divisions. In the northern Puritan regions, the Congregational Church was organized, and received support from the colonies. In the South, the Church of England was widespread. In the more ethnically diverse Middle Colonies, a more diverse religious group existed. The Quakers, who had been driven out of the Puritan regions, settled in Rhode Island and Pennsylvania. Immigrants from Scotland founded Presbyterian churches. Baptist churches began to emerge after the Great Awakening of the 1740s and ignited religious sentiments among many Protestants. Other denominations also took hold in the colonies, including Lutherans, Mennonites, and Dutch Reformed churches.

In the Puritan regions, personal responsibility toward one's community was a basic value that was based on the religious commitment one made to the church. The earliest settlements were centered on the church and the meetings among church members to decide public matters eventually transformed into the New England town meeting, a community-based system of government that is still used today. In educational matters, Puritans felt it important that everyone be able to study the Bible and ensured that their children received an elementary education.

Publicly funded grammar schools were established in New England to provide secondary education. The country's first college, Harvard, was established in Cambridge, Massachusetts. Other colleges, including Yale, Dartmouth, and Brown were established in other parts of New England.

In the Middle Colonies, the more diverse population led to a less homogenous region in terms of community relationships. The large number of Germans in the area meant that the German language remained in common use in many small communities. Marriage within these communities was encouraged. The Quaker Church was more inclusive than the Congregationalist church in the North, holding that all people were equal before God, and that women had an equal position in the church. Presbyterian Church members were arranged into synods and were able to make decisions on church matters without an authoritarian hierarchy. These "democratic" systems of church organizations supported democratic values that made their way into civic matters. A public responsibility toward the less fortunate was another Quaker tenet that culminated in the establishment of institutions such as public hospitals.

Education in the Middle Colonies was influenced largely by the Enlightenment movement, which emphasized scholarly research and public service. Benjamin Franklin embodied these principles in Philadelphia, which became a center of learning and culture, owing largely to its economic success and ease of access to European books and tracts.

In the South, the wealthy, elite landowners looked to England for culture. The Church of England was legally established throughout the colonies, and received public money in support. Wealthy planters were able to exercise their influence over their local regions through their authority over the local church organization. A hierarchical social system developed, with the wealthy planters at the top, followed by merchants, smaller farmers, and slaves. In the back country, Scots-Irish settlers lived in small farm communities outside of this system. During the Great Awakening, the hierarchy was threatened as Baptist congregations formed. Many planters sought to disrupt these congregations, sometimes with violence.

In education, as in many things, wealthy southerners looked to England. Some would send their sons to London for schooling and to learn the manners of British gentlemen. British tutors were hired for wealthy, southern children. Among the Roman Catholic communities in Maryland, some families sent their sons to Jesuit schools in France. Education for less wealthy southerners was not as widely available as it was in the North. As other groups moved into the area, such as the German Lutherans, elementary education became more common.

Skill 1.6　　Know and understand the growing social and political divergence of the colonies from England

As the proportion of English-born colonists decreased and the diversity of settlers increased, fewer and fewer colonists felt a cultural tie to the country that held so much influence over the colonies' trade and government. Divisions between the colonies became more pronounced as settlers of differing religious and national groups established themselves.

Government of the colonies differed depending on the type of colony. Each colony had a lower legislative assembly that was elected and a higher council and governor that were elected or appointed in different ways depending on how the colony was organized initially. In most colonies, the councils and governors were appointed by the King of England or by British property owners or agencies. In corporate colonies, the council and governors were elected by colonial property owners who maintained a close connection to England.

Thus, while the colonies were allowed to tax themselves and regulate much of their daily lives through representation in the colonial assemblies, Britain maintained control of international affairs and international trade by controlling the upper levels of colonial government. In practice, Britain allowed the colonies to go about their business without interference, largely because the colonies were providing important raw materials to the home country.

The first glimmers of dissent from the colonies came during the French and Indian War, in which colonial militias were raised to fight the French in America. Conflict arose with Britain over who should control these militias, with the colonies wanting the assemblies to have authority. Following the British victory over the French, Britain found itself in debt from the war and looked to the colonies to provide revenue. Britain began enforcing taxes on colonial trade that it had ignored prior to the war and began passing new regulations.

The war's effect on the colonies was to provide them with a sense of unity that they had lacked before. This newfound unity was to prove important in the growth of dissent against Britain's increased involvement in colonial affairs. In 1764, Parliament passed the Sugar Act in an attempt to stop colonists' smuggling of molasses. England strictly enforced the act but the colonists objected to the act even though the tax rate was lower than the earlier Sugar Act.

Feelings reached a peak with the passage of the **Stamp Act** the following year. The tax was a direct tax on colonists. Nine colonies assembled in New York to call for the repeal of the Act. At the same time, a group of New York merchants organized a protest to stop the importation of British goods. Similar protests arose in Philadelphia and Boston and other merchant cities, often erupting in violence. As Britain's representatives in the colonies, the governors and members of the cabinet and council were sometimes the targets of these protests.

The same year, 1765, Parliament passed the first Quartering Act. This purpose of this act was to protect colonists from a possible French threat after the French and Indian War. The act required colonists to house (quarter) the troops. A year later, colonists were required to feed the troops that they quartered. The second quartering act was passed in 1774 and was in existence for two years. This act removed the requirement that colonists provide the troops provisions (food). There was resistance to both laws, and, at one point, British soldiers needed to remain on their ships in New York harbor because the government refused to provide housing for them. Both acts caused dissention among the colonists.

Britain repealed the Stamp Act, but continued to tax external trade items such as tea through the **Townshend Act**, provoking the growth of the movement to halt importation of British goods. This boycott eventually led Britain to repeal much of the Townshend Act.

Meanwhile, increased contact between colonials had allowed a growing patriot movement to gain a foothold and the issue of independence arose in common thought. When Britain proposed that the East India Company be allowed to import tea to the colonies without customs duty, the colonists were faced with a dilemma. They could purchase the tea at a much lower price than the smuggled Dutch tea they had been drinking, however, tea was still subject to the Townshend Act, and purchasing it would be an acceptance of this act. The **Boston Tea Party** was the result, where a group of colonists seized a shipment of British tea in Boston Harbor and dumped it into the sea.

Britain responded with a series of even more restrictive acts, driving the colonies to come together in the **First Continental Congress** to make a unified demand that Britain remove these **Intolerable Acts**, as they were called by the colonists.

Britain stood firm and sought to dissolve the colonial assemblies that were coming forth in opposition to British policies, stockpiling weapons, and preparing militias. When the British military in America were ordered to break up the illegal meeting of the Massachusetts' assembly outside Boston, they were met with armed resistance at **Lexington and Concord**, and the Revolutionary War was underway.

COMPETENCY 2.0   CAUSES AND KEY EVENTS OF THE REVOLUTIONARY WAR AND MAJOR DEVELOPMENTS OF U.S. HISTORY THROUGH THE JACKSONIAN ERA

Skill 2.1   Understand the events, interests, and issues of the American Revolution

By the 1750s in Europe, Spain was no longer the most powerful nation and the remaining rivalry was between Britain and France. For nearly twenty-five years, between 1689 and 1748, a series of armed conflicts involving these two powers had been taking place. These conflicts had spilled over into North America. The War of the League of Augsburg in Europe, 1689 to 1697, had been King William's War. The War of the Spanish Succession, 1702 to 1713, had been Queen Anne's War. The War of the Austrian Succession, 1740 to 1748, was called King George's War in the colonies. The two nations fought for possession of colonies—especially in Asia and North America—and for control of the seas, but none of these conflicts was decisive.

The final conflict, which decided once and for all who was the most powerful, began in North America in 1754, in the Ohio River Valley. It was known in America as the **French and Indian War** and in Europe as the **Seven Years' War**, since it began there in 1756. In America, both sides had advantages and disadvantages. The British colonies were well established and consolidated in a smaller area. British colonists outnumbered French colonists 23 to 1. Except for a small area in Canada, French settlements were scattered over a much larger area—roughly half of the continent—and were smaller. However, the French settlements were united under one government and were quick to act and cooperate when necessary. In addition, the French had many more Indian allies than the British. The British colonies had separate, individual governments and very seldom cooperated, even when cooperation was needed. In Europe, at that time, France was the more powerful of the two nations.

Both sides had stunning victories and humiliating defeats. If there was one person who could be given the credit for British victory, it would have to be **William Pitt**. He was a strong leader, enormously energetic, supremely self-confident, and determined on a complete British victory. Despite the advantages and military victories of the French, Pitt succeeded. In the army, he got rid of the incompetents and replaced them with men who could do the job. He sent more troops to America, strengthened the British navy, and gave to the officers of the colonial militias equal rank to the British officers—in short, he saw to it that Britain took the offensive and kept it until victorious. Of all the British victories, perhaps the most crucial and important was winning Canada.

The French depended on the St. Lawrence River for transporting supplies, soldiers, and messages. It was the link between New France and the Mother

Country. Tied into this waterway system were the connecting links of the Great Lakes, and the Mississippi River and its tributaries along which were scattered French forts, trading posts, and small settlements. When, in 1758, the British captured Louisburg on Cape Breton Island, New France was doomed. Louisburg gave the British navy a base of operations, preventing French reinforcements and supplies getting to their troops. Other forts fell to the British: Frontenac, Duquesne, Crown Point, Ticonderoga, and Niagara, those in the upper Ohio Valley, Montreal, and, most importantly, Quebec. Spain entered the war in 1762 to aid France but it was too late. British victories occurred all around the world: in India, in the Mediterranean, and in Europe.

In 1763, France and Britain met in Paris to draw up the **Treaty of Paris.** Great Britain received most of India and all of North America east of the Mississippi River, except for New Orleans. Britain gained control of Florida from Spain and returned Cuba and the islands of the Philippines, taken during the war, to Spain. France lost nearly all of its possessions in America and India but was allowed to keep four islands: Guadeloupe, Martinique, Haiti on Hispaniola, and St. Pierre and Miquelon. France gave New Orleans and the vast territory of Louisiana, west of the Mississippi River, to Spain. Britain was now the most powerful nation, bar none.

Where did all of this leave the British colonies? Their colonial militias had fought with the British so they also benefited. The militias and their officers gained much fighting experience which was very valuable later. The thirteen colonies also began to realize that cooperating with each other was the only way to defend themselves. That last lesson wouldn't be fully implemented until the time came for the war for independence and establishing a national government, but a start had been made. Shortly after the start of the war in 1754, the French and their Indian allies had defeated Major George Washington and his militia at Fort Necessity. This left the entire northern frontier of the British colonies vulnerable and open to attack. In the wake of this, Benjamin Franklin proposed to the thirteen colonies that they unite permanently to be able to defend themselves.

Delegates from seven of the thirteen colonies met in Albany, New York, along with representatives from the Iroquois Confederation and British officials. Franklin's proposal, known as the Albany Plan of Union, was rejected by the colonists, along with a similar proposal from the British. Delegates simply did not want each of the colonies to lose the right to act independently. However, the seed of union was planted.

Before 1763, with the exception of trade and supplying raw materials, the colonies had mostly been left to themselves. England looked on them merely as part of an economic or commercial empire. Little consideration was given as to how they were to conduct their daily affairs, so the colonists became very independent, self-reliant, and extremely skillful at handling those daily affairs. This, in turn, gave rise to leadership, initiative, achievement, and vast experience. In fact, there was a far greater degree of independence and self-government in America than could be found in Britain or the major countries on the Continent or any other colonies anywhere. There were a number of reasons for this:

1. The religious and scriptural teachings of previous centuries put forth the worth of the individual and equality in God's sight. Freedom of worship and freedom from religious persecution were major reasons to live in the New World.

2. European Protestants, especially Calvinists, believed and taught the idea that government originates from those governed, that rulers are required to protect individual rights and that the governed have the right and privilege to choose their rulers.

3. Trading companies put into practice the principle that their members had the right to make the decisions and shape the policies affecting their lives.

4. The colonists believed and supported the idea that a person's property should not be taken without his consent, based on the English document, the Magna Carta, and English common law.

5. From about 1700 to 1750, population increases in America came about through immigration and generations and generations of descendants of the original settlers. The immigrants were mainly Scots-Irish who hated the English, Germans who cared nothing about England, and black slaves who knew nothing about England. The descendants of the original settlers had never been out of America at any time.

6. In America, as new towns and counties were formed, there began the practice of representation in government. Representatives to the colonial legislative assemblies were elected from the district in which they lived, chosen by qualified property-owning male voters, and represented the interests of the political district from which they were elected. Each of the 13 colonies had a royal governor appointed by the king, representing the king's interests in the colonies. Nevertheless, the colonial legislative assemblies controlled the purse strings by having the power to vote on all issues involving money to be spent by the colonial governments.

Contrary to this was the established government in England. Members of Parliament were not elected to represent their own districts. They were considered representative of classes, not individuals. If some members of a professional or commercial class or some landed interests were able to elect representatives, then those classes or special interests were represented. It had nothing at all to do with numbers or territories. Some large population centers had no direct representation at all, yet the people there considered themselves represented by men elected from their particular class or interest somewhere else. Consequently, it was extremely difficult for the English to understand why the American merchants and landowners claimed they were not represented because they themselves did not vote for members of Parliament.

The colonists' protest of "**No taxation without representation**" was meaningless to the English. Parliament represented the entire nation, was completely unlimited in legislation, and had become supreme. The colonists were incensed at this English attitude and considered their colonial legislative assemblies equal to Parliament, a position which was totally unacceptable in England. There were now two different environments: the older, traditional British system in the Mother Country, and the American system with its new ideas and different ways of doing things. In a new country, a new environment has little or no tradition, institutions or vested interests. New ideas and traditions grew extremely fast, pushing aside what was left of the old ideas and old traditions. By 1763, Britain had changed its perception of the American colonies to their being a "territorial" empire. The stage was set and the conditions were right for a showdown.

It all began in 1763 when Parliament decided to have a standing army in North America to reinforce British control. In 1765, the **Quartering Act** was passed requiring the colonists to provide supplies and living quarters for the British troops. In addition, efforts by the British were made to keep the peace by establishing good relations with the Indians. Consequently, a proclamation was issued that prohibited any American colonists from making any settlements west of the Appalachians until provided for through treaties with the Indians.

The **Sugar Act of 1764** required efficient collection of taxes on any molasses that was brought into the colonies and gave British officials free license to conduct searches of the premises of anyone suspected of violating the law. The colonists were taxed on newspapers, legal documents, and other printed matter under the **Stamp Act of 1765**. Although a stamp tax was already in use in England, the colonists would have none of it and after the ensuing uproar of rioting and mob violence, Parliament repealed the tax.

Of course, great exultation resulted when news of the repeal reached America. However, what no one noticed was the small, quiet Declaratory Act attached to the repeal. This act plainly, unequivocally stated that Parliament still had the right to make all laws for the colonies and denied their right to be taxed only by their own colonial legislatures—a very crucial, important piece of legislation, virtually overlooked and unnoticed at the time. Other acts leading up to armed conflict included the Townshend Acts passed in 1767 taxing lead, paint, paper, and tea brought into the colonies. This, too, increased anger and tension resulting in the British sending troops to New York City and Boston.

In Boston, mob violence provoked retaliation by the troops thus bringing about the deaths of five people and the wounding of eight others. The so-called **Boston Massacre** shocked Americans and British alike. Subsequently, in 1770, Parliament voted to repeal all the provisions of the Townshend Acts with the exception of the tea tax. In 1773, the tax on tea sold by the British East India Company was substantially reduced, fueling colonial anger once more. This gave the company an unfair trade advantage and forcibly reminded the colonists of the

British right to tax them. Merchants refused to sell the tea, colonists refused to buy and drink it, and a shipload of it was dumped into Boston Harbor—a most violent Tea Party.

Skill 2.2   Describe the conflicts between British and American ideas of sovereignty and significant leaders, events, and turning points of the Revolutionary War

In 1774, the passage of the **Quebec Act** extended the limits of that Canadian colony's boundary southward to include territory located north of the Ohio River. However, the punishment for Boston's Tea Party came in the same year with the Intolerable Acts. Boston's port was closed; the royal governor of the colony of Massachusetts was given increased power, and the colonists were compelled to house and feed the British soldiers. The propaganda activities of the patriot organizations **Sons of Liberty** and **Committees of Correspondence** kept the opposition and resistance before everyone.

Delegates from twelve colonies met in Philadelphia September 5, 1774, in the **First Continental Congress**. They defiantly opposed acts of lawlessness and wanted some form of peaceful settlement with Britain. They still maintained American loyalty to the Mother Country, however, and affirmed Parliament's power over colonial foreign affairs. They did insist on repeal of the **Intolerable Acts** and demanded ending all trade with Britain until this took place. The reply from George III, the last king of America, was an insistence of colonial submission to British rule or be crushed. With the start of the Revolutionary War on April 19, 1775, the Second Continental Congress began meeting in Philadelphia on May 10th of that year to conduct the business of war and government for the next six years. On August 23, 1775, George III declared that the colonies were in rebellion and warned them to stop or else.

The British were interested only in raising money to pay war debts, regulate the trade and commerce of the colonies, and look after business and financial interests between the Mother Country and the rest of her empire. The establishment of overseas colonies was first and foremost a commercial enterprise, not a political one. The political aspect was secondary and assumed. The British took it for granted that Parliament was supreme, was recognized so by the colonists, and were very resentful of the colonial challenge to Parliament's authority. They were contemptuously indifferent to politics in America and had no wish to exert any control over it but as resistance and disobedience swelled and increased in America, the British increased their efforts to punish them and put them in their place.

The British had been extremely lax and inconsistent in enforcement of the mercantile or trade laws passed in the years before 1754. The government itself was not particularly stable so actions against the colonies occurred in anger and the attitude was one of a moral superiority, that Parliament knew how to manage

America better than the Americans did themselves. This of course points to a lack of sufficient knowledge of conditions and opinions in America. The colonists had been left on their own for nearly 150 years and by the time the Revolutionary War began, they were quite adept at self-government and adequately handling the affairs of their daily lives, with no one looking over their shoulders telling them what to do or how to do it.

The Americans equated ownership of land or property with the right to vote. Property was considered the foundation of life and liberty and, in the colonial mind and tradition, these went together. Therefore, when an indirect tax on tea was made, the British felt since it wasn't a direct tax, there should be no objection to it. The colonists viewed any tax, direct or indirect, as an attack on their property. They felt that as a representative body, the British Parliament should protect British citizens, including the colonists, from arbitrary taxation. Since they felt they were not represented, Parliament, in their eyes, gave them no protection.

By 1776, the colonists and their representatives in the Second Continental Congress realized that things were past the point of no return. The **Declaration of Independence** was drafted and declared July 4, 1776. George Washington labored against tremendous odds to wage a victorious war. During the winter of 1777–78, George Washington's troops were encamped at Valley Forge, Pennsylvania. Weather conditions were very bad and the soldiers suffered from a lack of adequate clothing and supplies. It was during this time that Baron von Steuben trained the American troops to help turn them into more of a disciplined army. The turning point in the Americans' favor occurred in 1777 with the American victory at Saratoga. General Francis Marion, who was known as the Swamp Fox, and his soldiers fought guerilla warfare in the South Carolina area and drove the British from the area. In 1779, John Paul Jones won an important naval victory over the British, capturing the British ship Serapis. This victory led to the French to aligning themselves with the Americans against the British. With the aid of Admiral deGrasse and French warships blocking the entrance to Chesapeake Bay, British General Cornwallis was trapped at Yorktown, Virginia, and surrendered in 1781, ending the war. The Treaty of Paris officially ending the war was signed in 1783.

During the war, and after independence was declared, the former colonies now found themselves independent states. The Second Continental Congress conducted the war with representation by delegates from thirteen separate states. Yet the Congress had no power to act for the states or to require them to accept and follow its wishes. A permanent united government was desperately needed. On November 15, 1777, the **Articles of Confederation** were adopted, creating a league of free and independent states.

Skill 2.3   Know the strengths and weaknesses of the Articles of Confederation

Articles of Confederation - This was the first political system under which the newly independent colonies tried to organize themselves. It was drafted after the Declaration of Independence in 1776, was passed by the Continental Congress on November 15, 1777, ratified by the thirteen states, and took effect on March 1, 1781.

The newly independent states were unwilling to give too much power to a national government. They were already fighting Great Britain. They did not want to replace one harsh ruler with another. After many debates, the form of the Articles was accepted. Each state agreed to send delegates to the Congress. Each state had one vote in the Congress. The Articles gave Congress the power to declare war, appoint military officers, and coin money. The Congress was also responsible for foreign affairs. The Articles of Confederation limited the powers of Congress by giving the states final authority. Although Congress could pass laws, at least nine of the thirteen states had to approve a law before it went into effect. Congress could not pass any laws regarding taxes. To get money, Congress had to ask each state for it, but no state could be forced to pay.

Thus, the Articles created a loose alliance among the thirteen states. The national government was weak, in part, because it didn't have a strong chief executive to carry out laws passed by the legislature. This weak national government might have worked if the states had been able to get along with each other. However, many different disputes arose and there was no way of settling them. Thus, the delegates went to meet again to try to fix the Articles; instead, they ended up scrapping them and created a new Constitution that corrected earlier mistakes.

The central government of the new United States of America consisted of a Congress of two to seven delegates from each state, with each state having just one vote. The government under the Articles solved some of the postwar problems but had serious weaknesses. Some of its powers included: borrowing and coining money, directing foreign affairs, declaring war and making peace, building and equipping a navy, regulating weights and measures, and asking the states to supply men and money for an army. The delegates to Congress had no real authority as each state carefully and jealously guarded its own interests and limited powers under the Articles. Also, the delegates to Congress were paid by their states and had to vote as directed by their state legislatures. The serious weaknesses were the lack of power to regulate finances, manage interstate and foreign trade, enforce treaties, and have military power. Something better and more efficient was needed.

In May of 1787, delegates from all states except Rhode Island began meeting in Philadelphia. At first, they met to revise the Articles of Confederation as instructed by Congress; but they soon realized much more was needed. Abandoning the instructions, they set out to write a new Constitution—a new document, the foundation of all government in the United States, and a model for representative government throughout the world.

The first order of business was the agreement among all the delegates that the convention would be kept secret. No discussion of the convention outside of the meeting room would be allowed. They wanted to be able to discuss, argue, and agree among themselves before presenting the completed document to the American people.

The delegates were afraid that if the people were aware of what was taking place before it was completed the entire country would be plunged into argument and dissension. It would be extremely difficult, if not impossible, to settle differences and come to an agreement. Between the official notes kept and the complete notes of future President James Madison, an accurate picture of the events of the Convention is part of the historical record.

The delegates went to Philadelphia representing different areas and different interests. They all agreed on a strong central government, but not one with unlimited powers. They also agreed that no one part of government could control the rest. It would be a republican form of government (sometimes referred to as representative democracy) in which the supreme power was in the hands of the voters who would elect the men who would govern for them.

One of the first serious controversies involved the small states versus the large states over representation in Congress. Virginia's Governor Edmund Randolph proposed that state population determine the number of representatives sent to Congress, also known as the **Virginia Plan**. New Jersey delegate William Paterson countered with what is known as the **New Jersey Plan**, each state having equal representation.

After much argument and debate, the **Great Compromise** was devised, known also as the Connecticut Compromise, as proposed by Roger Sherman. It was agreed that Congress would have two houses. The Senate would have two Senators from each state, giving equal powers in the Senate. The House of Representatives would have its members elected based on each state's population. Both houses could draft bills to debate and vote on with the exception of bills pertaining to money, which must originate in the House of Representatives.

Another controversy involved economic differences between North and South. One concerned the counting of the African slaves for determining representation in the House of Representatives. The southern delegates wanted the slaves to be counted but didn't want them counted to determine taxes to be paid. The northern delegates argued the opposite: count the slaves for taxes but not for representation. The resulting agreement was known as the **"three-fifths" compromise**. Three-fifths of the slaves would be counted for both taxes and determining representation in the House.

The last major compromise, also between North and South, was the **Commerce Compromise**. The economic interests of the northern part of the country were ones of industry and business whereas the South's economic interests were primarily in farming. Northern merchants wanted the government to regulate and control commerce with foreign nations and with the states. Southern planters opposed this idea as they felt that any tariff laws passed would be unfavorable to them.

The acceptable compromise to this dispute was that Congress was given the power to regulate commerce with other nations and the states, including levying tariffs on imports. However, Congress did not have the power to levy tariffs on any exports. This increased Southern concern about the effect it would have on the slave trade. The delegates finally agreed that the importation of slaves would continue for 20 more years with no interference from Congress. Any import tax could not exceed 10 dollars per person. After 1808, Congress would be able to decide whether to prohibit or regulate any further importation of slaves.

Once work was completed and the document was presented, nine states needed to approve for it to go into effect. There was a large amount of discussion, arguing, debating, and haranguing. The opposition had three major objections:

1. The states felt they were being asked to surrender too much power to the national government.
2. The voters did not have enough control and influence over the men who would be elected by them to run the government.
3. The lack of a "bill of rights" guaranteeing hard-won individual freedoms and liberties.

Eleven states finally ratified the document and the new national government went into effect. It was no small feat that the delegates were able to produce a workable document which satisfied all opinions, feelings, and viewpoints. The separation of powers in the three branches of government and the built-in system of checks and balances to keep power balanced, was a stroke of genius. It provided for the individuals and the states, as well as an organized central authority, to keep the new and inexperienced young nation on track.

They created a system of government so flexible that it has continued in its basic form to this day. As Benjamin Franklin said, *"though it may not be the best there is"*; he said that he, *"wasn't sure that it could be possible to create one better"*. A fact which might be true considering that the Constitution has lasted through civil war, foreign wars, economic depression, and social revolution for more than 200 years. It is truly a living document because of its ability to remain wholly intact while allowing itself to be changed with changing times.

Skill 2.4   Know and understand the debate over the ratification of the U.S. Constitution

Ratification of the **U.S. Constitution** was by no means a foregone conclusion. The representative government had powerful enemies, especially those who had seen firsthand the failure of the Articles of Confederation. The strong central government had powerful enemies, including some of the guiding lights of the American Revolution.

Those who wanted to see a strong central government were called **Federalists**, because they wanted to see a federal government reign supreme. Among the leaders of the Federalists were Alexander Hamilton and John Jay. These two, along with James Madison, wrote a series of letters to New York newspapers, urging the state to ratify the Constitution. These became known as the **Federalist Papers**.

In the Anti-Federalist camp were Thomas Jefferson and Patrick Henry. These men and many others like them were worried that a strong national government would descend into the kind of tyranny that they had just worked so hard to abolish. In the same way that they took their name from their foes, they wrote a series of arguments against the Constitution called the **Anti-Federalist Papers.**

In the end, both sides got most of what they wanted. The Federalists got their strong, national government, which was held in place by the famous "checks and balances." The Anti-Federalists got the **Bill of Rights**, the first ten Amendments to the Constitution and a series of laws that protect some of the most basic human rights. The states that were in doubt about ratification of the Constitution signed on when the Bill of Rights was promised.

Skill 2.5   Know the significance of the major political and economic developments of the early Republic

In 1789 the Electoral College unanimously elected George Washington as the first President and the new nation was on its way. One of the most urgent and pressing problems of the new nation's government was to raise money to pay salaries and war debts. The early presidential administrations established much of the form and many of the procedures still present today, including the development of the party system. George Washington, the first U.S. President, established a cabinet form of government with individual advisors who oversee the various functions of the executive branch and advise the President, who makes a final decision. Divisions within his cabinet and within Congress during his administration eventually led to the development of political parties, which Washington, himself, opposed. Washington was also instrumental in establishing the power of the federal government when he rode at the head of militia forces to put down a rebellion in Pennsylvania. Washington was elected to two terms and served from 1789 to 1797.

Washington's Vice President, John Adams, was elected to succeed him. Adams' administration was marked by the new nation's first entanglement in international affairs. Britain and France were at war, with Adams' Federalist Party supporting the British and Vice President Thomas Jefferson's Republican Party supporting the French. The nation was brought nearly to the brink of war with France, but Adams managed to negotiate a treaty that avoided full conflict. In the process, however, he lost the support of his party and was defeated after one term by Thomas Jefferson.

Under President Adams, a minor diplomatic upset occurred with the government of France. By this time, the two major political parties, the Federalists and the Democratic-Republicans, had fully developed. Hamilton and his mostly northern followers had formed the Federalist Party, which favored a strong central government and was sympathetic to Great Britain and its interests. The Democratic-Republican Party had been formed by Jefferson and his mostly Southern followers and they wanted a weak central government and stronger relations with and support of France. In 1798, the Federalists, in control of Congress, passed the **Alien and Sedition Acts**, written to silence vocal opposition. These acts made it a crime to voice any criticism of the President or Congress and unfairly treated all foreigners.

The legislatures of Kentucky and Virginia protested these laws, claiming they attacked freedoms and challenged their constitutionality. These Resolutions stated mainly the states had created the federal government which was considered merely an agent of the states and was limited to certain powers and could be criticized by the states, if warranted. They went further, stating that states' rights included the power to declare any act of Congress null and void if the states felt it unconstitutional. The controversy died down as the Alien and Sedition Acts expired, one by one, but the doctrine of states' rights was not finally settled until the Civil War.

Through the early 1790s, the two parties that developed were led by Jefferson as the Secretary of State and Alexander Hamilton as the Secretary of the Treasury. Jefferson and Hamilton were different in many ways. Not the least was their view on what should be the proper form of government of the United States. This difference helped to shape the parties that formed around them.

Hamilton wanted the federal government to be stronger than the state governments. Jefferson believed that the state governments should be stronger. Hamilton supported the creation of the first Bank of the United States. Jefferson opposed it because he felt that it gave too much power to wealthy investors who would help run it.

Jefferson interpreted the Constitution strictly; he argued that nowhere did the Constitution give the federal government the power to create a national bank. He believed that the common people, especially the farmers, were the backbone of the nation. He thought that the rise of big cities and manufacturing would corrupt American life.

Hamilton interpreted the Constitution much more loosely. He pointed out that the Constitution gave Congress the power to make all laws "necessary and proper" to carry out its duties. He reasoned that since Congress had the right to collect taxes, then Congress had the right to create the bank. Hamilton wanted the government to encourage economic growth. He favored the growth of trade, manufacturing, and the rise of cities as the necessary parts of economic growth. He favored the business leaders and mistrusted the common people.

Up to this point, Hamilton and Jefferson had their disagreements only in private. When Congress began to pass many of Hamilton's ideas and programs, however, Jefferson and his friend, James Madison, decided to organize support for their own views. They moved quietly and very cautiously in the beginning. In 1791, they went to New York telling people that they were just going to study its wildlife.

Actually, Jefferson was more interested in meeting with several important New York politicians such as its governor George Clinton and Aaron Burr, a strong critic of Hamilton. Jefferson asked Clinton and Burr to help defeat Hamilton's program by getting New Yorkers to vote for Jefferson's supporters in the next election. Before long, leaders in other states began to organize support for either Jefferson or Hamilton. Jefferson's supporters called themselves **Democratic-Republicans** (often this was shortened just to Republicans, though, in actuality, it was the forerunner of today's Democratic Party, not the Republican). Hamilton and his supporters were known as **Federalists**, because they favored a strong federal government. The Federalists had the support of the merchants and ship owners in the Northeast and some planters in the South. Small farmers, craft workers, and some of the wealthier landowners supported Jefferson and the Democratic-Republicans.

Early developments occurred in the courts, too. The **Judiciary Act** set up the U.S. **Supreme Court** by providing for a Chief Justice and five associate justices. It also established federal district and circuit courts that had original jurisdiction over serious crimes and appellate jurisdiction over the district courts. The Supreme Court, under **Chief Justice John Marshall,** made extremely significant contributions to the American judiciary. He set or established three basic principles of law, which became the foundation of the judicial system and the federal government:

1. It established the power of judicial review; the right of the Supreme Court to determine the constitutionality of laws passed by Congress.

2. It held that only the Supreme Court had the power to set aside laws passed by state legislatures when they contradicted the U.S. Constitution.
3. It established the Court's right to reverse decisions of state courts that violated the Constitution.

The United States' unintentional and accidental involvement in what was known as the **War of 1812** came about due to the political and economic struggles between France and Great Britain. Napoleon's goal was complete conquest and control of Europe, including and—especially—Great Britain. Although British troops were temporarily driven off the mainland of Europe, the navy still controlled the seas; the seas across which France had to bring the products needed. America traded with both nations, especially with France and its colonies. The British decided to destroy the American trade with France, mainly for two reasons. First, products and goods from the U.S. gave Napoleon what he needed to keep up his struggle with Britain. He and France were the enemy and it was felt that the Americans were aiding the Mother Country's enemy. Second, Britain felt threatened by the increasing strength and success of the U.S. merchant fleet. They were becoming major competitors with the ship owners and merchants in Britain.

The British issued the **Orders in Council** which were a series of measures prohibiting American ships from entering any French ports, not only in Europe but also in India and the West Indies. At the same time, Napoleon began efforts for a coastal blockade of the British Isles. He issued a series of orders prohibiting all nations, including the United States, from trading with the British. He threatened seizure of every ship entering French ports after they stopped at any British port or colony, even threatening to seize every ship inspected by British cruisers or that paid any duties to their government. The British were stopping American ships and impressing American seamen to service on British ships. Americans were outraged.

In 1807, Congress passed the **Embargo Act** forbidding American ships from sailing to foreign ports. It couldn't be completely enforced and it also hurt business and trade in America so it was repealed in 1809. Two additional acts passed by Congress after James Madison became president attempted to regulate trade with other nations and to get Britain and France to remove the restrictions they had put on American shipping. The catch was that whichever nation removed restrictions, the U.S. would agree not to trade with the other one. Napoleon was the first to do this, prompting Madison to issue orders prohibiting trade with Britain, ignoring warnings from the British not to do so. Although Britain eventually rescinded the Orders in Council, war came in June of 1812.

During the war, Americans were divided over not only whether or not it was necessary to even fight, but also over what territories should be fought for and taken. The nation was still young and just not prepared for war. The primary American objective to conquer Canada ended in failure. Two naval victories and one military victory stand out for the United States. Oliver Perry gained control of Lake Erie and Thomas MacDonough fought on Lake Champlain. Both of these naval battles successfully prevented the British invasion of the United States from Canada. Nevertheless, British troops did land below Washington on the Potomac, marched into the city, and burned the public buildings, including the White House. Andrew Jackson's victory at New Orleans was a great morale booster to Americans, giving them the impression the U.S. had won the war. The battle actually took place after Britain and the United States had reached an agreement and it had no impact on the war's outcome.

The war ended Christmas Eve, 1814, with the signing of the Treaty of Ghent. The peace treaty did little for the United States other than bringing peace, releasing prisoners of war, restoring all occupied territory, and setting up a commission to settle boundary disputes with Canada. Interestingly, the war proved to be a turning point in American history.

Previously, European events had profoundly shaped U.S. policies, especially foreign policies. In President Monroe's message to Congress on December 2, 1823, he delivered what we have always called the Monroe Doctrine. The United States was informing the powers of the Old World that the American continents were no longer open to European colonization, and that any effort to extend European political influence into the New World would be considered by the United States "as dangerous to our peace and safety." The United States would not interfere in European wars or internal affairs, and expected Europe to stay out of American affairs.

Skill 2.6   Be knowledgeable about the rise of popular politics during the Jacksonian era

European events had profoundly shaped U.S. policies. After 1815, the U.S. became much more independent from European influence and began to be treated with growing respect by European nations who were impressed by the fact that the young United States showed no hesitancy in going to war with the world's greatest naval power.

The election of Andrew Jackson as President signaled a swing of the political pendulum from government influence of the wealthy, aristocratic Easterners to the interests of the Western farmers and pioneers and the era of the "common man." Jacksonian democracy was a policy of equal political power for all.

After the War of 1812, Henry Clay and supporters favored economic measures that came to be known as the American System. This involved tariffs protecting American farmers and manufacturers from having to compete with foreign products, stimulating industrial growth and employment. With more people working, more farm products would be consumed, prosperous farmers would be able to buy more manufactured goods, and the additional monies from tariffs would make it possible for the government to make the needed internal improvements. To get all of this going, in 1816, Congress not only passed a high tariff, but also chartered a second Bank of the United States. Upon becoming President, Jackson fought to get rid of the bank.

One of the many duties of the bank was to regulate the supply of money for the nation. The President believed that the bank was a monopoly that favored the wealthy. Congress voted in 1832 to renew the bank's charter but Jackson vetoed the bill, withdrew the government's money, and the bank finally collapsed.

Jackson also faced the "null and void," or nullification issue from South Carolina. Congress, in 1828, passed a law placing high tariffs on goods imported into the United States. Southerners, led by South Carolina's then Vice-President of the U.S., John C. Calhoun, felt that the tariff favored the manufacturing interests of New England and denounced it as an abomination, claiming that any state could nullify any of the federal laws it considered unconstitutional. The tariff was lowered in 1832, but not low enough to satisfy South Carolina, which promptly threatened to secede from the Union. Although Jackson agreed with the rights of states, he also believed in preservation of the Union. A year later, the tariffs were lowered and the crisis was averted.

Skill 2.7   Describe the origins and accomplishments of the antebellum reform movements

Many social reform movements began during this period, including education, women's rights, labor and working conditions, temperance, prisons, and insane asylums. But the most intense and controversial was the abolitionists' efforts to end slavery, an effort alienating and splitting the country, hardening the South's defense of slavery, and leading to four years of bloody war. The abolitionist movement had political fallout, affecting admission of states into the Union and the government's continued efforts to keep a balance between total numbers of free and slave states. Congressional legislation after 1820 reflected this.

The **Industrial Revolution** had spread from Great Britain to the United States. Before 1800, most manufacturing activities were done in small shops or in homes. However, starting in the early 1800s, factories with modern machines were built, making it easier to produce goods faster. The eastern part of the country became a major industrial area although some developed in the West. At about the same time, improvements began to be made in building roads, railroads, canals, and steamboats. The increased ease of travel facilitated the westward movement as well as boosted the economy with faster and cheaper shipment of goods and products, covering larger and larger areas. Some of the innovations included the Erie Canal connecting the interior and the Great Lakes with the Hudson River and the coastal port of New York. Many other natural waterways were connected by canals.

Robert Fulton's **Clermont**, the first commercially successful steamboat, led the way in commercial shipping, thus making the steamboat one of the most important ways to ship goods at the time. Later, steam-powered railroads soon became the biggest rival of the steamboat as a means of shipping, and, eventually, became the most important transportation method opening the West. With expansion into the interior of the country, the United States became the leading agricultural nation in the world. The hardy pioneer farmers produced a vast surplus and emphasis went to producing products with a high-sale value. Implements such as the cotton gin and reaper aided in production efficiencies. Travel and shipping were greatly assisted in areas not yet touched by railroad or, by improved or new roads, such as the National Road in the East and in the West the Oregon and Santa Fe Trails. It was the railroad, however, that sped communications and settlement of the West after the Civil War.

People were exposed to works of literature, art, newspapers, drama, live entertainment, and political rallies. With better communication and travel, more information was desired about previously unknown areas of the country, especially the West. The discovery of gold and other mineral wealth resulted in a literal surge of settlers and even more interest.

More industries and factories required more and more labor. Women, children, and, at times, entire families worked the long hours and days, until the 1830s. By that time, the factories were getting even larger and employers began hiring immigrants who were coming to America in huge numbers. Before then, efforts were made to organize a labor movement to improve working conditions and increase wages. It never really caught on until after the Civil War, but the seed had been sown, and the labor union movement gained momentum after the Civil War.

Public schools were established in many of the states with more and more children being educated. With more literacy and more participation in literature and the arts, the young nation was developing its own unique culture becoming less and less influenced by and dependent on that of Europe.

Horace Mann grew up a poor child with little opportunity for education except for his small community library. He took full advantage of it, however, and was admitted to Brown University, from which he graduated in 1819. Mann practiced law for several years and served in the Massachusetts House of Representatives. He served on the committee of the first school funded by public tax dollars in Dedham, Massachusetts, and, in 1837, was appointed secretary to the newly formed State Board of Education. Mann became an outspoken proponent of educational reform, and fought for better resources for schools and teachers. Mann planned the Massachusetts Normal School system for training new teachers. The compulsory public education that is taken for granted today was a new idea in antebellum America, and Mann faced opposition to his ideas.

Shortly after Massachusetts adopted this system, New York followed suit, laying the foundation for the present state-based educational system.

Dorothea Dix was an advocate for public treatment and care for the mentally ill. In the early 1840s, Dix called attention to the deplorable treatment and conditions to which the mentally ill in Massachusetts were subjected in a pamphlet entitled *Memorial.* Her efforts resulted in a bill that expanded the state hospital. Dix traveled to several other states, encouraging and overseeing the founding of state mental hospitals. Dix proposed federal legislation that would have sold public land with the proceeds being distributed to the states to fund care for the mentally ill. The legislation was approved by Congress, however, using public money for social welfare was a contentious issue, and President Franklin Pierce vetoed it on these grounds.

The **Seneca Falls Convention** was a gathering of women and men in 1848, in the New York mill town of Seneca Falls, to address the rights of women in the United States. The growing momentum of the anti-slavery movement and discussion over the rights of black citizens had drawn attention to the rights of female citizens, who could not vote or hold important positions in American government. Some 300 people attended the convention, which culminated in the publication of a "Declaration of Sentiments," which was modeled on the Declaration of Independence and called for equal participation for women. The Seneca Falls Convention is considered an early milestone in the feminist movement.

The following is just a partial list of well-known Americans who contributed their leadership and talents in various fields and reforms:

- Lucretia Mott and Elizabeth Cady Stanton for **women's rights**
- Emma Hart Willard, Catharine Esther Beecher, and Mary Lyon for **education for women**
- Dr. Elizabeth Blackwell, the **first woman doctor**
- Antoinette Louisa Blackwell, the **first female minister**
- Dorothea Lynde Dix for **reforms in prisons and insane asylums**
- Elihu Burritt and William Ladd for **peace movements**
- Robert Owen for a **Utopian society**
- Horace Mann, Henry Barmard, Calvin E. Stowe, Caleb Mills, and John Swett for **public education**
- Benjamin Lundy, David Walker, William Lloyd Garrison, Isaac Hooper, Arthur and Lewis Tappan, Theodore Weld, Frederick Douglass, Harriet Tubman, James G. Birney, Henry Highland Garnet, James Forten, Robert Purvis, Harriet Beecher Stowe, Wendell Phillips, and John Brown for **abolition of slavery and the Underground Railroad**
- Louisa Mae Alcott, James Fenimore Cooper, Washington Irving, Walt Whitman, Henry David Thoreau, Ralph Waldo Emerson, Herman Melville,

Richard Henry Dana, Nathaniel Hawthorne, Henry Wadsworth Longfellow, John Greenleaf Whittier, Edgar Allan Poe, Oliver Wendell Holmes, **famous writers**

- John C. Fremont, Zebulon Pike, Kit Carson, **explorers**
- Henry Clay, Daniel Webster, Stephen Douglas, John C. Calhoun, American **statesmen**
- Robert Fulton, Cyrus McCormick, Eli Whitney, **inventors**
- Noah Webster, American **dictionary and spellers**

The list goes on but the contributions of these and many, many others greatly enhanced the unique American culture.

COMPETENCY 3.0   WESTWARD EXPANSION, THE CIVIL WAR, AND RECONSTRUCTION

Skill 3.1   Understand the key events and issues related to westward expansion

As the nation extended its borders into the lands west of the Mississippi, thousands of settlers streamed into this part of the country bringing with them ideas and concepts adapting them to the development of the unique characteristics of the region. Equality for everyone, as stated in the Declaration of Independence, did not yet apply to minority groups, black Americans, or American Indians. Voting rights and the right to hold public office were restricted, in varying degrees, in each state. All of these factors decidedly affected the political, economic, and social life of the country and all three were focused in the attitudes of the three sections of the country on slavery.

After the U.S. purchased the Louisiana Territory from France in 1803 under the terms of the **Louisiana Purchase**, Jefferson appointed Captains Meriwether Lewis and William Clark to explore it, in order to find out exactly what had been bought. With the help of local guides, including a Native American woman named **Sacagawea**, the expedition went all the way to the Pacific Ocean. Having been presumed long since dead, Lewis and Clark returned two years later with maps, journals, and artifacts. This led the way for future explorers to make available more knowledge about the territory and resulted in the Westward Movement and the later belief in the doctrine of Manifest Destiny.

The Red River cession was the next acquisition of land and came about as part of a treaty with Great Britain in 1818. It included parts of North and South Dakota and Minnesota. In 1819, Florida, both East and West, was ceded to the U.S. by Spain along with parts of Alabama, Mississippi, and Louisiana. Texas was annexed in 1845 and after the war with Mexico in 1848, the government paid $15 million for what would become the states of California, Utah, and Nevada, and parts of four other states.

In 1846, the **Oregon Country** was ceded to the U.S., which extended the western border to the Pacific Ocean. The northern U.S. boundary was established at the 49th parallel. The states of Idaho, Oregon, and Washington were formed from this territory. In 1853, the **Gadsden Purchase** rounded out the present boundary of the 48 conterminous states with payment to Mexico of $10 million for land that makes up the present states of New Mexico and Arizona.

Westward expansion occurred for a number of reasons, the most important being economic. Cotton had become most important to the people who lived in the southern states. The effects of the Industrial Revolution, which began in England, were now being felt in the United States. With the invention of power-driven machines, the demand for cotton fiber greatly increased the yarn needed in spinning and weaving. Eli Whitney's cotton gin made the separation of the seeds from the cotton much more efficient and faster. This, in turn, increased the demand and more farmers became involved in the raising and selling of cotton.

The innovations and developments of better methods of long-distance transportation moved the cotton in greater quantities to textile mills in England as well as the areas of New England and Middle Atlantic States in the U.S. As prices increased along with increased demand, southern farmers began expanding by clearing increasingly more land to grow cotton. Movement, settlement, and farming headed west to utilize the fertile soils. This, in turn, demanded increased need for a large supply of cheap labor. The system of slavery expanded, both in numbers and in the movement to lands "west" of the South.

Cotton farmers and slave owners were not the only ones heading west. Many, in other fields of economic endeavor, began the migration: trappers, miners, merchants, ranchers, and others were all seeking their fortunes. The Lewis and Clark expedition stimulated the westward push. Fur companies hired men, known as "Mountain Men", to go westward, searching for animal pelts to supply the market and meet the demands of the East and Europe. These men explored and discovered the many passes and trails that would eventually be used by settlers in their trek to the west. The California gold rush also had a very large influence on the movement west.

There were also religious reasons for westward expansion. Increased settlement was encouraged by missionaries who traveled west with the fur traders. They sent word back east for more settlers and the results were tremendous. By the 1840s, the population increases in the Oregon country alone were at a rate of about a thousand people a year. People of many different religions and cultures, as well as Southerners with black slaves, made their way west which leads to a third reason for westward migration: political.

It was the belief of many that the United States was destined to control all of the land between the two oceans, or as one newspaper editor termed it, "**Manifest Destiny**." This mass migration westward put the U.S. government on a collision course with the Indians, Great Britain, Spain, and Mexico. The fur traders and missionaries ran against the Indians in the Northwest and the claims of Great Britain for Oregon country. The U.S. and Britain had shared the Oregon country up until this time, but by the 1840s, with increases in the free and slave populations and the demand from settlers for control of government by the U.S., the conflict had to be resolved. In a treaty, signed in 1846 by both nations, a peaceful resolution occurred with Britain giving up its claims south of the 49th parallel.

In the American Southwest, the results were exactly the opposite. Spain had claimed this area since the 1540s, had spread northward from Mexico City, and, in the 1700s, had established missions, forts, villages, towns, and very large ranches. After the purchase of the Louisiana Territory in 1803, Americans began moving into Spanish territory. A few hundred American families in what is now Texas were allowed to live there, but had to agree to become loyal subjects to Spain. In 1821, Mexico successfully revolted against Spanish rule, won independence, and chose to be more tolerant towards the American settlers and traders. The Mexican government encouraged and allowed extensive trade and settlement, especially in Texas. Many of the new settlers were southerners and brought their slaves with them. Slavery was outlawed in Mexico and technically illegal in Texas, although the Mexican government looked the other way.

With the influx of so many Americans and the liberal policies of the Mexican government, there came to be concern over the possible growth and development of an American state within Mexico. Settlement restrictions, cancellation of land grants, the forbidding of slavery, and increased military activity brought everything to a head. The order of events included the fight for Texas independence, the brief Republic of Texas, eventual annexation of Texas, statehood, and finally **war with Mexico**. The Texas controversy was not the sole reason for war. Since American settlers had begun pouring into the Southwest, cultural differences played a prominent role. Language, religion, law, customs, and government were opposite between the two groups. A clash was bound to occur.

The impact of the entire westward movement resulted in the completion of the borders of the present-day conterminous United States; the bloody war with Mexico; the ever-growing controversy over slave versus free states affecting the balance of power or influence in the U.S. Congress, especially the Senate; and finally, the Civil War itself.

Skill 3.2   Describe the differences between the northern and southern economic systems and way of life

See Skill 3.3

Skill 3.3   Show an understanding of the sources of sectional conflict

In between the growing economy, expansion westward of the population, and improvements in travel and mass communication, the federal government did face periodic financial depressions. Contributing to these downward spirals were land speculations, availability and soundness of money and currency, failed banks, failing businesses, and unemployment. Sometimes conditions outside the nation would help trigger it; at other times, domestic politics and presidential elections affected it. The growing strength and influence of two major political parties with opposing philosophies and methods of conducting government did not ease matters.

The drafting of the Constitution, as well as its ratification and implementation, united thirteen different, independent states into a union under one central government. The two crucial compromises of the convention delegates concerning slaves pacified Southerners, especially slave owners, but the issue of slavery was not settled and from then on, **sectionalism** became stronger and more apparent, putting the entire country on a collision course.

Slavery in the English colonies began in 1619 when twenty Africans arrived in the colony of Virginia at Jamestown. From then on, slavery had a foothold, especially in the agricultural South, where a large amount of slave labor was needed for the extensive plantations. Free men refused to work for wages on the plantations when land was available for settling on the frontier. Therefore, slave labor was the only recourse left. If it had been profitable to use slaves in New England and the Middle Colonies, then without doubt slavery would have been more widespread. Profit, or the lack thereof, confined slavery to the South.

The West was involved in the controversy of slavery as well as the North and South. By 1860, the country was made up of these three major regions. The people in all three sections or regions had a number of beliefs and institutions in common. Of course, there were major differences with each region having its own unique characteristics. The basic problem was their development occurred along very different lines.

The North was industrial with towns and factories growing and increasing at a very fast rate. The South had become agricultural, eventually becoming increasingly dependent on the one crop of cotton. In the West, restless pioneers moved into new frontiers seeking land, wealth, and opportunity. Many were from the South and were slave owners, bringing their slaves with them. So, between these three different parts of the country, the views on tariffs, public lands, internal improvements at federal expense, banking and currency, and the issue of slavery were decidedly different, to say the least.

This period of U.S. history was one of compromises, breakdowns of the compromises, desperate attempts to restore and retain harmony among the three sections, short-lived intervals of the uneasy balance of interests, and ever-increasing conflict.

At the Constitutional Convention, one of the slavery compromises concerned counting slaves for deciding the number of representatives for the House and the amount of taxes to be paid. Southerners pushed for counting the slaves for representation but not for taxes. The Northerners pushed for the opposite. The resulting compromise, sometimes referred to as the **"three-fifths compromise,"** was that both groups agreed that three-fifths of the slaves would be counted for both taxes and representation.

The other compromise involving slavery was part of the dispute over how much regulation the central government would control of commercial activities, such as trade with other nations and the slave trade. It was agreed that Congress would regulate commerce with other nations including taxing imports. Southerners were worried about taxing slaves coming into the country and the possibility of Congress prohibiting the slave trade altogether. The agreement reached allowed the states to continue importation of slaves for the next twenty years until 1808, at which time Congress would make the decision as to the future of the slave trade. During the 20-year period, no more than $10 per person could be levied on slaves coming into the country.

These two slavery compromises were a necessary concession to have Southern support as well as approval for the new document and new government. Many Americans felt that the system of slavery would eventually die out in the U.S., but by 1808, cotton was becoming increasingly important in the primarily agricultural South and the institution of slavery had become firmly entrenched in Southern culture. It is also evident that as early as the Constitutional Convention, active anti-slavery feelings and opinions were very strong, leading to extremely active groups and societies.

As the nation extended its borders into lands west of the Mississippi, thousands of settlers streamed into the West and brought their ideas and adapted them to the development of the unique characteristics of the region. Equality for everyone, as stated in the Declaration of Independence, did not yet apply to minority groups, black Americans, or American Indians. Voting rights and the right to hold public office were restricted in varying degrees in each state. All of these factors decidedly affected the political, economic, and social life of the country and all three were focused in the attitudes of the three sections of the country on slavery.

The first serious clash between the North and South occurred from 1819 to1820, when James Monroe was in office as President, and it was over whether or not Missouri should be admitted as a state. In 1819, the U.S. consisted of 21 states: 11 free states and 10 slave states. Alabama was admitted as a slave state which consequently balanced the Senate with the North and South, each having twenty-two senators. Missouri petitioned for statehood in 1819. The Missouri Territory allowed slavery, and if Missouri were admitted, it would cause an imbalance in the number of U.S. Senators. The first **Missouri Compromise** resolved the conflict by approving admission of Maine as a free state along with Missouri as a slave state, thus continuing to keep a balance of power in the Senate with the same number of free and slave states.

An additional provision of this compromise was that with the admission of Missouri, slavery would not be allowed in the rest of the Louisiana Purchase territory north of latitude 36 degrees 30'. This was acceptable to the Southern Congressmen since it was not profitable to grow cotton on land north of this latitude line anyway. It was thought that the crisis had been resolved but in the next year, Missouri drafted its state constitution and included a provision that discriminated against the free blacks. Anti-slavery supporters in Congress wanted to exclude Missouri from the Union. Henry Clay, known as the **Great Compromiser**, then proposed a second Missouri Compromise which was acceptable to everyone. His proposal stated that the Constitution of the United States guaranteed protections and privileges to citizens of states and that Missouri's proposed constitution could not deny these rights to any of its citizens. The acceptance in 1820 of this second compromise opened the way for Missouri's statehood in 1821. The second compromise was only a temporary reprieve.

The issue of tariffs also was a divisive factor during this period, especially between 1829 and 1833. The Embargo Act of 1807 and the War of 1812 had completely cut off the source of manufactured goods for Americans, so it was necessary to build factories to produce what was needed. After 1815 when the war had ended, Great Britain proceeded to get rid of its industrial rivals by unloading its goods in America. To protect and encourage its own industries and their products, Congress passed the Tariff of 1816, which required high duties to be levied on manufactured goods coming into the United States. Southern leaders, such as John C. Calhoun of South Carolina, supported the tariff with the assumption that the South would develop its own industries.

For a about a ten year period (from 1815 to 1825), after the War of 1812, the nation enjoyed the **"Era of Good Feelings."** People were moving into the West; industry and agriculture were growing; a feeling of national pride united Americans in their efforts and determination to strengthen the country. However, over-speculation in stocks and lands for quick profits backfired. Cotton prices were rising so many Southerners bought land for cultivation at inflated prices. Manufacturers in the industrial North purchased land to build more plants and factories as an attempt to have a part of this prosperity. Settlers in the West rushed to buy land to reap the benefits of the increasing prices of meat and grain. To have the money for all of these economic activities, all of these groups were borrowing heavily from the banks and the banks themselves encouraged this by giving loans on inadequate security.

In late 1818, the Bank of the United States and its branches stopped renewal of personal mortgages and required state banks to immediately pay their bank notes in gold, silver, or in national bank notes. The state banks were unable to do this so they closed their doors and were unable to do any business at all. Since mortgages could not be renewed, people lost all their properties and foreclosures ran rampant throughout the country. At the same time, as all of this was occurring, cotton prices collapsed in the English market. Its high price had caused the British manufacturers to seek cheaper cotton from India for their textile mills. With the fall of cotton prices, the demand for American manufactured goods declined, revealing how fragile the economic prosperity had been.

In 1824, a higher tariff was passed by Congress, favoring the financial interests of the manufacturers in New England and the Middle Atlantic States. In addition, the 1824 tariff was closely tied to the presidential election of that year. Before the tariff was enacted into law, Calhoun had proposed the very high tariffs in an effort to get Eastern business interests to vote with the agricultural interests in the South (who were against it) with supporters of candidate Andrew Jackson siding with whichever side served their best interests. Jackson himself would not be involved in any of this scheming.

The bill became law, to Calhoun's surprise, due mainly to the political maneuverings of Martin van Buren and Daniel Webster. By the time the higher 1828 tariff was passed, feelings were extremely bitter in the South, where the populace believed that the New England manufacturers would greatly benefit from it. Vice-President Calhoun, also speaking for his home state of South Carolina, promptly declared that if any state felt that a federal law was unconstitutional, that state could nullify it. In 1832, Congress took the action of lowering the tariffs to a degree but not enough to please South Carolina, which promptly declared the tariff null and void, threatening to secede from the Union.

In 1833, Congress lowered the tariffs again, this time to a level acceptable to South Carolina. Although President Jackson believed in states' rights, he also firmly believed in and was determined to preserve the Union. A constitutional crisis had been averted but sectional divisions were becoming deeper and more pronounced. The **abolition movement** was growing rapidly, becoming an important issue in the North. The slavery issue was at the root of every problem, crisis, event, decision, and struggle from then on.

The next crisis involved the issue concerning Texas. By 1836, Texas was an independent republic with its own constitution. During its fight for independence, Americans were sympathetic to and supportive of the Texans and some recruited volunteers who crossed into Texas to help the struggle. Problems arose when the state petitioned Congress for statehood. Texas wanted to allow slavery but Northerners in Congress opposed the admission of Texas to the Union because it would disrupt the balance between free and slave states and give Southerners in Congress increased influence. There were others who believed that granting statehood to Texas would lead to a war with Mexico, which had refused to recognize Texas' independence. For the time being, Texas statehood was put on hold.

Friction increased between land-hungry Americans swarming into western lands and the Mexican government, which controlled these lands. The clash was not only political but also cultural and economic. The Spanish influence permeated all parts of southwestern life: law, language, architecture, and customs. By this time, the doctrine of Manifest Destiny was in the hearts and on the lips of those seeking new areas of settlement and a new life. Americans were demanding U.S. control of not only the Mexican Territory but, also, Oregon. Peaceful negotiations with Great Britain secured Oregon but it took two years of war to gain control of the southwestern U.S.

In addition, the Mexican government owed debts to U.S. citizens whose property was damaged or destroyed during its struggle for independence from Spain. By the time war broke out in 1845, Mexico had not paid its war debts. The government was weak, corrupt, irresponsible, torn by revolutions, and not in decent financial shape. Mexico was also bitter over American expansion into Texas and the 1836 Revolution, which resulted in Texas independence. In the 1844 Presidential election, the Democrats pushed for annexation of Texas and Oregon. After winning, they started the procedure to admit Texas into Union.

When statehood occurred, diplomatic relations between the U.S. and Mexico ended. President Polk wanted U.S. control of the entire Southwest, from Texas to the Pacific Ocean. He sent a diplomatic mission with an offer to purchase New Mexico and Upper California but the Mexican government refused to even receive the diplomat. Consequently, in 1846, each nation claimed aggression on the part of the other and war was declared. The treaty signed in 1848 and a subsequent one in 1853 completed the southwestern boundary of the United States, reaching to the Pacific Ocean, as President Polk wished.

The slavery issue flared again and would not to be done away with until the end of the Civil War. It was obvious that the newly acquired territory would be divided up into territories that would later become states. In addition to the two factions of Northerners who advocated prohibition of slavery and of Southerners who favored slavery existing there, a third faction arose supporting the doctrine of "popular sovereignty" which stated that people living in territories and states should be allowed to decide for themselves whether or not slavery should be permitted. In 1849, California applied for admittance into the Union and the furor began.

The result was the **Compromise of 1850**, a series of laws designed as a final solution to the slavery issue. Concessions made to the North included the admission of California as a free state and the abolition of slave trading in Washington, D.C. The laws also provided for the creation of the New Mexico and Utah territories. As a concession to Southerners, the residents there would decide whether to permit slavery when these two territories became states. In addition, Congress authorized implementation of stricter measures to capture runaway slaves.

A few years later, Congress took up consideration of new territories between Missouri and present-day Idaho. Again, heated debate over permitting slavery in these areas flared up. Those opposed to slavery used the Missouri Compromise to prove their point showing that the land being considered for territories was part of the area the Compromise had designated as banned to slavery. But on May 25, 1854, Congress passed the infamous **Kansas-Nebraska Act** which nullified this provision, created the territories of Kansas and Nebraska, and provided for the people of these two territories to decide for themselves whether or not to permit slavery to exist there. Feelings were so deep and divided that any further attempts to compromise would meet with little, if any, success. Political and social turmoil swirled everywhere. Kansas was called "Bleeding Kansas" because of the extreme violence and bloodshed throughout the territory because two governments existed there, one pro-slavery and the other anti-slavery.

Skill 3.4   Understand issues and events leading to the secession crisis

In 1857 the Supreme Court handed down a decision guaranteed to cause explosions throughout the country. **Dred Scott** was a slave whose owner had taken him from slave state Missouri, then to free state Illinois, into Minnesota Territory, free under the provisions of the Missouri Compromise, then, finally, back to Missouri. Abolitionists pursued the dilemma by presenting a court case, stating that since Scott had lived in a free state and free territory, he was in actuality a free man. Two lower courts had ruled before the Supreme Court became involved, one ruling in favor and one against freedom for Scott. The Supreme Court decided that residing in a free state and free territory did not make Scott a free man because Scott and all other slaves were not U.S. citizens and Scott was not a state citizen of Missouri. Therefore, he did not have the right to sue in state or federal courts. The Court went a step further and ruled that the old Missouri Compromise was now unconstitutional because Congress did not have the power to prohibit slavery in the territories.

Anti-slavery supporters were stunned. They had just recently formed the new Republican Party and one of its platforms was keeping slavery out of the territories. Now, according to the decision in the Dred Scott case, this basic party principle was unconstitutional. The only way to ban slavery in new areas was by a Constitutional amendment, requiring ratification by three-fourths of all states. At this time, this was out of the question because the supporters would be unable to get a majority due to Southern opposition.

In 1858, **Abraham Lincoln** and Stephen A. Douglas were running for the office of U.S. Senator from Illinois and participated in a series of debates, which directly affected the outcome of the 1860 Presidential Election. Douglas, a Democrat, was up for re-election and knew that if he won this race, he had a good chance of becoming President in 1860. Lincoln, a Republican, was not an abolitionist but he believed that slavery was wrong morally and he firmly believed in and supported the Republican Party principle that slavery must not be allowed to extend any further.

Douglas, on the other hand, originated the doctrine of "popular sovereignty" and was responsible for supporting and getting through Congress the inflammatory Kansas-Nebraska Act. In the course of the debates, Lincoln challenged Douglas to show that popular sovereignty reconciled with the Dred Scott decision. Either way he answered Lincoln, Douglas would lose crucial support from one group or the other. If he supported the Dred Scott decision, Southerners would support him but he would lose Northern support. If he stayed with popular sovereignty, Northern support would be his but Southern support would be lost. His reply to Lincoln, stating that territorial legislatures could exclude slavery by refusing to pass laws supporting it, gave him enough support and approval to be re-elected to the Senate, but cost him the Democratic nomination for President in 1860.

Southerners came to the realization that Douglas supported and was devoted to popular sovereignty but not necessarily to the expansion of slavery. On the other hand, two years later, Lincoln received the nomination of the Republican Party for President.

In 1859, abolitionist **John Brown** and his followers seized the federal arsenal at Harper's Ferry in what is now West Virginia. His purpose was to take the guns stored in the arsenal, give them to nearby slaves, and lead them in a widespread rebellion. He and his men were captured by Colonel Robert E. Lee of the United States Army. After his trial ended with a guilty verdict, Brown was hanged. Most Southerners felt that the majority of Northerners approved of Brown's actions but, in actuality, most of them were stunned and shocked. Southern newspapers took great pains to quote a small but well-known minority of abolitionists who applauded and supported Brown's actions. This merely served to widen the gap between the two sections.

The final straw came with the election of Lincoln to the presidency the next year. Due to a split in the Democratic Party, there were four candidates from four political parties. With Lincoln receiving a minority of the popular vote and a majority of electoral votes, the Southern states, one by one, voted to secede from the Union as they had promised they would do if Lincoln and the Republicans were victorious. The die was cast.

As 1860 began, the nation had extended its borders north, south, and west. Industry and agriculture were flourishing. Although the U.S. did not involve itself actively in European affairs, the relationship with Great Britain was much improved and it and other nations that dealt with the young nation accorded it more respect and admiration. Nevertheless, the country was deeply divided along political lines concerning slavery and the election of Abraham Lincoln. War was on the horizon.

The colonies had won independence and written a Constitution forming a union of those states under a central government. A newly formed United States had fought wars and signed treaties, purchased and explored vast areas of land. It had developed industry and agriculture, improved transportation, and seen the population expand westward. It had increased the number of states admitted to the Union annually. Despite all that, one issue remained: the issue of human slavery had to be settled once and for all. One historian has stated that before

1865, the nation referred to itself as "the United States are...." but after 1865, "the United States is..." It took the Civil War to finally, completely unify all states into one Union.

Skill 3.5   Be able to recall significant leaders, strategies, battles and turning points of the Civil War

South Carolina was the first state to **secede** from the Union and the first shots of the war were fired on Fort Sumter in Charleston Harbor. Both sides quickly prepared for war. The North had the advantage: a larger population; superiority in finances and transportation facilities; manufacturing, agricultural, and natural resources. The North possessed most of the nation's gold, had about 92% of all industries, and almost all known supplies of copper, coal, iron, and various other minerals. Since most of the nation's railroads were in the North and mid-West, men and supplies could be moved wherever needed; food could be transported from the farms of the mid-West to workers in the East and to soldiers on the battlefields. Trade with nations overseas could go on as usual due to control of the navy and the merchant fleet. The Northern states numbered 24 and included western (California and Oregon) and border (Maryland, Delaware, Kentucky, Missouri, and West Virginia) states.

The Southern states numbered eleven and included South Carolina, Georgia, Florida, Alabama, Mississippi, Louisiana, Texas, Virginia, North Carolina, Tennessee, and Arkansas, making up the Confederacy. Although outnumbered in population, the South was completely confident of victory. They knew that all they had to do was fight a defensive war, protecting their own territory until the North, who had to invade and defeat an area almost the size of Western Europe, was tired of the struggle and gave up. Another advantage of the South was that a number of its best officers had graduated from the U.S. Military Academy at West Point and had had long years of army experience, some even exercising varying degrees of command in the Indian wars and the war with Mexico. Men from the South were conditioned to living outdoors and were more familiar with horses and firearms than many men from Northeastern cities. Since cotton was such an important crop, Southerners felt that British and French textile mills were so dependent on raw cotton that they would be forced to help the Confederacy in the war.

The South had specific reasons and goals for fighting the war—more so than the North. The major aim of the Confederacy never wavered: to win independence, the right to govern themselves as they wished, and to preserve slavery. The Northerners were not as clear in their reasons for conducting war. At the beginning, most believed, along with Lincoln, that preservation of the Union was paramount. Only a few extremely fanatical abolitionists looked on the war as a way to end slavery. However, by war's end, more and more northerners had come to believe that freeing the slaves was just as important as restoring the Union.

The war strategies for both sides were relatively clear and simple. The South planned a defensive war, wearing down the North until it agreed to peace on Southern terms. The exception was to gain control of Washington, D.C., go north through the Shenandoah Valley into Maryland and Pennsylvania in order to drive a wedge between the Northeast and mid-West, interrupt the lines of communication, and end the war quickly. The North had three basic strategies:

1. Blockade the Confederate coastline in order to cripple the South.
2. Seize control of the Mississippi River and interior railroad lines to split the Confederacy in two.
3. Seize the Confederate capital of Richmond, Virginia, then driving southward to join up with Union forces coming east from the Mississippi Valley.

The South won decisively until the Battle of Gettysburg, July 1–3, 1863. Prior to Gettysburg, Lincoln's commanders, **McDowell and McClellan**, were less than desirable, and **Burnside and Hooker** had not been what was needed. **Lee**, on the other hand, had many able officers, **Jackson and Stuart** were depended on heavily by him. Jackson died at Chancellorsville and was replaced by **Longstreet**. Lee decided to invade the North and depended on **J.E.B. Stuart** and his cavalry to keep him informed of the location of Union troops and their strengths. Four things worked against Lee at Gettysburg:

1. The Union troops gained the best positions and the best ground first, making it easier to make a stand there.
2. Lee's move into Northern territory put him and his army a long way from food and supply lines. They were more or less on their own.
3. Lee thought that his Army of Northern Virginia was invincible and could fight and win under any conditions or circumstances.
4. Stuart and his men did not arrive at Gettysburg until the end of the second day of fighting and by then, it was too little too late. He and the men had had to detour around Union soldiers and he was delayed getting the information Lee needed.

Consequently, Lee made the mistake of failing to listen to Longstreet and followed the strategy of regrouping back into Southern territory to the supply lines. Lee felt that regrouping was retreating and almost an admission of defeat. He was convinced the army would be victorious. Longstreet was concerned about the Union troops occupying the best positions and felt that regrouping to a better position would be an advantage. He was also very concerned about the distance from supply lines.

It was not the intention of either side to fight there but the fighting began when a Confederate brigade stumbled into a unit of Union cavalry while looking for shoes. On the third and last day, Lee launched the final attempt to break Union lines. **General George Pickett** sent his division of three brigades under Generals

Garnet, Kemper, and Armistead against Union troops on Cemetery Ridge under command of General Winfield Scott Hancock. Union lines held and Lee and the defeated Army of Northern Virginia made their way back to Virginia. Although Lincoln's commander George Meade successfully turned back a Confederate charge, he and the Union troops failed to pursue Lee and the Confederates. This battle was the turning point for the North. After this, Lee never again had the troop strength to launch a major offensive.

The day after Gettysburg, on July 4, Vicksburg, Mississippi surrendered to Union **General Ulysses Grant**, thus severing the western Confederacy from the eastern part. In September 1863, the Confederacy won its last important victory at Chickamauga. In November, the Union victory at Chattanooga made it possible for Union troops to go into Alabama and Georgia, splitting the eastern Confederacy in two. Lincoln gave Grant command of all Northern armies in March of 1864. Grant led his armies into battles in Virginia while Phil Sheridan and his cavalry did as much damage as possible. In a skirmish at a place called Yellow Tavern, Virginia, Sheridan's and Stuart's forces met, with Stuart being fatally wounded. The Union won the Battle of Mobile Bay and in May 1864, **William Tecumseh Sherman** began his march to successfully demolish Atlanta, then his troops moved on to Savannah. He and his troops turned northward through the Carolinas to meet Grant in Virginia. On April 9, 1865, Lee formally surrendered to Grant at **Appomattox Courthouse**, Virginia.

The Civil War took more American lives than any other war in history. The South lost one-third of its soldiers in battle compared to about one-sixth for the North. More than half of the total deaths were caused by disease and the horrendous conditions of field hospitals. Both sections paid a tremendous economic price but the South suffered more severely from direct damages. Destruction was pervasive with towns, farms, trade, industry, lives and homes of men, women, children all destroyed and an entire Southern way of life was lost. The deep resentment, bitterness, and hatred that remained for generations gradually lessened as the years went by but legacies of it surface and remain to this day. The South had no voice in the political, social, and cultural affairs of the nation, lessening to a great degree the influence of the more traditional Southern ideals. The Northern Yankee Protestant ideals of hard work, education, and economic freedom became the standard of the United States and helped influence the development of the nation into a modem industrial power.

The effects of the Civil War were tremendous. It changed the methods of waging war and has been called the first modern war. It introduced weapons and tactics that, when improved later, were used extensively in wars of the late 1800s and 1900s. Civil War soldiers were the first to fight in trenches, first to fight under a unified command, first to wage a defense called "major cordon defense," a strategy of advance on all fronts. They were also the first to use repeating and breech loading weapons. Observation balloons were first used during the war along with submarines, ironclad ships, and mines. Telegraphy and railroads were put to use first in the Civil War. It was considered a modern war because of the vast destruction and was a "total war," involving the use of all resources of the opposing sides. There is little possibility it could have ended any way other than the total defeat and unconditional surrender of one side or the other.

By executive proclamation and constitutional amendment, slavery was officially and finally ended. There remained deep prejudice and racism, the vestiges of which still remain today. Also, the Union was preserved and the states were finally truly united. **Sectionalism**, especially in the area of politics, remained strong for another 100 years, but not to the degree of intensity or violence that existed before 1861. It has been noted that the Civil War may have been American democracy's greatest failure as between 1861 to 1865, calm reason, basic to democracy, fell to human passion. However, democracy did survive.

The victory of the North established that no state has the right to end or leave the Union. Because of unity, the U.S. became a major global power. Lincoln never proposed to punish the South. He was most concerned with restoring the South to the Union in a program that was flexible and practical rather than rigid and unbending. In fact, he never really felt that the states had succeeded in leaving the Union but that they had left the 'family circle" for a short time. His plans consisted of two major steps:

All Southerners taking an oath of allegiance to the Union, promising to accept all federal laws and proclamations dealing with slavery, would receive a full pardon. The only ones excluded from this were men who had resigned from civil and military positions in the federal government to serve in the Confederacy, those who were part of the Confederate government, those in the Confederate army above the rank of lieutenant, and Confederates who were guilty of mistreating prisoners of war and blacks.

A state would be able to write a new constitution, elect new officials, and return to the Union fully equal to all other states on certain conditions: a minimum number of persons (at least 10% of those who were qualified voters in their states before secession from the Union who had voted in the 1860 election) must take an oath of allegiance.

As the war had dragged on to its bloody, destructive conclusion, Lincoln had been very concerned and anxious to get the states restored to the Union and showed flexibility in his thinking as he made changes to his Reconstruction program to make it as easy and painless as possible. Of course, Congress had final approval of many actions and it would be interesting to know how differently things might have turned out if Lincoln had lived to see some or all of his kind policies, supported by fellow moderates, put into action. Unfortunately, it didn't turn out that way. After Andrew Johnson became President and the Radical Republicans gained control of Congress, the harsh measures of radical Reconstruction were implemented.

The economic and social chaos in the South after the war was overrun with starvation and rampant disease, especially in the cities. The U.S. Army provided some relief of food and clothing for both white and blacks but the major responsibility fell to the Freedmen's Bureau. Though the bureau agents to a certain extent helped southern whites, their main responsibility was to the freed slaves. They were to assist the freedmen to become self-supporting and protect them from being taken advantage of by others. Northerners looked on it as a real, honest effort to help the South out of the chaos it was in. Most white Southerners charged the bureau with causing racial friction, deliberately encouraging the freedmen to consider former owners as enemies.

As a result, as southern leaders began to be able to restore life as it had once been, they adopted a set of laws known as "black codes", containing many of the provisions of the prewar "slave codes." There were certain improvements in the lives of freedmen, but the codes denied the freedmen their basic civil rights. In short, except for the condition of freedom and a few civil rights, white Southerners made every effort to keep the freedmen in a way of life subordinate to theirs.

Radicals in Congress pointed out these illegal actions by white Southerners as evidence that they were unwilling to recognize, accept, and support the complete freedom of black Americans and could not be trusted. Therefore, Congress drafted its own program of Reconstruction, including laws that would protect and further the rights of blacks. Three amendments were added to the Constitution: the **13th Amendment** of 1865 outlawed slavery throughout the entire United States. The **14th Amendment** of 1868 made blacks American citizens. The **15th Amendment** of 1870 gave black Americans the right to vote and made it illegal to deny anyone the right to vote based on race.

Federal troops were stationed throughout the South and protected Republicans who took control of Southern governments. Bitterly resentful, white Southerners fought the new political system by joining a secret society called the **Ku Klux Klan**, using violence to keep black Americans from voting and getting equality. However, before being allowed to rejoin the Union, the Confederate states were required to agree to all federal laws. Between 1866 and 1870, all of them had returned to the Union, but Northern interest in Reconstruction was fading. Reconstruction officially ended when the last Federal troops left the South in 1877. It can be said that Reconstruction had broad success as it set up public school systems and expanded legal rights of black Americans. Nevertheless, white supremacy came to be in control again and its bitter fruitage is still with us today.

Lincoln and Johnson had considered the conflict of Civil War as a "rebellion of individuals," but Congressional Radicals, such as Charles Sumner in the Senate, considered the Southern states as complete political organizations and were now in the same position as any unorganized Territory and should be treated as such.

Radical House leader Thaddeus Stevens considered the Confederate States, not as Territories, but as conquered provinces and felt they should be treated that way. President Johnson refused to work with Congressional moderates, insisting on having his own way. As a result, the Radicals gained control of both houses of Congress and when Johnson opposed their harsh measures they came within one vote of impeaching him.

General Grant was elected President in 1868, serving two scandal-ridden terms. He himself was an honest, upright person, but he greatly lacked political experience and his greatest weakness was a blind loyalty in his friends. He absolutely refused to believe that his friends were not honest and stubbornly would not admit to their using him to further their own interests. One of the sad results of the war was the rapid growth of business and industry with large corporations controlled by unscrupulous men. However, after 1877, some degree of normalcy returned and there was time for rebuilding, expansion, and growth.

COMPETENCY 4.0   **THE MAJOR DEVELOPMENTS THAT SHAPED U.S HISTORY FROM 1877 TO 1920**

Skill 4.1   Know the effects of the continued westward expansion

The post-Reconstruction era represents a period of great transformation and expansion for the United States, both economically and geographically, particularly for the South, which was recovering from the devastation of the Civil War and migration west of the Mississippi River. Great numbers of former slaves moved west, away from their former masters, lured by the promise of land. White migration was also spurred by similar desires for land and resources, leading to boom economies of cotton, cattle and grain starting in Kansas and spreading westward. Although industrial production grew fastest in the South during this period, it was still predominantly agricultural, which featured land tenancy and sharecropping, which did not really advance the remaining freed slaves economically since most of the land was still owned by the large plantation landowners who retained their holdings from before the Civil War. The economic chasm dividing white landowners and black freedmen only widened as the tenants sank further into debt to their landlords.

Westward movement of significant populations from the eastern United States originated with the discovery of gold in the West in the 1840s and picked up greater momentum after the Civil War. Settlers were lured by what they perceived as unpopulated places with land for the taking. However, when they arrived, they found that the lands were populated by earlier settlers of Spanish descent and Native Americans, who did not particularly welcome the newcomers. These original and earlier inhabitants frequently clashed with those who were moving west.

Despite having signed treaties with the United States government years earlier, virtually all were ignored and broken as westward settlement accelerated and the government was called upon to protect settlers who were en route and when they had reached their destinations. This led to a series of wars between the United States and the various Native American Nations that were deemed hostile. Although the bloodshed during these encounters was great, it paled in comparison to the number of Native Americans who died from epidemics of deadly diseases for which they had no resistance. Eventually, the government sought to relocate inconveniently located peoples to Indian reservations, and to Oklahoma, which lacked the resources they needed and was geographically remote from their home range. The justification for this westward expansion at the expense of the previous inhabitants was that it was America's "Manifest Destiny" to "tame" and settle the continent from coast-to-coast.

Another major factor affecting the opening of the West to migration of Americans and displacement of native peoples was the expansion of the railroad. The **transcontinental railroad** was completed in 1869, joining the West Coast with the existing rail infrastructure terminating at Omaha, Nebraska, its westernmost point. This not only enabled unprecedented movement of people and goods, it also hastened the near extinction of bison, which the Indians of the Great Plains, in particular, depended on for their survival.

Skill 4.2   Show knowledge of the causes and consequences of industrialization

There was a marked degree of industrialization before and during the Civil War, but at war's end, industry in America was small. Of course, industry before, during, and after the Civil War was centered mainly in the North, especially the tremendous industrial growth after. Yet post-war, dramatic changes took place: machines replaced hand labor, extensive nationwide railroad service made possible the wider distribution of goods, new products were invented and made available in large quantities, and large amounts of money from bankers and investors was made available for the expansion of business operations.

Cities became the centers of this new business activity resulting in mass population movements there and tremendous growth. This new boom in business resulted in huge fortunes for some Americans and extreme poverty for many others. The discontent this caused resulted in a number of new reform movements from which came measures controlling the power and size of big business and helping the poor.

The use of machines in industry enabled workers to produce a large quantity of goods much faster than by hand. With the increase in business, hundreds of workers were hired, assigned to perform a certain job in the production process. This was a method of organization called "**division of labor**" and by its increasing the rate of production, businesses lowered prices for their products making the products affordable for more people. As a result, sales and businesses were increasingly successful and profitable.

A great variety of new products or inventions such as the typewriter, the telephone, barbed wire, the electric light, the phonograph, and the automobile became available. From this list, the one that had the greatest effect on America's economy was the automobile.

The increase in business and industry was greatly affected by the many rich natural resources that were found throughout the nation. The industrial machines were powered by the abundant water supply. The construction industry, as well as products made from wood, depended heavily on lumber from the forests. Coal and iron ore in abundance were needed for the steel industry, which profited and increased from the use of steel in such things as skyscrapers, automobiles, bridges, railroad tracks, and machines. Other minerals such as silver, copper, and petroleum played a large role in industrial growth, especially petroleum, from which gasoline was refined as fuel for the increasingly popular automobile.

Skill 4.3   Be able to explain the business and labor in an era of industrial expansion

As business grew, new methods of sales and promotion were developed. Salesmen (as they were all male back then) went to all parts of the country, promoting the varied products, opening large department stores in the growing cities, offering the varied products at reasonably affordable prices. People who lived too far from the cities, making it impossible to shop there, had the advantage of using a mail order service, buying what they needed from catalogs furnished by the companies. Developments in communication, such as the telephone and telegraph, increased the efficiency and prosperity of big business.

Investments in corporate stocks and bonds resulted from business prosperity. In their eager desire to share in the profits, individuals began investing heavily. Their investments made available the needed capital for companies to expand their operations. From this, banks increased in number throughout the country, making loans to businesses and significant contributions to economic growth. At the same time, during the 1880s, government made little effort to regulate businesses. This gave rise to **monopolies** where larger businesses were rid of their smaller competitors and assumed complete control of their industries.

Some owners in the same business would join or merge to form one company. Others formed what were called "**trusts**," a type of monopoly in which rival businesses were controlled but not formally owned. Monopolies had some good effects on the economy. Out of them grew the large, efficient corporations, which made important contributions to the growth of the nation's economy. Also, the monopolies enabled businesses to keep their sales steady and avoid sharp fluctuations in price and production.

At the same time, the downside of monopolies was the unfair business practices of the business leaders. Some acquired so much power that they took unfair advantage of others. Those who had little or no competition would require their suppliers to supply goods at a low cost, sell the finished products at high prices, and reduce the quality of the product to save money.

Skilled laborers were organized into a labor union called the **American Federation of Labor** in an effort to gain better working conditions and wages for its members. Farmers joined organizations such as the National Grange and Farmers Alliances. Farmers were producing more food than people could afford to buy. This was the result of both new farmlands, rapidly sprouting on the plains and prairies, and the development and availability of new farm machinery and newer and better methods of farming. They tried selling their surplus abroad but faced stiff competition from other nations selling the same farm products. Other problems contributed significantly to their situation. Items they needed for daily life were priced exorbitantly high. Having to borrow money to carry on farming activities kept them constantly in debt. Higher interest rates, shortage of money, falling farm prices, dealing with the so-called middlemen, and the increasingly high charges by the railroads to haul farm products to large markets all contributed to the desperate need for reform to relieve the plight of American farmers.

Skill 4.4   Compare and contrast the effect of immigration, internal migration and urbanization

Between 1870 and 1916, more than 25 million immigrants came into the United States, adding to the phenomenal population growth taking place. This tremendous growth aided business and industry in two ways. First, the number of consumers increased creating a greater demand for products, thus enlarging the markets for the products. And second, with increased production and expanding business, more workers were available for newly created jobs. The completion of the nation's transcontinental railroad, in 1869, contributed greatly to the nation's economic and industrial growth. Some examples of the benefits of using the railroads include: raw materials were shipped quickly by the mining companies and finished products were sent to all parts of the country. Many wealthy industrialists and railroad owners saw tremendous profits steadily increasing due to this improved method of transportation.

Innovations in new industrial processes and technology grew at a pace unmatched at any other time in American history. **Thomas Edison** was the most prolific inventor of that time, using a systematic and efficient method to invent and improve on current technology in a profitable manner. The abundance of resources, together with growth of industry and the pace of capital investments led to the growth of cities. Populations were shifting from rural agricultural areas to urban industrial areas and by the early 1900s a third of the nation's population lived in cities. Industry needed workers in its factories, mills, and plants and rural workers were being displaced by advances in farm machinery and their increasing use and other forms of automation.

The dramatic growth of population in cities was fueled by growing industries, more efficient transportation of goods and resources, and the people who migrated to those new industrial jobs, either from rural areas of the United States or immigrants from foreign lands. Increased urban populations, frequently packed into dense tenements, often without adequate sanitation or clean water, led to public health challenges that required cities to establish sanitation, water and public health departments to cope with and prevent epidemics. Political organizations also saw the advantage of mobilizing the new industrial working class and created vast patronage programs that sometimes became notorious for corruption in big-city machine politics, such as **Tammany Hall** in New York.

Skill 4.5   Show an understanding of Populism and the Progressive Era

Populism is the philosophy concerned with the common sense needs of average people. Populism often finds expression as a reaction against perceived oppression of the average people by the wealthy elite in society. The prevalent claim of populist movements is that they will put the people first. Populism is often connected with religious fundamentalism, racism, or nationalism. Populist movements claim to represent the majority of the people and call them to stand up to institutions or practices that seem detrimental to their well-being.

Populism flourished in the late 19th and early 20th centuries. Several political parties were formed out of this philosophy, including the Greenback Party, the Populist Party, the Farmer-Labor Party, the Single Tax movement of Henry George, the Share Our Wealth movement of Huey Long, the Progressive Party, and the Union Party. In the 1890s, the People's Party won the support of millions of farmers and other working people. This party challenged the social ills of the monopolists of the "Gilded Age."

The tremendous change that resulted from the industrial revolution led to a demand for reform that would control the power wielded by big corporations. The gap between the industrial moguls and the working people was growing. This disparity between rich and poor resulted in a public outcry for reform at the same time that there was an outcry for governmental reform that would end the political corruption and elitism of the day.

The late 1800s and early 1900s was a period of the efforts of many to make significant reforms and changes in the areas of politics, society, and the economy. There was a need to reduce the levels of poverty and to improve the living conditions of those affected by it. Regulations of big business, and ridding governmental corruption and making it more responsive to the needs of the people were also on the list of reforms to be accomplished. Until 1890, there was very little success, but from 1890 on, the reformers gained increased public support and were able to achieve some influence in government. Since some of these individuals referred to themselves as "**progressives**," and the period of 1890 to 1917 is referred to by historians as the **Progressive Era**.

This fire was fueled by the writings of investigative journalists known as "**muckrakers**" who published scathing exposés of political and business wrongdoing and corruption. The result was the rise of a group of politicians and reformers who supported a wide array of populist causes. Although these leaders came from many different backgrounds and were driven by different ideologies, they shared a common fundamental belief that government should be eradicating social ills and promoting the common good and the equality guaranteed by the Constitution.

The reforms initiated by these leaders and the spirit of **Progressivism** were far-reaching. Politically, many states enacted the initiative and the referendum. The adoption of the recall occurred in many states. Several states enacted legislation that would undermine the power of political machines. On a national level the two most significant political changes were firstly, the ratification of the 17th amendment, which required that all U.S. Senators be chosen by popular election, and secondly, the ratification of the **19th Amendment**, which granted women the right to vote.

Major economic reforms of the period included aggressive enforcement of the **Sherman Antitrust Act**, passage of the Elkins Act, and the Hepburn Act, which gave the Interstate Commerce Commission greater power to regulate the railroads. The Pure Food and Drug Act prohibited the use of harmful chemicals in food. The Meat Inspection Act regulated the meat industry to protect the public against tainted meat. Over 2/3 of the states passed laws prohibiting child labor. Workmen's compensation was mandated and the **Department of Commerce and Labor** was created.

Responding to concern over the environmental effects of the timber, ranching, and mining industries, President Theodore Roosevelt set aside 238 million acres of federal lands to protect them from development. Wildlife preserves were established, the national park system was expanded, and the National Conservation Commission was created. The Newlands Reclamation Act also provided federal funding for the construction of irrigation projects and dams in semi-arid areas of the country.

The Wilson Administration carried out additional reforms. The Federal Reserve Act created a national banking system, providing a stable money supply. The Sherman Act and the Clayton Antitrust Act defined unfair competition, made corporate officers liable for the illegal actions of employees, and exempted labor unions from antitrust lawsuits. The Federal Trade Commission was established to enforce these measures. Finally, the 16th amendment was ratified, establishing an income tax. This measure was designed to relieve the poor of a disproportionate burden in funding the federal government and make the wealthy pay a greater share of the nation's tax burden.

Skill 4.6   Discuss the movement for African American civil rights

After the Civil War, the Emancipation Proclamation in 1863, together with the 13th Amendment in 1865, ended slavery in the United States, but these measures did not erase the centuries of racial prejudices among whites that held blacks to be inferior in intelligence and morality. These prejudices, along with fear of economic competition from newly freed slaves, led to a series of state laws that permitted or required businesses, landlords, school boards and others to physically segregate blacks and whites in their everyday lives.

Segregation laws were foreshadowed in the **Black Codes**, strict laws proposed by some southern states during the Reconstruction period which sought to essentially recreate the conditions of pre-war servitude. Under these codes, blacks were to remain subservient to their white employers, and were subject to fines and beatings if they failed to work.

Freedmen, as newly freed slaves were called, were afforded some civil rights protection during the Reconstruction period; however, beginning around 1876, so-called Redeemer governments began to take office in southern states after the removal of Federal troops that had supported Reconstruction goals. The Redeemer state legislatures began passing segregation laws which came to be known as **Jim Crow** laws.

The Jim Crow laws varied from state to state, but the most significant of them required separate school systems and libraries for blacks and whites. Ticket windows, waiting rooms and seating areas on trains and, later, other public transportation were also segregated. Restaurant owners were permitted or sometimes required to provide separate entrances and tables and counters for blacks and whites, so that the two races would not see one another while dining. Public parks and playgrounds were constructed for each race. Landlords were not allowed to mix black and white tenants in apartment houses in some states.

The Jim Crow laws were given credibility in 1896 when the Supreme Court handed down its decision in the case *Plessy vs. Ferguson*. In 1890, Louisiana had passed a law requiring separate train cars for blacks and whites. Homer Plessy, a man who had a black great grandparent and, so, was considered legally "black" in that state, challenged this law in 1892 when he purchased a ticket in the white section and took his seat. Upon informing the conductor that he was black, he was told to move to the black car. He refused and was arrested. His case was eventually elevated to the Supreme Court.

The Court ruled against Plessy, thereby ensuring that the Jim Crow laws would continue to proliferate and be enforced. The Court held that segregating races was not unconstitutional as long as the facilities for each were identical. This became known as the **"separate but equal"** principle. In practice, facilities were seldom equal. Black schools were not funded at the same level, for instance. Streets and parks in black neighborhoods were not maintained. This trend continued throughout the following decades. Even the federal government adopted segregation as official policy when President Woodrow Wilson segregated the civil service in the 1910s.

The 13th Amendment abolished slavery and involuntary servitude, except as punishment for crime. The amendment was proposed on January 31, 1865. It was declared ratified by the necessary number of states on December 18, 1865. The Emancipation Proclamation had freed slaves held in states that were considered to be in rebellion. This amendment freed slaves in states and territories controlled by the Union. The Supreme Court has ruled that this amendment does not bar mandatory military service.

The 14th Amendment provides for **Due Process and Equal Protection** under the Law. It was proposed on June 13, 1866 and ratified on July 28, 1868. The drafters of the Amendment took a broad view of national citizenship. The law requires that states provide equal protection under the law to all persons—not just all citizens. This amendment also came to be interpreted as overturning the Dred Scott case, which stated that blacks were not and could not become citizens of the United States. The full potential of interpretation of this amendment was not realized until the 1950s and 1960s, when it became the basis of ending segregation in the ruling of the Supreme Court in the case of *Brown v. Board of Education*. The 14th amendment includes the stipulation that all children born on American soil, with very few exceptions, are U.S. citizens. There have been recommendations that this guarantee of citizenship be limited to exclude the children of illegal immigrants and tourists, but this has not yet occurred. There is no provision in this amendment for loss of citizenship.

After the Civil War, many Southern states passed laws that attempted to restrict the movements of blacks and prevent them from bringing lawsuits or testifying in court. In **the Slaughterhouse Cases** (1871), the Supreme Court ruled that the Amendment applies only to rights granted by the federal government. In the **Civil Rights Cases**, the Court held that the guarantee of rights did not outlaw racial discrimination by individuals and organizations. In the next few decades the Court overturned several laws barring blacks from serving on juries and discriminating against the Chinese immigrants in regulating the laundry businesses.

The Fifteenth Amendment grants voting rights regardless of race, color, or previous condition of servitude. It was ratified on February 3, 1870.

(See Skill 6.5 for additional information)

Skill 4.7   Major developments in arts and literature

Expressionism refers to German art, literature and film-making which elicits a specific emotional response from the viewer, mirroring the expression of the artist. Fauvism is closely related to expressionism, marked by bizarre use of color and wild distortion.

Cubism seeks to redefine space in relation to the subject matter and time, usually resulting in a fragmented image. Abstract art begins with a real subject or image, which is then distorted for any number of reasons, depending on the artist. **Dadaism** and **Surrealism** are related styles that focus on disgust and satire of the arts, and the role of the subconscious in art, respectively. Absurdity, hostility, and the effects of a mechanical universe marked Dadaism during the early years of the century. Surrealism is characterized by intrigue with the intuitive mind. Mimicking the nightmarish quality of dreams by the juxtaposition of bizarre objects, and using a panoramic, hazy backdrop to represent the human "mindscape" were favorite techniques of the surrealist artists.

Abstract expressionism is an umbrella-label for a collection of diverse artistic styles. All, however, are characterized by freedom of the artist from traditional subject matter and techniques, resulting in powerful, highly personal expressions. **Pop** and **Op** art, products mostly of the 1950s and 60s, stem from the words "popular" and "optical", respectively. Pop art deals with imagery from popular culture and often carries a message decrying the superficial quality of modern society. Optical art deals with illusionary art, most often utilizing non-representational designs to stimulate eye movement.

Twentieth-century music contrasts with prior music in several ways, including the elimination of meter, inclusion of dissonance to a higher degree, and refusal to use traditional tonality. A proliferation of styles marks modern music. **Jazz** centers around improvised variations on a theme, rendered with an emotional quality that is mimicked by the instruments. Offshoots such as ragtime, blues, swing and bebop, emerged as the century progressed.

In an attempt to control musical elements more tightly in a composition, serialism as a musical style was developed. It involved the creation of the structure of the piece before the actual piece itself.

Aleatory music was an effort in the opposite direction, incorporating randomness in many aspects of the composition. The development of new technologies in instruments and recording has also significantly contributed to the changes in twentieth-century music, although not to changes in style itself.

(See Skill 10.5 for additional information)

COMPETENCY 5.0   THE EMERGENCE OF THE UNITED STATES AS A
                     WORLD POWER AND THE EFFECTS OF MAJOR
                     CONFLICTS ON THE UNITED STATES FROM 1898
                     TO THE PRESENT

Skill 5.1   Know the key events and issues related to U.S. expansionism

Once the American West was subdued and firmly under United States control did the United States start looking beyond its shores. Overseas markets were becoming important as American industry produced goods more efficiently and manufacturing capacity grew. Out of concern for the protection of shipping, the United States modernized and built up its Navy, which by 1900 ranked third in the world. This gave the U.S. the means to become an imperial power. The first overseas possession was **Midway Island** annexed in 1867.

By the 1880s, Secretary of State James G. Blaine pushed for expanding U.S. trade and influence to Central and South America and, in the 1890s, President Grover Cleveland invoked the **Monroe Doctrine** to intercede in Latin American affairs when it looked as if Great Britain was going to exert its influence and power in the Western Hemisphere. In the Pacific, the United States lent its support to American sugar planters who overthrew the Kingdom of **Hawaii** and eventually annexed it as a U.S. territory.

During the 1890s, Spain controlled such overseas possessions as Puerto Rico, the Philippines, and Cuba. Cubans rebelled against Spanish rule and the U.S. government found itself besieged by demands from Americans to assist the Cubans in their revolt. The event that proved a turning point was the **Spanish-American War** in 1898, which used the explosion of the USS Maine as a pretext for the United States to invade Cuba, though the underlying reason was the ambition for empire and economic gain. Two months later, Congress declared war on Spain and the U.S. quickly defeated them. The war with Spain also triggered the dispatch of the fleet under Admiral George Dewey to the Philippines, followed up by sending Army troops.

Victory over the Spanish proved fruitful for American territorial ambitions. Although Congress passed legislation renouncing claims to annex Cuba, in a rare moment of idealism, the United States gained control of the island of **Puerto Rico**, a permanent deep-water naval harbor at Guantanamo Bay, Cuba, the Philippines and various other Pacific islands formerly possessed by Spain. The decision to occupy the **Philippines**, rather than grant it immediate independence, led to a guerrilla war, the "Philippines Insurrection" that lasted until 1902. U.S. rule over the Philippines lasted until 1942, but unlike the guerrilla war years, American rule was relatively benign. The peace treaty gave the U.S. possession of **Puerto Rico, the Philippines, Guam, and Hawaii**, which was annexed during the war.

This success enlarged and expanded the U.S. role in foreign affairs. Under the administration of Theodore Roosevelt, the U.S. armed forces were built up, greatly increasing its strength. Roosevelt's foreign policy was summed up in the slogan of "**Speak softly and carry a big stick**," backing up the efforts in diplomacy with a strong military. During the years before the outbreak of World War I, evidence of U.S. emergence as a world power could be seen in a number of actions.

Using the Monroe Doctrine of non-involvement of Europe in the affairs of the Western Hemisphere, President Roosevelt forced Italy, Germany, and Great Britain to remove their blockade of Venezuela, gained the rights to construct the **Panama Canal** by threatening force, and assumed the finances of the Dominican Republic to stabilize it and prevent any intervention by Europeans. In 1916, under President Woodrow Wilson, U.S. troops were sent to the Dominican Republic to keep order.

In Europe, Italy and Germany were each united into one nation from many smaller states. The key events in Europe at this time were revolutions in Austria and Hungary, the Franco-Prussian War, the dividing of Africa among the strong European nations, interference and intervention of Western nations in Asia, and the breakup of Turkish dominance in the Balkans.

In Africa, the nations of France, Great Britain, Italy, Portugal, Spain, Germany, and Belgium controlled the entire continent except Liberia and Ethiopia. In Asia and the Pacific Islands, only China, Japan, and present-day Thailand (Siam) kept their independence. The others were controlled by the strong European nations. Before the 1890s, the U.S. had little to do with foreign affairs, was not a strong nation militarily, and had inconsequential influence on international political affairs. In fact, the Europeans looked on the American diplomats as inept and bungling in their diplomatic efforts and activities. However, all of this changed and the Spanish-American War of 1898 saw the entry of the United States as a world power.

Skill 5.2   Know the causes and consequences of U.S. intervention of World War I

U.S. involvement in the war did not occur until 1917. When the war began in 1914, triggered by the assassination of Austrian Archduke Francis Ferdinand and his wife in Sarajevo, President Woodrow Wilson declared that the U.S. was neutral. Most Americans were opposed to any involvement anyway and were content to stay out of the matter as Europe marched off to war.

In 1916, Wilson was reelected to a second term based on a slogan proclaiming his efforts at keeping America out of the war. For a few months after, he put forth most of his efforts to stopping the war but German submarines began unlimited warfare against American merchant shipping. The development of the German *unterseeboat* or **U-boat** allowed them to efficiently attack merchant ships that were supplying their European enemies from Canada and the U.S. In 1915, a German U-boat sank the passenger liner RMS **Lusitania**, killing more than 1,000 civilians, including more than 100 Americans. This attack outraged the American public and turned public opinion against Germany. The attack on the Lusitania became a rallying point for those advocating U.S. involvement in the European conflict.

Great Britain intercepted and decoded a secret message from Germany to Mexico urging Mexico to go to war against the U.S. The publishing of this information, known as the **Zimmerman Note,** along with continued German destruction of American ships resulted in the eventual entry of the U.S. into the conflict, the first time the country prepared to fight in a conflict not on American soil. Though unprepared for war, governmental efforts and activities resulted in massive defense mobilization with America's economy directed to the war effort. Though America made important contributions of war materials, its greatest contribution to the war was manpower, soldiers desperately needed by the Allies.

Some ten months before the war ended, President Wilson had proposed a program called the **Fourteen Points** as a method of bringing the war to an end with an equitable peace settlement. In these Fourteen Points he had five points setting out general ideals; there were eight pertaining to immediately working to resolve territorial and political problems; and the fourteenth point counseled establishing an organization of nations to help keep world peace.

When Germany agreed in 1918 to an armistice, it assumed that the peace settlement would be drawn up on the basis of these Fourteen Points. However, the peace conference in Paris ignored these points and Wilson had to be content with efforts at establishing the **League of Nations**. Italy, France, and Great Britain, having suffered and sacrificed far more in the war than America, wanted retribution. The treaties punished severely the Central Powers, taking away arms and territories and requiring payment of reparations. Germany was punished more than the others and, according to one clause in the treaty, was forced to assume the responsibility for causing the war.

President Wilson lost in his efforts to get the U.S. Senate to approve the peace treaty. The Senate at the time was a reflection of American public opinion and its rejection of the treaty was a rejection of Wilson. The approval of the treaty would have made the U.S. a member of the League of Nations but Americans had just come off a bloody war to ensure that democracy would exist throughout the world. Americans just did not want to accept any responsibility that resulted from its new position of power and were afraid that membership in the League of Nations would embroil the U.S. in future disputes in Europe.

The harsh treatment of Germany would not be forgotten, especially by the Germans themselves as they sought to rebuild their nation. World War I left

European leaders skittish of another major conflict, and the United States once again adopted a policy of isolationism. It seemed as though few real lessons had been learned, and the seeds were sown for another conflict.

(See Skill 11.1 for additional information)

Skill 5.3   Understand the importance and impact of events, and consequences of U.S. participation in World War II

After war began in Europe in 1939, U.S. **President Franklin D. Roosevelt** announced that the United States was neutral. Most Americans, although hoping for an Allied victory, wanted the U.S. to stay out of the war. President Roosevelt and his supporters, called "interventionists," favored all aid except war to the Allied nations fighting Axis aggression. They were fearful that an Axis victory would seriously threaten and endanger all democracies. On the other hand, the "isolationists" were against any U.S. aid being given to the warring nations, accusing President Roosevelt of leading the U.S. into a war very much unprepared to fight. Roosevelt's plan was to defeat the Axis nations, Germany, Italy, and Japan, by sending the Allied nations the equipment needed to fight. This equipment included ships, aircraft, tanks, and other war materials.

In Asia, the U.S. had opposed Japan's invasion of Southeast Asia, an effort to gain Japanese control of that region's rich resources. Consequently, the U.S. stopped all important exports to Japan, whose industries depended heavily on petroleum, scrap metal, and other raw materials. Later Roosevelt refused the Japanese withdrawal of its funds from American banks. General Tojo became the Japanese premier in October 1941 and quickly realized that the U.S. Navy was powerful enough to block Japanese expansion into Asia. Deciding to cripple the Pacific Fleet, the Japanese aircraft, without warning, bombed the Fleet December 7, 1941, while the American fleet was at anchor in **Pearl Harbor** in Hawaii. Temporarily the attack was a success. It destroyed many aircraft and disabled much of the U.S. Pacific Fleet. In the end, it was a costly mistake for Japan as it quickly motivated the Americans to prepare for and wage war.

Military strategy in the European theater of war as developed by **Roosevelt, Churchill, and Stalin** was to concentrate on Germany's defeat first, then Japan's. The start was made in North Africa, pushing Germans and Italians off the continent, beginning in the summer of 1942 and ending successfully in May 1943. Before the war, Hitler and Stalin had signed a non-aggression pact in 1939, which Hitler violated in 1941 by invading the Soviet Union. The German defeat at Stalingrad, which marked a turning point in the war, was brought about by a combination of entrapment of German troops by Soviet troops and the death of many more Germans by starvation and freezing due to the horrendous winter conditions. All of this occurred at the same time the Allies were driving them out of North Africa.

The liberation of Italy began in July 1943 and ended May 2, 1945. The third part of the strategy was **D-Day, June 6, 1944,** with the Allied invasion of France at Normandy. At the same time, starting in January, 1943, the Soviets began pushing the German troops back into Europe (greatly assisted by supplies from Britain and the United States). By April, 1945, Allies occupied positions beyond the Rhine and the Soviets moved on to Berlin, surrounding it by April 25. Germany surrendered May 7 and the war in Europe was finally over.

The years between WWI and WWII had produced significant advancement in aircraft technology. But the pace of aircraft development and production was dramatically increased during WWII. Major developments included flight-based weapon delivery systems such as the long-range bomber, the first jet fighter, the first cruise missile, and the first ballistic missile, although the cruise and ballistic missiles were not widely used during the war. Glider planes were heavily used in WWII because they were silent upon approach. Another significant development was the broad use of paratrooper units. Finally, hospital planes came into use to extract the seriously wounded from the front and transport them to hospitals for treatment.

Weapons and technology in other areas also improved rapidly during the war. These advances were critical in determining the outcome of the war. Used for the first time were devices such as radar and electronic computers. More new inventions were registered for patents than ever before. Most of these new ideas were aimed to either kill or prevent soldiers from being killed.

The war began with essentially the same weaponry that had been used in WWI. The aircraft carrier joined the battleship on the seas. Light tanks were developed to meet the needs of a changing battlefield, and other armored vehicles were developed. Submarines were also perfected during this period. Numerous other weapons of modern warfare were also developed or invented to meet the needs of battle during WWII: the bazooka, the rocket propelled grenade, anti-tank weapons, assault rifles, cruise missiles, rocket artillery, guided weapons, torpedoes, self-guiding weapons and napalm.

The **Yalta Conference** took place in Yalta in February 1945, between the Allied leaders Winston Churchill, Franklin Roosevelt, and Joseph Stalin. With the defeat of Nazi Germany within sight, the three allies met to determine the shape of post-war Europe. Germany was to be divided into four zones of occupation, as was the capital city of Berlin. Germany was also to undergo demilitarization and to make reparations for the war. Poland was to remain under control of Soviet Russia. Roosevelt also received a promise from Stalin that the Soviet Union would join the new United Nations.

Following the surrender of Germany in May, 1945, the Allies called the Potsdam Conference in July. Winston Churchill met with Harry Truman and Stalin and, later in July, Clement Atlee replaced Mr. Churchill at the conference. **The**

Potsdam Conference addressed the administration of post-war Germany and provided for the forced migration of millions of Germans from previously occupied regions.

Meanwhile, in the Pacific, in the six months after the attack on Pearl Harbor, Japanese forces moved across Southeast Asia and the western Pacific Ocean. By August, 1942, the Japanese Empire was at its largest size and stretched northeast to Alaska's Aleutian Islands, west to Burma, south to what is now Indonesia. Invaded and controlled areas included Hong Kong, Guam, Wake Island, Thailand, part of Malaysia, Singapore, the Philippines, and Darwin on the north coast of Australia.

The raid of **General Doolittle**'s bombers on Japanese cities and the American naval victory at **Midway** along with the fighting in the **Battle of the Coral Sea** helped turn the tide against Japan. **Island-hopping** by U.S. Seabees and Marines and the grueling bloody battles fought resulted in gradually pushing the Japanese back toward Japan. After victory was attained in Europe, concentrated efforts were made to secure Japan's surrender, but it took dropping two atomic bombs on the cities of **Hiroshima** and **Nagasaki** to finally end the war in the Pacific.

The development and use of the atomic bomb during WWII was probably the most profound military development of the war years. This invention made it possible for a single plane to carry a single bomb that was sufficiently powerful to destroy an entire city. It was believed that possession of the bomb would serve as a deterrent to any nation because it would make aggression against a nation with a bomb a decision for mass suicide.

Two nuclear bombs were dropped in 1945 on the cities of Nagasaki and Hiroshima. They caused the immediate deaths of between 100,000 and 200,000 people, and far more deaths over time. This was (and still is) a controversial decision. Those who opposed the use of the atom bomb argued that it was an unnecessary act of mass killing, particularly of non-combatants. Proponents argued that it ended the war sooner, thus resulting in fewer casualties on both sides. The development and use of nuclear weapons marked the beginning of a new age in warfare that created greater distance from the act of killing and eliminated the ability to minimize the effect of war on non-combatants.

Japan formally surrendered on September 2, 1945, aboard the U.S. battleship Missouri, anchored in Tokyo Bay. The war was finally ended.

After Japan's defeat, the Allies began a military occupation, directed by American **General Douglas MacArthur**, that introduced a number of reforms and eventually ridded Japan of its military institutions and transformed it into a democracy. A constitution was drawn up in 1947 transferring all political rights from the emperor to the people, granting women the right to vote, and denying

Japan the right to declare war. War crimes trials of twenty-five war leaders and government officials were also conducted. The U.S. did not sign a peace treaty with Japan until 1951. The treaty permitted Japan to rearm but took away its overseas empire.

Again, after a major world war came efforts to prevent war from occurring again throughout the world. Preliminary work began in 1943 when the U.S., Great Britain, the Soviet Union, and China sent representatives to Moscow where they agreed to set up an international organization that would work to promote peace around the earth. In 1944, the four Allied powers met again and made the decision to name the organization the **United Nations**. In 1945, a charter for the UN was drawn up and signed, taking effect in October of that year.

Skill 5.4   Be able to describe the U.S. foreign policy during the Cold War and the impact of the Cold War on U.S. politics

After the end of the Second World War, the United States perceived its greatest threat to be the expansion of Communism in the world. To that end, it devoted a larger and larger share of its foreign policy, diplomacy, and both economic and military might to combating it.

In the aftermath of the Second World War, with the Soviet Union having emerged as the *second* strongest power on Earth, the United States embarked on a policy known as "**Containment**" of the Communist menace. This involved what came to be known as the "**Marshall Plan**" and the "**Truman Doctrine**." The Marshall Plan involved the economic aid that was sent to Europe in the aftermath of the Second World War aimed at preventing the spread of communism.

The Truman Doctrine offered military aid to those countries that were in danger of communist upheaval. This led to the era known as the **Cold War** in which the United States took the lead along with the Western European nations against the Soviet Union and the Eastern Bloc countries. It was also at this time that the United States finally gave up on George Washington's' advice against "European entanglements" and joined the **North Atlantic Treaty Organization** or **NATO**. This was formed in 1949 and was composed of the United States and several Western European nations for the purposes of opposing communist aggression.

In the 1950s, the United States embarked on what was called the **Eisenhower Doctrine**, named after the then President Eisenhower. This aimed at trying to maintain peace in a troubled area of the world, the Middle East. However, unlike the Truman Doctrine in Europe, it would have little success. Soviet countries signed the Warsaw Pact in 1955 as a treaty of cooperation, mutual assistance, and friendship.

The introduction and possession of nuclear weapons by the United States quickly led to the development of similar weapons by other nations, proliferation of the most destructive weapons ever created, massive fear of the effects of the use of these weapons, including radiation poisoning and **nuclear winter**, and led to much of the paranoia of the Cold War.

(See Skill 12.1 for additional information)

Skill 5.5   **Understand the importance and impact of causes, key events and consequences of U.S. intervention in Korea, Vietnam, and the Cuban missile crisis**

The first "hot war" in the post-World War II era was the **Korean War**, which began June 25, 1950, and ended with a truce on July 27, 1953. Troops from Communist North Korea invaded democratic South Korea in an effort to unite both sections under Communist control. The United Nations organization asked its member nations to furnish troops to help restore peace. Many nations responded and President Truman sent American troops to help the South Koreans. The war dragged on for three years and ended with a truce, not a peace treaty. Like Germany then, Korea remained divided and does so to this day, with the two Koreas facing each other across the longest militarized border in the world, the Demilitarized Zone, or **DMZ**.

In 1954, the French were forced to give up their colonial claims in Indochina, the present-day countries of **Vietnam**, **Laos**, and **Cambodia**. Afterwards, the Communist northern part of Vietnam began battling with the democratic southern part over control of the entire country. In the late 1950s and early 1960s, U.S. Presidents Eisenhower and Kennedy sent to Vietnam a number of military advisers and military aid to assist and support South Vietnam's non-Communist government. During Lyndon Johnson's presidency, the war escalated with thousands of American troops being sent to participate in combat with the South Vietnamese. The war was extremely unpopular in America and caused such serious divisiveness among its citizens that Johnson decided not to seek reelection in 1968. It was in President Richard Nixon's second term in office that the U.S. signed an agreement ending war in Vietnam and restoring peace. This was done January 27, 1973, and by March 29, the last American combat troops and American prisoners of war left Vietnam for home. It was the longest war in U.S. history and to this day carries the perception that it was a "lost war."

In 1962, during the administration of President **John F. Kennedy**, Premier Khrushchev and the Soviets decided, as a protective measure for Cuba against an American invasion, to install nuclear missiles on the island. In October, American U-2 spy planes photographed over Cuba what were identified as missile bases under construction. The decision for the White House was how to handle the situation without starting a war. The only recourse was removal of the missile sites and preventing more being set up. Kennedy announced that the U.S. had set up a "quarantine" of Soviet ships heading to Cuba. It was in reality a blockade but the word itself could not be used publicly as a blockade was actually considered an act of war.

A week of incredible tension and anxiety gripped the entire world until Khrushchev capitulated. Soviet ships carrying missiles for the Cuban bases turned back and the crisis eased. What precipitated the crisis was Khrushchev's underestimation of President Kennedy. The President made no effort to prevent the erection of the Berlin Wall and was reluctant to commit American troops to invade Cuba and overthrow Fidel Castro. The Soviets assumed this was a weakness and decided they could install the missiles without any interference. As tensions eased in the aftermath of the crisis, several agreements were made. The U.S. missiles in Turkey that were directed toward the Soviet Union were removed as were the Cuban missiles. A telephone "hot line" was set up between Moscow and Washington to make it possible for the two heads of government to have instant contact with each other. The U.S. agreed to sell its surplus wheat to the Soviets.

Skill 5.6   Be knowledgeable about the end of the Cold War and the emergence of new foreign policy challenges

Probably the highlight of the foreign policy of **President Richard Nixon**, after the end of the Vietnam War and withdrawal of troops, was his 1972 trip to China. Since 1949, when the Communists gained control of China, the policy of the U.S. government had been to refuse to recognize the Communist government. Instead, the U.S. regarded the legitimate government of **China** to be that of Chiang Kai-shek, exiled on the island of Taiwan.

In 1971, Nixon sent Henry Kissinger on a secret trip to Peking to investigate whether or not it would be possible for America to give recognition to China. In February 1972, President and Mrs. Nixon spent a number of days in the country visiting well-known Chinese landmarks, dining with the two leaders, Mao Zedong and Chou En-lai. Agreements were made for cultural and scientific exchanges, eventual resumption of trade, and future unification of the mainland with Taiwan. In 1979, formal diplomatic recognition was achieved. With this one visit, the pattern of the Cold War was essentially shifted.

During the administration of **President Jimmy Carter**, Egyptian President Anwar el-Sadat and Israeli Prime Minister Menachem Begin met at presidential retreat **Camp David** and agreed, after a series of meetings, to sign a formal treaty of peace between the two countries. In 1979, the Soviet invasion of Afghanistan was perceived by Carter and his advisers as a threat to the rich oil fields in the Persian Gulf but at the time, U.S. military capability to prevent further Soviet aggression in the Middle East was weak. The last year of Carter's presidential term was taken up with the fifty-three American hostages held in Iran. The shah had been deposed and control of the government and the country was in the hands of Muslim leader, Ayatollah Ruhollah Khomeini.

Khomeini's extreme hatred for the U.S. was the result of the 1953 overthrow of Iran's Mossadegh government, sponsored by the CIA. To make matters worse, the CIA proceeded to train the shah's ruthless secret police force. So, when the terminally ill exiled shah was allowed into the U.S. for medical treatment, a fanatical mob stormed into the American embassy taking the fifty-three Americans as prisoners, supported and encouraged by Khomeini.

President Carter froze all Iranian assets in the U.S., set up trade restrictions, and approved a risky rescue attempt, which failed. He had appealed to the UN for aid in gaining release for the hostages and to European allies to join the trade embargo on Iran. Khomeini ignored UN requests for releasing the Americans and Europeans refused to support the embargo so as not to risk losing access to Iran's oil. American prestige was damaged and Carter's chances for reelection were doomed. The hostages were released on the day of Ronald Reagan's inauguration as President when Carter released Iranian assets as ransom.

The foreign policy of **President Ronald Reagan** was, in his first term, focused primarily on the Western Hemisphere, particularly in Central America and the West Indies. U.S. involvement in the domestic revolutions of El Salvador and Nicaragua continued into Reagan's second term when Congress held televised hearings on what came to be known as the **Iran-Contra Affair**. A cover-up was exposed showing that profits from secretly selling military hardware to Iran had been used to give support to rebels, called Contras, who were fighting in Nicaragua.

In 1983, in Lebanon, 241 American Marines were killed when an Islamic suicide bomber drove an explosive-laden truck into U.S. Marines headquarters located at the airport in Beirut. This tragic event came as part of the unrest and violence between the Israelis and the Palestinian Liberation Organization (PLO) forces in southern Lebanon.

In the same month, 1,900 U.S. Marines landed on the island of **Grenada** to rescue a small group of American medical students at the medical school and depose the leftist government.

Perhaps the most intriguing and far-reaching event toward the end of Reagan's second term was the arms-reduction agreement Reagan reached with Soviet General Secretary **Mikhail Gorbachev**. Gorbachev began easing East-West tensions by stressing the importance of cooperation with the West and easing the harsh and restrictive life of the people in the Soviet Union. Though regarded as a fierce Cold Warrior, having compared the Soviet Union to an "evil empire," Reagan proved willing to talk repeatedly with the Soviets, and a new level of accord was reached. In retrospect, it was clearly a prelude to the events that would occur during the administration of **President George Bush.**

After Bush took office it appeared, for a brief period, that democracy would gain a hold and influence in China with democracy protests in **Tiananmen Square**, but the brief movement was quickly and decisively crushed. The biggest surprise was the fall of the **Berlin Wall**, resulting in the unification of all of Germany, the loss of power of the Communists in other Eastern European countries, and the fall of Communism in the Soviet Union and the breakup of its republics into independent nations. The countries of Poland, Hungary, Romania, Czechoslovakia, Albania, and Bulgaria replaced Communist rule for a democratic one.

The former **Yugoslavia** broke apart into individual ethnic enclaves with the republics of Serbia, Croatia, and Bosnia-Herzegovina embarking on wars of ethnic cleansing between Catholics, Orthodox, and Muslims. In Russia, as in the other former republics and satellites, democratic governments were put into operation and the difficult task of changing communist economies into ones of capitalistic free enterprise began. For all practical purposes, it appeared that the tensions and dangers of the post-World War II "Cold War" between the U.S. and Soviet-led Communism were over.

President Bush, in December of 1989, sent U.S. troops to invade **Panama** and arrest the Panamanian dictator Manuel Noriega. Although he had periodically assisted CIA operations with intelligence information, at the same time, Noriega laundered money from drug smuggling and gunrunning through Panama's banks. When a political associate tried unsuccessfully to depose him and an off-duty U.S. Marine was shot and killed at a roadblock, Bush acted. Noriega was brought to the U.S. where he stood trial on charges of drug distribution and racketeering.

During the time of the American hostage crisis, Iraq and Iran fought a war in which the U.S. and most of Iraq's neighbors supported Iraq. In a five-year period, **Saddam Hussein** received from the U.S. $500 million worth of American technology, including lasers, advanced computers, and special machine tools used in missile development. The Iraq-Iran war was a bloody one resulting in a stalemate with a UN truce ending it. Deeply in debt from the war and totally dependent on oil revenues, Saddam invaded and occupied Kuwait. The U.S. made extensive plans to put into operation a strategy to successfully carry out **Operation Desert Storm**, the liberation of Kuwait. In four days, February 24–28, 1991, the war was over and Iraq had been defeated, its troops driven back into their country. Saddam remained in power although Iraq's economy was seriously damaged.

President Bill Clinton sent U.S. troops to Haiti to protect the efforts of Jean-Bertrand Aristide to gain democratic power and to Bosnia to assist UN peacekeeping forces. He also inherited from the Bush administration the problem of Somalia in East Africa, where U.S. troops had been sent in December 1992 to support UN efforts to end the starvation of the Somalis and restore peace. The efforts were successful at first, but eventually failed due to the severity of the intricate political problems within the country. After U.S. soldiers were killed in an ambush, along with 300 Somalis, American troops were withdrawn and returned home.

**COMPETENCY 6.0   THE MAJOR DEVELOPMENTS THAT SHAPED
U.S. HISTORY FROM 1920 TO THE PRESENT**

**Skill 6.1   Be able to describe the major cultural, social, and economic
developments of the 1920s**

The end of World War I and the decade of the 1920s saw tremendous changes
in the United States, signifying the beginning of its development into its modern
society today. The shift from farm to city life was occurring in tremendous
numbers. Social changes and problems were occurring at such a fast pace that it
was extremely difficult and perplexing for many Americans to adjust to them.
Politically, the 18th Amendment to the Constitution, the so-called Prohibition
Amendment that prohibited selling alcoholic beverages throughout the U.S.,
resulted in problems affecting all aspects of society. The passage of the 19th
Amendment gave to women the right to vote in all elections. The decade of the
1920s also showed a marked change in roles and opportunities for women with
more and more of them seeking and finding careers outside the home. They
began to think of themselves as equals of men rather than just housewives and
mothers.

The U.S. economy experienced a tremendous period of boom. Restrictions on
business because of war no longer existed and the conservatives in control
adopted policies that helped and encouraged big business. To keep foreign
goods from competing with American goods, tariffs were raised to the highest
level. New products were developed by American manufacturers and many
different items became readily available to the people. These included
refrigerators, radios, washing machines, and, most importantly, the automobile.

The influence of the automobile, the entertainment industry, and the rejection of
the morals and values of pre-World War I life, resulted in the fast-paced **Roaring
Twenties**, and had significant effects on events leading to the Depression-era
1930s and another world war. Many Americans greatly desired the pre-war life
and supported political policies and candidates in favor of the return to what was
considered normal. It was desired to end government's strong role and adopt a
policy of isolating the country from world affairs, a result of the war.

Americans in the 1920s heavily invested in corporation stocks, providing
companies a large amount of capital for expanding their businesses. The more
money investors put into the stock market, the more the value of the stocks
increased. This, in turn, led to widespread speculation that increased stock value
to a point beyond the level that was justified by earnings and dividends.

Prohibition of the sale of alcohol had caused the increased activities of
bootlegging and the rise of underworld **gangs** and the illegal **speakeasies**, and
the **jazz** music and dances they promoted. The customers of these clubs were
considered "modern," reflected by extremes in clothing, hairstyles, and attitudes

toward authority and life. Movies and, to a certain degree, other types of entertainment, along with increased interest in sports figures and the accomplishments of national heroes, such as Lindbergh, influenced Americans to admire, emulate, and support individual accomplishments.

As wild and uninhibited modern behavior became, this decade witnessed an increase in a religious tradition known as "**revivalism**," emotional preaching. Although law and order were demanded by many Americans, the administration of President Warren G. Harding was marked by widespread corruption and scandal, not unlike the administration of Ulysses S. Grant, except Grant was honest and innocent. The decade of the 1920s also saw the resurgence of such racist organizations as the **Ku Klux Klan.**

As African Americans left the rural South and migrated to the North in search of opportunity, many settled in Harlem in New York City. By the 1920s Harlem had become a center of life and activity for persons of color. The music, art, and literature of this community gave birth to a cultural movement known as **the Harlem Renaissance**. The artistic expressions that emerged from this community in the 1920s and 1930s celebrated the black experience, black traditions, and the voices of black America. Major writers and works of this movement included: Langston Hughes (*The Weary Blues),* Nella Larsen (*Passing),* Zora Neale Hurston (*Their Eyes Were Watching God),* Claude McKay, Countee Cullen, and Jean Toomer.

Many refer to the decade of the 1920s as **The Jazz Age**. The decade was a time of optimism and exploration of new boundaries. It was a clear movement in many ways away from conventionalism. Jazz music, uniquely American, was the country's popular music at the time. The jazz musical style perfectly typified the mood of society. Jazz is essentially free-flowing improvisation on a simple theme with a four-beat rhythm. Jazz originated in the poor districts of New Orleans as an outgrowth of the Blues. The leading jazz musicians of the time included: Buddy Bolden, Joseph "King" Oliver, Duke Ellington, Louis Armstrong, and Jelly Roll Morton.

As jazz grew in popularity and in the intricacy of the music, it gave birth to **Swing** and the era of **Big Band** Jazz by the mid-1920s. Some of the most notable musicians of the Big Band era were: Bing Crosby, Frank Sinatra, Don Redman, Fletcher Henderson, Count Basie, Benny Goodman, Billie Holiday, Ella Fitzgerald, and The Dorsey Brothers, among others.

In painting and sculpture, the new direction of the decade was **realism**. In the early years of the twentieth century, American artists had developed several realist styles, some of which were influenced by modernism, others that reacted against it. Several groups of artists of this period are particularly notable.

The Eight or **The Ashcan School** developed around the work and style of Robert Henri. Their subjects were everyday urban life that was presented without adornment or glamour. **The American Scene Painters** produced a tight, detailed style of painting that focused on images of American life that were understandable to all. In the Midwest, a school within this group was called **regionalism**. One of the leading artists of regionalism was Grant Wood, best known for *American Gothic.* Other important realists of the day were Edward Hopper and Georgia O'Keeffe.

Marcus Garvey, an English-educated Jamaican, established an organization call the *Universal Negro Improvement and Conservation Association and African Communities League* (usually called the Universal Negro Improvement Association). In 1919 this "Black Moses" claimed followers numbering about two million. He spoke of a "new Negro" who was proud to be black. He published a newspaper in which he taught about the "heroes" of the race and the strengths of African culture. He told blacks that they would be respected only when they were economically strong. He created a number of businesses by which he hoped to achieve this goal. He then called blacks to work with him to build an all-black nation in Africa. His belief in racial purity and black separatism was not shared by a number of black leaders. In 1922 he and other members of the organization were jailed for mail fraud. His sentence was commuted and he was deported to Jamaica as an undesirable alien.

The **Ku Klux Klan** (KKK) is a name that has been used by several white supremacist organizations throughout history. Their beliefs encompass white supremacy, anti-Semitism, racism, anti-Catholicism and nativism. Their typical methods of intimidation have included terrorism, violence, cross burning and the like. The birth of the organization was in 1866. At that time, members were veterans of the Confederate Army seeking to resist Reconstruction and the "carpetbaggers."

The Klan entered a second period beginning in 1915. Using the new film medium, this group tried to spread its message with ***The Birth of a Nation***. They also published a number of anti-Semitic newspaper articles. The group became a structured membership organization. Membership during the 1920s reached approximately four million—twenty percent of the adult white male population in many regions and as high as forty percent in some areas. Its numbers did not begin to decline until the Great Depression.

Although the KKK began in the South, its membership, at its peak, extended into the Midwest, the Northern states, and even into Canada. The political influence of the group was significant. The group essentially controlled the governments of Tennessee, Indiana, Oklahoma, and Oregon as well as some Southern legislatures.

The **motion picture industry** made its home in southern California. Most of the early movies were brief. But in 1913, Samuel Goldfish and Archibald Selwyn formed the feature motion picture company Goldwyn. They then partnered with Louis B. Mayer to form Metro-Goldwyn Mayer, the leading studio in Hollywood for more than a quarter of a century. The industry grew, and with it the need for mansions for the stars and all of the workers who were needed.

Early efforts at reform began with movements to organize farmers and laborers, to push to give women the right to vote, and to push for the successful passage of Congressional legislation establishing merit as the basis for federal jobs rather than political favoritism. Other efforts were directed toward improvements in education, living conditions in city slums, and breaking up trusts and monopolies in big businesses.

After World War I ended, the 18th Amendment to the U.S. Constitution, commonly referred to as **Prohibition**, was ratified, forbidding the sale of alcoholic beverages. The violence and upheaval it caused was a major characteristic of the wild decade of the 1920s. The wild financial speculations came to an abrupt end with the stock market crash of October 1929, plunging the U.S. into the **Great Depression**.

Skill 6.2   Know the causes and consequences of the Great Depression, Franklin D. Roosevelt and the New Deal

The **1929 Stock Market crash** was a powerful event and is generally interpreted as the beginning of the Great Depression in America. Although the crash of the Stock Market was unexpected, it was not without identifiable causes. The 1920s had been a decade of social and economic growth and hope. But the attitudes and actions of the 1920s regarding wealth, production, and investment created several trends that quietly set the stage for the 1929 disaster.

Much of the stock speculation of the 1920's involved paying a small part of the cost and borrowing the rest. This led eventually to the stock market crash of 1929, financial ruin for many investors, a weakening of the nation's economy, and the **Great Depression** of the 1930s. The Depression hit the United States tremendously hard resulting in bank failures, loss of jobs due to cut-backs in production, and a lack of money leading to a sharp decline in spending which in turn affected businesses, factories and stores, and higher unemployment. Farm products were not affordable so the farmers suffered even more. Foreign trade sharply decreased and in the early 1930s, the U.S. economy was effectively paralyzed. Europe was affected even more so.

The revival of political liberalism in the twentieth century can be traced to the policies of **Franklin Roosevelt** beginning in the Great Depression of the 1930s. Roosevelt's "**New Deal**" programs aimed, in part, to provide relief to hard-hit workers by offering government sponsored work programs such as the Civilian

Conservation Corps. This step was in stark contrast to prior administrations, particularly that of President Herbert Hoover, who believed that the government should not provide direct aid to citizens or be directly involved in the economy.

Many of Roosevelt's policies faced strong opposition, and some programs were struck down by the Supreme Court. Roosevelt was a tremendously popular president, however, and was elected to four terms. Numerous like-minded Democrats were swept into office in the wake of Roosevelt's popularity.

The election of Franklin Roosevelt to the office of President in 1932, largely on his promise to the American people of a "new deal," was the start of the social and economic recovery and reform of legislative acts designed to gradually ease the country back to more prosperity. Upon assuming the office, Roosevelt and his advisers immediately launched a massive program of innovation and experimentation to try to bring the Depression to an end and get the nation back on track. Congress gave the President unprecedented power to act to save the nation. The legislation was intended to accomplish three goals: **relief, recovery, and reform**.

The first step in the "**New Deal**" was to relieve suffering. This was accomplished through a number of job-creation projects. The second step, the recovery aspect, was to stimulate the economy. The third step was to create social and economic change through innovative legislation.

The National Recovery Administration attempted to accomplish several goals:

- Restore employment
- Increase general purchasing power
- Provide character-building activity for unemployed youth
- Encourage decentralization of industry and thus divert population from crowded cities to rural or semi-rural communities
- Develop river resources in the interest of navigation and cheap power and light
- Complete flood control on a permanent basis
- Enlarge the national program of forest protection and to develop forest resources.
- Control farm production and improve farm prices
- Assist home builders and home owners
- Restore public faith in banking and trust operations
- Recapture the value of physical assets, whether in real property, securities, or other investments.

These objectives and their accomplishment implied a restoration of public confidence and courage.

To provide economic stability and prevent another crash, Congress passed the **Glass-Steagall Act**, which separated banking and investing. The **Securities and Exchange** Commission was created to regulate dangerous speculative practices on Wall Street. **The Wagner Act** guaranteed a number of rights to workers and unions in an effort to improve worker-employer relations. The **Social Security Act of 1935** established pensions for the aged and infirm as well as a system of unemployment insurance.

During the next eight years, the most extensive and broadly based legislation in the nation's history was enacted. These acts included relief for the nation's farmers, regulation of banks, public works providing jobs for the unemployed, and giving aid to manufacturers. Some of the agencies set up to implement these measures included the **Works Progress Administration** (WPA), **Civilian Conservation Camps** (CCC), the **Farm Credit Administration** (FCA), and the **Social Security Board**. These last two agencies gave credit to farmers and set up the nation's social security system.

Among the "alphabet organizations" set up to work out the details of the recovery plan, the most prominent were:

- **Agricultural Adjustment Administration** (AAA), designed to readjust agricultural production and prices thereby boosting farm income.
- **Civilian Conservation Corps** (CCC), designed to give wholesome, useful activity in the forestry service to unemployed young men.
- **Civil Works Administration** (CWA) and the **Public Works Administra**tion (PWA), designed to give employment in the construction and repair of public buildings, parks, and highways.
- **Works Progress Administration** (WPA), whose task was to move individuals from relief rolls to work projects or private employment.

Skill 6.3 Understand the importance of the growth and decline of organized labor

The charter of the National Recovery Administration included a statement defending the right of labor unions to exist and to negotiate with employers. This was interpreted by thousands as support for unions. But the Supreme Court declared this unconstitutional, and there would be several major events or actions that were particularly important to the history of organized labor during the decade.

The **Wagner Act** (The National Labor Relations Act) established a legal basis for unions, set collective bargaining as a matter of national policy required by the law, provided for secret ballot elections for choosing unions, and protected union members from employer intimidation and coercion. This law was later amended by the Taft-Hartley Act (1947) and by the Landrum Griffin Act (1959). The Wagner Act itself was upheld by the Supreme Court in 1937.

One of the most common tactics of the union was the **strike**. Half a million Southern mill workers walked off the job in the Great Uprising of 1934, establishing the precedent that without workers, industry could not move forward. Then, in 1936, the United Rubber Workers staged the first **sit-down strike** where, instead of walking off the job, they stayed at their posts but refused to work. The United Auto Workers used the sit-down strike against General Motors in 1936.

Strikes were met with varying degrees of resistance by the companies. Sometimes, "**scabs**" were brought in to replace the striking workers. In 1936, the Anti-Strikebreaker Act (the Byrnes Act) made it illegal to transport or aid strikebreakers in interstate or foreign trade. In part this was an attempt to stem the violence often associated with management's attempts to bully the workers back into their jobs.

As the leaders of industry were often powerful community figures, they sometimes employed law enforcement to disrupt the strikes. During a strike in 1937 of the Steel Workers Organizing Committee against Republic Steel, police attacked a crowd gathered in support of the strike, killing ten and injuring eighty. This came to be called **The Memorial Day Massacre**.

A number of acts were designed to provide fair compensation and other benefits to workers. The Davis-Bacon Act was passed in 1931 and provided that employers of contractors and subcontractors on public construction should be paid the prevailing wages. The states sometimes took matters into their own hands. Wisconsin created the first unemployment insurance act in the country in 1932. The Public Contracts Act (the **Walsh-Healey Act**) of 1936 established labor standards, including minimum wages, overtime pay, child and convict labor provisions and safety standards on federal contracts. The **Fair Labor Standards** Act created a $0.25 minimum wage, stipulated time-and-a-half pay for hours over 40 per week. The Social Security Act was approved in 1935.

There were also efforts to clean up or unionize particular industries. The Supreme Court upheld the Railway Labor Act in 1930, including its prohibition of employer interference or coercion in the choice of bargaining representatives which was later applied to other organize labor unions. The Guffey Act stabilized the coal industry and improved labor conditions in 1935, though a year later it was declared unconstitutional. General Motors recognized the **United Auto Workers** and US Steel recognized the **Steel Workers Organizing Committee**, both in 1937. Then in 1938 Merchant Marine Act created a Federal Maritime Labor Board.

One of labor's biggest unions was formed in 1935. The Committee for Industrial Organization (**CIO**) was formed within the AFL to carry unionism to the industrial sector. By 1937, however, the CIO had been expelled from the AFL over charges of dual unionism or competition. It then became known as the Congress of Industrial Organizations.

Federal labor efforts included:

- The Anti-Injunction Act of 1932 which prohibited federal injunctions in most labor disputes.
- The Wagner-Peyser Act which created the United States Employment Service within the Department of Labor in 1933.
- The Secretary of Labor calling for the first National Labor Legislation Conference to get better cooperation between the federal government and the states in defining a national labor legislation program in 1934.
- The U.S. joining the International Labor Organization, also in 1934.
- And the National Apprenticeship Act establishing the Bureau of Apprenticeship within the Department of Labor in 1937.

Skill 6.4   Know and understand the major postwar developments

The impact of the Cold War on migration patterns was very significant. Until the middle of the twentieth century, voluntary migrations to America were primarily Europeans. After WWII, a large number of Europeans were admitted to the U.S. and Canada. These were considered the most desirable immigrants. Indeed, immigration policies based upon ethnicity or country of origin were not eliminated until the 1960s.

American policies toward immigration became more open to political escapees from communist countries, partly out of a desire to embarrass these nations. The number of immigrants from third-world nations was also increasing dramatically. The end of the Cold War marked a shift in migration patterns such that migrations from south to north came to predominate global migration.

A significant change in immigration policy occurred after WWII. Both the U.S. and Canada began to distinguish between economically motivated, voluntary immigrants and **political refugees**. The conditions that existed after the war made it clear that some immigrants must be treated differently on the basis of humanitarian concerns. Fear of persecution caused massive migrations. The United Nations created the International Refugee Organization in 1946. In the next three years, this organization relocated over a million European refugees.

Immigration policy in the U.S. was carefully aligned with foreign policy. President Truman introduced the **Displaced Persons Act in 1948** which facilitated the admission of more than 400,000 persons from Europe. During the 1950s, however, the immigration policy became very restrictive. The McCarran-Walter Immigration Nationality Act of 1952 established a quota system and was clearly anti-Asian. The number of refugees from Eastern Europe far exceeded these quotas. Both President Truman and President Eisenhower urged extension of the quotas, and in time they were abandoned. Refugees from communist Europe were admitted under the President's Escapee Program of 1952 and the Refugee Relief Act of 1953.

Immigration by Asians had been restricted for some time and this policy did not change after WWII. The changes in immigration policies and the great influx of Europeans brought a wide variety of people into the U.S. To be sure, some were farmers and laborers, but many were highly trained and skilled scientists, teachers, inventors, and executives. This migration added to the American "melting pot" experience. The immigrants provided new sources of labor for a booming economy and the introduction of new cultural ideas and contributions to science and technology. The acceptance and assimilation of European immigrants was, for the most part, easier than the prejudiced assimilation of persons of Asian descent, particularly after the recent hostilities with Japan.

McCarthyism is a term that came to be used to describe the anti-communist movement within the federal government in the late 1940s and 1950s. The movement is named after Senator Joseph McCarthy of Wisconsin, who was one of its prime movers. Several congressional committees convened to investigate and interrogate citizens on their possible sympathies for or connections to the Communist Party. Failure to cooperate with these committees often resulted in the loss of one's job and placement on a "**blacklist**," which prevented one from being hired for many positions. After targeting the entertainment industry and educational institutions, McCarthy turned his sights on the Army. This proved unpopular with the American public, and his influence began to wane. McCarthy was eventually censured by the Senate for his overzealous attacks.

In 1960, **John F. Kennedy** was elected President. Kennedy espoused an ethic of national service, establishing the **Peace Corps** and similar programs in the mold of Roosevelt. He fostered the growing civil rights movement, and introduced a bill in Congress that proposed the end to legal discrimination against blacks and the abolition of Jim Crow segregation laws.

Kennedy was assassinated before the bill was completely through Congress. His Vice President, Lyndon Johnson, carried on support for the bill. The bill was enacted as the **Civil Rights Act of 1964**, which President Johnson signed. The **Civil Rights Acts of 1964 and 1968** prohibited discrimination in housing sales and rentals, employment, public accommodations, and voter registration.

Johnson was elected to his own full term as President in 1964, defeating the very conservative Barry Goldwater. Johnson had been a Roosevelt democrat during the 1930s, and proposed legislation and programs that were based on the principles of the New Deal. Once again, war interrupted domestic business as the United States became more fully involved in Vietnam. Controversy over the war led to a splintering of the Democratic Party during the run up to the presidential election of 1968, and several viable candidates emerged, including

Robert Kennedy. Johnson decided not to run for re-election.

Republican **Richard Nixon** won the election against Democratic nominee Hubert Humphrey. Nixon was more moderate than Goldwater, and, indeed, many of the liberal policies implemented by Kennedy and Johnson found their way into the Nixon administration.

Skill 6.5   Be knowledgeable about the struggle for African American civil rights

The economic boom following the war led to prosperity for many Americans in the 1950s. This prosperity did not extend to the poor blacks of the south, however, and the economic disparities between the races became more pronounced. After World War II and the Korean War, efforts began to relieve the problems of millions of African-Americans, including ending discrimination in education, housing, jobs, and the grinding widespread poverty.

Taking inspiration from similar struggles in India at the time led by Mahatma Ghandi, a burgeoning civil rights movement began to gain momentum under such leaders as **Dr. Martin Luther King, Jr**. The phrase "the civil rights movement" generally refers to the nation-wide effort made by black people and those who supported them to gain equal rights to whites and to eliminate segregation. Discussion of this movement is generally understood in terms of the period of the 1950s and 1960s.

The **key people** in the civil rights movement are:

Rosa Parks – A black seamstress from Montgomery Alabama who, in 1955, refused to give up her seat on the bus to a white man. This event is generally understood as the spark that lit the fire of the Civil Rights Movement. She has been generally regarded as the "mother of the Civil Rights Movement."

Martin Luther King, Jr. – the most prominent member of the Civil Rights movement. King promoted nonviolent methods of opposition to segregation. The "**Letter from Birmingham Jail**" explained the purpose of nonviolent action as a way to make people notice injustice. He led the march on Washington in 1963, at which he delivered the "**I Have a Dream**" speech. He received the 1968 Nobel Prize for Peace.

James Meredith – the first African American to enroll at the University of Mississippi.

Emmett Till – a teenage boy who was murdered in Mississippi while visiting from Chicago. The crime of which he was accused was "whistling at a white woman in a store." He was beaten and murdered, and his body was dumped in a river. His two white abductors were apprehended and tried. They were acquitted by an all-white jury. After the acquittal, they admitted their guilt, but remained free because of double jeopardy laws. His death became one of the key events in the movement.

Ralph Abernathy – A major figure in the Civil Rights Movement who succeeded Martin Luther King, Jr. as head of the Southern Christian Leadership Conference

Malcolm X – a political leader and part of the Civil Rights Movement. Unlike Dr King, Malcolm X did not take a pacifist stance and maintained the view that African Americans should do everything that was necessary to secure their rights. He was a prominent Black Muslim.

Stokeley Carmichael – one of the leaders of the Black Power movement that called for independent development of political and social institutions for blacks. Carmichael called for black pride and maintenance of black culture. He was head of the Student Nonviolent Coordinating Committee.

Key events of the Civil Rights Movement include:

Brown vs. Board of Education, 1954 – This Supreme Court case decision began the desegregation of public schools in the United States.

Rosa Parks and the Montgomery Bus Boycott, 1955–56 – After refusing to give up her seat on a bus in Montgomery, Alabama, Parks was arrested, tried, and convicted of disorderly conduct and violating a local ordinance. When word reached the black community a bus boycott was organized to protest the segregation of blacks and whites on public buses. The boycott lasted 381 days, until the ordinance was lifted.

Strategy shift to "direct action" – nonviolent resistance and civil disobedience, 1955–1965. This action consisted mostly of bus boycotts, sit-ins, freedom rides.

Formation of the Southern Christian Leadership Conference, 1957. This group was formed by Martin Luther King, Jr., John Duffy, Rev. C. D. Steele, Rev. T. J. Jemison, Rev. Fred Shuttlesworth, Ella Baker, A. Philip Randolph, Bayard Rustin, and Stanley Levison. The group provided training and assistance to local efforts to fight segregation. Non-violence was its central doctrine and its major method of fighting segregation and racism.

The Desegregation of Little Rock, 1957. Following up on the decision of the Supreme Court in Brown vs. Board of Education, the Arkansas school board voted to integrate the school system. The NAACP chose Arkansas as the place to push integration because it was considered a relatively progressive Southern state. However, the governor called up the National Guard to prevent nine black students from attending Little Rock's Central High School. President Eisenhower sent a division of the U.S. Army to Little Rock and federalized the state's National Guard, leading the way for the students to attend the high school.

Sit-ins – In 1960, students began to stage "sit-ins" at local lunch counters and stores as a means of protesting the refusal of those businesses to desegregate. The first was in Greensboro, NC. This led to a rash of similar campaigns throughout the South. Demonstrators began to protest parks, beaches, theaters, museums, and libraries. When arrested, the protesters made "jail-no-bail" pledges. This called attention to their cause and put the financial burden of providing jail space and food on the cities.

Freedom Rides – Activists traveled by bus throughout the Deep South to desegregate bus terminals (required by federal law). These protesters undertook extremely dangerous protests. Many buses were firebombed, and protestors were attacked by the KKK and beaten. They were crammed into small, airless jail cells and mistreated in many ways. Key figures in this effort included John Lewis, James Lawson, Diane Nash, Bob Moses, James Bevel, Charles McDew, Bernard Lafayette, Charles Jones, Lonnie King, Julian Bond, Hosea Williams, and Stokeley Carmichael.

The Birmingham Campaign, 1963–64. A campaign was planned to use sit-in, kneel-ins in churches, and a march to the county building to launch a voter registration campaign. The city obtained an injunction forbidding all such protests. The protesters, including Martin Luther King, Jr., believed the injunction was unconstitutional, and defied it. They were arrested. While in jail, King wrote his famous "Letter from Birmingham Jail." When the campaign began to falter, the "Children's Crusade" called students to leave school and join the protests. The events became news when more than 600 students were jailed. The next day more students joined the protest.

The media was present and broadcast vivid pictures to the nation, showing fire hoses being used to knock down children and dogs attacking some of them. The resulting public outrage led the Kennedy administration to intervene. About a month later, a committee was formed to end hiring discrimination, arrange for the release of jailed protesters, and establish normative communication between blacks and whites. Four months later, the KKK bombed the **Sixteenth Street Baptist Church**, killing four girls.

The March on Washington, 1963. This was a march on Washington for jobs and freedom. It was a combined effort of all major civil rights organizations. The goals of the march were: meaningful civil rights laws, a massive federal works program, full and fair employment, decent housing, the right to vote, and adequate integrated education. It was at this march that Martin Luther King, Jr. made the famous "I Have a Dream" speech.

Mississippi Freedom Summer, 1964. Students were brought from other states to Mississippi to assist local activists in registering voters, teaching in "Freedom Schools" and in forming the Mississippi Freedom Democratic Party. Three of the workers disappeared, murdered by the KKK. It took six weeks to find their bodies. The national uproar forced President Johnson to send in the FBI. Johnson was able to use public sentiment to effect passage in Congress of the Civil Rights Act of 1964.

Selma to Montgomery marches, 1965. Attempts to obtain voter registration in Selma, Alabama, had been largely unsuccessful due to opposition from the city's sheriff. M.L. King came to the city to lead a series of marches. He and more than 200 demonstrators were arrested and jailed. Each successive march was met with violent resistance by police. In March, a group of more than 600 intended to walk from Selma to Montgomery (54 miles). News media were on hand when, six blocks into the march, state and local law enforcement officials attacked the marchers with billy clubs, tear gas, rubber tubes wrapped in barbed wire, and bull whips. They were driven back to Selma. National broadcast of the footage provoked a nation-wide response. President Johnson again used public sentiment to achieve passage of the Voting Rights Act of 1965.

Key policies, legislation and court cases included the following:

Brown v. Board of Education, 1954 – the Supreme Court declared that Plessy v. Ferguson was unconstitutional. This was the ruling that had established "Separate but Equal" as the basis for segregation. With this decision, the Court ordered immediate desegregation in the public schools.

Civil Rights Act of 1964 – bars discrimination in public accommodations, employment and education.

Voting Rights Act of 1965 – suspended poll taxes, literacy tests, and other voter tests for voter registration. This law irrevocably changed the political landscape of the South.

Tragically, the Reverend Martin Luther King, Jr., an influential leader of the Civil Rights Movement and its most eloquent spokesman, was assassinated in Memphis, Tennessee, sparking racial riots in many American cities. Also, Senator Robert F. Kennedy of New York, the late President John F. Kennedy's younger brother, was assassinated in Los Angeles after winning the California Democratic Primary. Before he died, it looked very possible that he would have won the party's nomination, running on an anti-war platform.

Skill 6.6   Recognize and be able to discuss the political, economic and social issues of the 20th century to present

"**Minority rights**" encompasses two ideas: the first is the normal individual rights of members of ethnic, racial, class, religious, or sexual minorities; the second is collective rights of minority groups. Various civil rights movements have sought to guarantee that the individual rights of persons are not denied on the basis of being part of a minority group. The effects of these movements may be seen in guarantees of minority representation, affirmative action quotas, etc.

Since 1941, a number of anti-discrimination laws have been passed by Congress, many—if not most of which—were designed to protect the rights of minority or under-represented groups. These acts have protected the civil rights of several groups of Americans. These laws include:

- Fair Employment Act of 1941
- Civil Rights Act of 1964
- Immigration and Nationality Services Act of 1965
- Voting Rights Act of 1965
- Civil Rights Act of 1968
- Age Discrimination in Employment Act of 1967
- Age Discrimination Act of 1975
- Pregnancy Discrimination Act of 1978
- Americans with Disabilities Act of 1990
- Civil Rights Act of 1991
- Employment Non-Discrimination Act

Numerous groups have used various forms of protest, attempts to sway public opinion, legal action, and congressional lobbying to obtain full protection of their civil rights under the Constitution. The **disability rights** movement was a successful effort to guarantee access to public buildings and transportation, equal access to education and employment, and equal protection under the law in terms of access to insurance and other basic rights of American citizens. As a result of these efforts, public buildings and public transportation must be accessible to persons with disabilities, discrimination in hiring or housing on the basis of disability is also illegal.

A "prisoners' rights" movement has been working for many years to ensure the basic human rights of persons incarcerated for crimes. **Immigrant rights** movements have provided for employment and housing rights, as well as preventing abuse of immigrants through hate crimes. In some states, immigrant rights movements have led to bi-lingual education and public information access. Another group movement to obtain equal rights is the lesbian, gay, bisexual, and transgender social movement. This movement seeks equal housing, freedom from social and employment discrimination, and equal recognition of relationships under the law.

The **women's rights** movement is concerned with the freedoms of women as differentiated from broader ideas of human rights. These issues are generally different from those that affect men and boys because of biological conditions or social constructs. The rights the movement has sought to protect throughout history include:

- The right to vote
- The right to work
- The right to fair wages
- The right to bodily integrity and autonomy
- The right to own property
- The right to an education
- The right to hold public office
- Marital rights
- Parental rights
- Religious rights
- The right to serve in the military
- The right to enter into legal contracts

The movement for women's rights has resulted in many social and political changes. Many of the ideas that seemed very radical merely 100 years ago are now normative.

Some of the most famous leaders in the women's movement throughout American history are:

- Abigail Adams
- Gloria E. Anzaldua
- Betty Friedan
- Olympe de Gouges
- Gloria Steinem
- Harriet Tubman
- Mary Wollstonecraft
- Virginia Woolf
- Germaine Greer

Many within the women's movement are primarily committed to justice and the natural rights of all people. This has led many members of the women's movement to be involved in the Black Civil Rights Movement, the gay rights movement, and the recent social movement to protect the rights of fathers. It should be noted that many of these groups often support one another (though not always) as they seek similar goals of protection of rights and justice for minority or under-represented groups.

Students of American history should be familiar with the accomplishments and contributions of other American women. Previous mention has been made of the accomplishments of such nineteenth century women as: writer Louisa Mae Alcott; abolitionist Harriet Beecher Stowe; women's rights activists **Elizabeth Cady Stanton** and **Lucretia Mott**; physician Dr. Elizabeth Blackwell; women's education activists Mary Lyon, Catharine Esther Beecher, and Emma Hart Willard; prison and asylum reform activist **Dorothea Dix**; social reformer, humanitarian, pursuer of peace Jane Addams; aviatrix Amelia Earhart; women's suffrage activists **Susan B. Anthony**, Carrie Chapman Catt, and Anna Howard Shaw; Supreme Court Associate Justices **Sandra Day O'Connor** and Ruth Bader Ginsberg; and many, many more who have made tremendous contributions in science, politics and government, music and the arts (such as Jane Alexander who is National Chairperson of the National Endowment for the Arts), education, athletics, law, etc.

W.E.B. DuBois, another outstanding African-American leader and spokesman, believed that only continuous and vigorous protests against injustices and inequalities coupled with appeals to black pride would effect changes. The results of his efforts were the formation of the Urban League and the NAACP (the National Association for the Advancement of Colored People), which today continue to eliminate discriminations and secure equality and equal rights.

Others who made significant contributions were **Dr. George Washington Carver** who worked to improve agricultural techniques for both black and white farmers; the writers William Wells Brown, Paul L. Dunbar, Langston Hughes, and Charles W. Chesnutt; musicians Duke Ellington, W.C. Handy, Marion Anderson, Louis Armstrong, Leontyne Price, Jessye Norman, Ella Fitzgerald, and many, many others.

Inflation increased in the late 1960s, and the 1970s witnessed a period of high unemployment, the result of a severe recession. The decision of the OPEC (Organization of Petroleum Exporting Countries) ministers to cut back on oil production—thus raising the price of a barrel of oil—created a fuel shortage. This made it clear that energy and fuel conservation was necessary in the American economy, especially since fuel shortages created two energy crises during the decade of the 1970s. Americans experienced shortages of fuel oil for heating and gasoline for cars and other vehicles.

Skill 6.7   Discuss the Vietnam War and American society

U.S. involvement in the **Vietnam War** from 1957 to 1973 was the second phase of three in Vietnam's history. The first phase began in 1946 when the Vietnamese fought French troops for control of the country. Vietnam, prior to 1946, had been part of the French colony of Indochina since 1861 along with Laos and Kampuchea or Cambodia. In 1954, the defeated French left and the country became divided into Communist North and Democratic South. The United States' aid and influence continued as part of the U.S. "Cold War" foreign policy to help any nation threatened by Communism.

The second phase involved a much more direct U.S. commitment. The Communist Vietnamese considered the war one of national liberation, a struggle to avoid continual dominance and influence of a foreign power. Participants were the United States of America, Australia, New Zealand, South and North Vietnam, South Korea, Thailand, and the Philippines. With active U.S. involvement from 1957 to 1973, it was the longest war participated in by the U.S. to date. It was tremendously destructive and completely divided the American public in their opinions and feelings about the war. Many were frustrated and angered by the fact that it was the first war fought on foreign soil in which U.S. combat forces were totally unable to achieve their goals and objectives.

The Vietnam War also divided the Democratic Party, and the **1968 Democratic National Convention** in Chicago turned out to be a highly contentious and bitterly fought, both on the floor of the convention and outside, where thousands had gathered to protest the Vietnam War. Vice President Hubert H. Humphrey became the party's nominee, but he led a divided party.

In Vietnam, the forces of the **Viet Cong** and the **North Vietnamese Army (NVA)** launched a coordinated and devastating offensive on January 30, on the eve of Tet, the Lunar New Year, disproving the Johnson Administration officials who claimed that the Vietnamese Communists were no longer a viable military force. Although the **Tet Offensive** was a tactical defeat for the Viet Cong, it no longer could field a large enough military force to match American firepower in a set-piece engagement, it was a strategic defeat for the Americans, in public relations and the political will to continue in a seemingly endless conflict.

A cease-fire was arranged in January 1973 and a few months later, U.S. troops left for good. The third and final phase consisted of fighting between the Vietnamese but ended April 30, 1975, with the surrender of South Vietnam and the entire country being united under a Communist ruler.

Poverty remained a serious problem in the central sections of large cities resulting in riots and soaring crime rates, which ultimately found its way to the suburbs. The escalation of the war in Vietnam and the social conflict and upheaval of support vs opposition to U.S. involvement led to antiwar demonstrations, escalation of drug abuse, weakening of the family unit, homelessness, poverty, mental illness, along with increasing social, mental, and physical problems experienced by the Vietnam veterans returning to families, marriages, and a country all divided and torn apart.

Returning veterans faced not only readjustment to normal civilian life but also bitterness, anger, rejection, and no heroes' welcomes. Many suffered severe physical and deep psychological problems. The war set a precedent where both

Congress and the American people actively challenged U.S. military and foreign policy. The conflict, though tempered markedly by time, still exists and still has a definite effect on people.

Skill 6.8   Understand the conservative movement and the Reagan Revolution

In the decade preceding the election of Ronald Reagan in 1980, the United States had experienced increased inflation, an upswing in the crime rate, and a fuel shortage crisis. These factors contributed to a general dissatisfaction with the federal government, and a lack of confidence in the ability of the government to prevent or solve the nation's problems. It was a time of social division, as well. The 1973 Supreme Court decision in *Roe vs. Wade* upheld the legality of abortion, which angered many conservatives and became a rallying point for the right wing of the Republican Party, which had been out of favor for many years.

This conservative branch of the party had enjoyed prominence in 1964, when Barry Goldwater was selected to run for President on the Republican ticket. Goldwater was defeated, and the Republicans found more success four years later with the more moderate Richard Nixon. Then came the **Watergate** scandal, resulting in the first-ever resignation of a sitting American president, and was the most crucial domestic crisis of the 1970s. Nixon's presidency ended in disgrace with his resignation and in the meantime the Democrats retained their strong hold in both houses of Congress.

In 1976, Democrat Jimmy Carter was elected President, and it was on his watch that public dissatisfaction was to reach its peak. This dissatisfaction was to provide the conservative Republicans an opportunity to offer a new direction, and the American public was receptive. Bolstering the more conservative Republicans were large numbers of religious activists who gathered behind television evangelists **Jerry Falwell** and **Pat Robertson**. This large bloc not only opposed abortion but pressed for a conservative agenda that invoked religious doctrine in interpreting and proposing social legislation.

In **Ronald Reagan**, the rising conservative movement found an eloquent and charismatic representative. Reagan was a former movie star who was comfortable in front of a camera. He had entered politics in California, eventually becoming governor. He had supported the conservative Goldwater in 1964, and had delivered a speech on his behalf at the nominating convention. Reagan was confident, and carried a positive message of American strength that resonated with many voters. He won the presidential election of 1980 against Jimmy Carter in a landslide. He was elected to a second term against Walter Mondale in 1984.

Reagan brought with him a cabinet of conservative advisors who believed in a conservative social agenda, limited government involvement in the economy, and American strength abroad. In 1988, Reagan's vice president, **George H.W.**

Bush, was elected president and continued many of the conservative policies implemented by Reagan. The religious groups that had gained a foothold in the years surrounding Reagan's first election continued to grow and still maintains political influence, particularly in the Republican Party.

In 2000, conservative **George W. Bush**, the son of President George H.W. Bush, was elected President. George W. Bush populated his cabinet with many of the same people who had advised President Reagan twenty years earlier, thereby building on the conservative base that Ronald Reagan had laid.

Skill 6.9   Discuss the growth of Latino influence in American society

Although Puerto Rico became a territory of the U.S. at the end of the Spanish American War, there was little immigration during the first half of the century. The transition from Spanish colony to U.S. possession was not easy for the people of Puerto Rico. Residents have been U.S. citizens since 1917 but have no direct voting representation in the Congress. Technically, moving from the island to the U.S. mainland is considered internal migration rather than immigration. This does not, however, recognize that leaving an island with a distinct culture and identity involves the same cultural conflicts and intellectual, language, and other adjustments as those faced by most immigrants.

A severe economic depression created widespread poverty in the early part of the twentieth century. Few Puerto Ricans were able to afford the fare to travel by boat to the mainland. In 1910, there were only about 2,000 Puerto Ricans living on the mainland; most created small enclaves in New York City. By 1945, there were 13,000 Puerto Ricans in New York City. But by 1946, there were more than 50,000. And for each of the next ten years, more than 25,000 additional Puerto Ricans would immigrate each year. By the mid-1960s, there were more than a million Puerto Ricans on the mainland.

The primary factors that account for the sudden migration included a continuing economic depression in Puerto Rico, and the recruitment of workers from Puerto Rico by U.S. factory owners and employment agencies. Another factor was the return of thousands of war veterans to Puerto Rico who wanted more than the island could offer. Most important, however, was the sudden availability of air travel at an affordable cost.

Many of the immigrant Puerto Ricans established communities in major east coast cities, the mid-Atlantic farming regions, and also in the mill towns of New England. A very large number of these immigrants settled in the northeastern part of Manhattan that came to be known as **Spanish Harlem**. They quickly became an important factor in the city's political and cultural life. Although the first generation of migrants faced prejudice, unemployment, discrimination, and poverty, most remained and learned to thrive.

Today, Puerto Rican immigrants and their descendants have developed several means of preserving and teaching their heritage. Their communities are strong and integrated into the mainstream of the society. They have contributed to the growth of the nation and the inclusion within every area of American life from politics to education to sports and the arts.

Skill 6.10 Know the major developments in science, medicine, and mass culture

The population of the U.S. had greatly increased, and along with it the nation's industries, resulting in harmful pollution of the environment. Factory smoke, automobile exhaust, waste from factories and other sources all combined to create hazardous air, water, and ground pollution which, if not brought under control and significantly diminished, would severely endanger all life on earth.

The 1980s was the decade of the horrible **Exxon Valdez** oil spill off the Alaskan coast and the nuclear accident and melt-down at the Ukrainian nuclear power plant at Chernobyl. The U.S. had a narrow escape with the near disaster at **Three Mile Island** Nuclear Plant in Pennsylvania.

The 1980s also saw the difficulties of rising inflation, recession, recovery, and the insecurity of long-term employment. Foreign competition and imports, the use of robots and other advanced technology in industries, the opening and operation of American companies and factories in other countries to lower labor costs, all contributed to the economic and employment problems.

The Soviet Union was the first industrialized nation to successfully begin a program of **space flight and exploration,** launching Sputnik and putting the first man in space. The United States also experienced success in its space program successfully landing space crews on the moon.

On January 28, 1986, the United States suffered the loss of the seven crew members of the NASA space shuttle **Challenger**. The reliability and soundness of numerous savings and loans institutions were in serious jeopardy when hundreds of these failed and others went into bankruptcy due to customer default on loans and mismanagement. Congressional legislation helped rebuild the industry.

The deeper human problems have been more seriously addressed only since the end of the Cold War and the Arms Race. Only then could attention be given to the growing divide between the rich and the poor. The conditions of life in the cities and in third world countries have only begun to be addressed. The massive relocation from the farm to the city has changed the way people think about the environment, about values, and about other people.

In art and architecture, there has been a search for new forms, and for basic symbols, that would speak a universal language. This fragmentation and anxiety has found expression in cubism and surrealism. In painting, one need only consider the works of Cezanne, Picasso, and Dali. In sculpture, artists took one of two directions: either looking back and preserving the conventional ideals of beauty, or experimenting with distortion and the abstract concepts of time and force. Architecture tended to move toward more functional lines and expressions.

In religion and philosophy there have been great changes as well. For much of the period, religious interpretation tended to swing like a pendulum between the liberal and the conservative. By the end of the twentieth century, however, the struggle for meaning and identity had resulted in a generalized conservative trend. This tendency can be seen in most religions yet today. Religion and philosophy are, to be sure, the means of self-definition and the understanding of one's place in the universe. Recent conservative trends, however, have had a polarizing effect. Issues of the relationship of Church and State have arisen and been resolved in most countries during this period. Yet, at the same time there has been an increasing effort to understand the religious beliefs of others, either to create new ways to define one's religion over and against other religions, or as the basis of new attacks on the values and teachings of other religions.

COMPETENCY 7.0   **HUMAN BEGINNINGS, EARLY HUMAN SOCIETIES, AND THE ROOTS OF WESTERN CIVILIZATION: PREHISTORY TO A.D. 500**

Skill 7.1   Understand human origins and prehistory

Anthropology is the scientific study of human culture and humanity, the relationship between man and his culture. Anthropologists study different groups, how they relate to other cultures, and patterns of behavior, similarities and differences. Their research is two-fold: cross-cultural and comparative. Their major method of study is referred to as **participant observation**. The anthropologist studies and learns about the people being studied by living among them and participating with them in their daily lives. Other methods may be used but this is the most characteristic.

Archaeology is the scientific study of past human cultures by studying the remains they left behind—objects such as pottery, bones, buildings, tools, and artwork. Archaeologists locate and examine any evidence to help explain the way people lived in past times. They use special equipment and techniques to gather the evidence and make a special effort to keep detailed records of their findings since a lot of their research results in destruction of the remains being studied. The chemical process of radiocarbon dating is beneficial in studying this field.

The first step is to locate an archaeological site using various methods. Next, surveying the site takes place starting with a detailed description of the site with notes, maps, photographs, and collecting artifacts from the surface. **Excavating** follows either by digging for buried objects or by diving and working in submersible decompression chambers, when underwater. Archaeologists record and preserve the evidence for eventual classifying, dating, and evaluating of their find.

Although written records only go back about 4,500 years, scientists have pieced together evidence which documents the existence of humans (or "man-apes) as far back as 600,000 years ago. Knowledge about early humans comes from many different sources, including fossils derived from **burial pits**, the occasional bones found in rock deposits, and archaeological excavations of tools, pottery, and paintings. Even then study of living primitives can yield clues about ancient man.

The first manlike creatures arose in many parts of the world about one million years ago. By slow stages, these creatures developed into types of men who discovered fire and tools. These creatures had human-sized brains and inbred to produce **Cro-Magnon** type creatures circa 25,000 years ago, from which **homo sapiens** descended. These primitive humans demonstrated wide behavior patterns and great adaptability. Little is known in the way of details, including when language began to develop. They are believed to have lived in small communities that developed on the basis of the need to hunt. **Cave paintings** reveal a belief that magic pictures of animals could conjure up real ones. Some figurines seem to indicate belief in fertility gods and goddesses. Belief in some form of afterlife is indicated by burial formalities.

Fire and weapons were in use quite early. Archaeological evidence points to the use of hatchets, awls, needles, and cutting tools in the **Paleolithic**, or Old Stone Age, one million years ago. Artifacts of the **Neolithic** or New Stone Age, dating from 6000 to 8000 BCE, include indications of polished tools, domesticated animals, the wheel, and some agriculture. Pottery and textiles have been found dating to the end of the New Stone Age. The discovery of metals in the **Bronze Age**, 3000 BCE, is concurrent with the establishment of what are believed to be the first civilizations. The Iron Age followed quickly on the heels of the Bronze Age.

By 4000 BCE humans lived in villages, engaged in animal husbandry, grew grains, sailed in boats, and practiced religions. Civilizations arose earliest in the fertile river valleys of the Nile, Mesopotamia, the Indus, and the Hwang Ho.

There are four prerequisites of civilization:

- Use of metals rather than stone for tools and weapons
- A system of writing
- A calendar
- A territorial state organized on the basis of residence in the geographic region.

The earliest known civilizations developed in the Tigris-Euphrates valley of Mesopotamia (modern Iraq) and the Nile valley of Egypt between 4000 BCE and 3000 BCE. Because these civilizations arose in river valleys, they are known as **fluvial civilizations**.

Geography and the physical environment played a critical role in the rise and the survival of both of these civilizations. First, the rivers provided a source of water that would sustain life, including animal life. The hunters of the society had ample access to a variety of animals, initially for hunting to provide food, as well as hides, bones, antlers, etc. from which clothing, tools, and art could be made. Second, the proximity to water provided a natural attraction to animals that could be herded and husbanded to provide a stable supply of food and animal products. Third, the rivers of these regions overflowed their banks each year, leaving behind a deposit of very rich soil. As these early people began to experiment with growing crops rather than gathering food, the soil was fertile and water was readily available to produce sizeable harvests. In time, the people developed systems of irrigation that channeled water to the crops without significant human effort on a continuing basis.

The **Fertile Crescent** was bounded on the West by the Mediterranean, on the South by the Arabian Desert, on the north by the Taurus Mountains, and on the east by the Zagros Mountains. The designation "Fertile Crescent" was applied by the famous historian and Egyptologist James Breasted to the part of the Near East that extended from the Persian Gulf to the Sinai Peninsula. It included Mesopotamia, Syria, and Palestine. This region was marked by almost constant invasions and migrations. These invaders and migrants seemed to have destroyed the culture and civilization that existed. Upon taking a longer view, however, it becomes apparent that they actually absorbed and supplemented the civilization that existed before their arrival. This is one of the reasons the civilization developed so quickly and created such an advanced culture.

Skill 7.2 Identify political, economic, religious, and cultural characteristics of the early civilizations of Egypt, the Middle East, India, and China

Ancient civilizations were those cultures that developed to a greater degree and were considered advanced. There are a number of ancient civilizations worth examining, each with its own major accomplishments.

The ancient civilization of the **Sumerians** invented the wheel, developed irrigation through use of canals, dikes, and devices for raising water, devised the system of cuneiform writing, learned to divide time, and built large boats for trade. The **Babylonians** devised the famous **Code of Hammurabi**, the first written code of laws, which would later form the basis for our modern laws. **Egypt** made numerous significant contributions including construction of the great pyramids, development of hieroglyphic writing, preservation of bodies after death, making paper from papyrus, the invention of the method of counting in groups of 1 to 10 (the decimal system), completion of a solar calendar, and laying the foundation for science and astronomy.

The civilizations of the Sumerians, Amorites, Hittites, Assyrians, Chaldeans, and Persians controlled various areas of the land we call Mesopotamia. The culture of **Mesopotamia** was definitely autocratic in nature. The various civilizations that crisscrossed the Fertile Crescent were very much top-heavy, with a single ruler at the head of the government and, in many cases, also the head of the religion. The people followed his strict instructions or faced the consequences, which were usually dire and often life-threatening.

For example, each Sumerian city-state (and there were a few) had its own god, with the city-state's leader doubling as the high priest of worship of that local god. Subsequent cultures had a handful of gods as well, although they had more of a national worship structure, with high priests centered in the capital city as advisers to the tyrant. With few exceptions, tyrants and military leaders controlled the vast majority of aspects of society, including trade, religions, and the laws.

Trade was vastly important to these civilizations, since they had access to some but not all of the things that they needed to survive. Some trading agreements led to occupation, as was the case with the Sumerians, who didn't bother to build walls to protect their wealth of knowledge. Egypt and the Phoenician cities were powerful and regular trading partners of the various Mesopotamian cultures. Legacies handed down to us from these people include:

- The first use of writing, the wheel, and banking (Sumeria)
- The first epic story (*Gilgamesh*)
- The first library dedicated to preserving knowledge (instituted by the Assyrian leader Ashurbanipal)
- The Hanging Gardens of Babylon (built by the Chaldean Nebuchadnezzar)

One of the earliest civilizations to develop in the Nile River Valley, Kushite states rose to power before a period of Egyptian incursion into the area. The earliest historical record of **Kush** is in Egyptian sources. This civilization was characterized by a settled way of life in fortified mud-brick villages. They subsisted on hunting and fishing, herding cattle, and gathering grain. Skeletal remains suggest that the people were a blend of Negroid and Mediterranean peoples. This civilization appears to be the second oldest in Africa (after Egypt).

In government, the king ruled through a law of custom that was interpreted by priests. The king was elected from members of the royal family. As in Egypt, descent was determined through the mother's line, but unlike the Egyptians, the Kushites were ruled by a series of female monarchs. The Kushite religion was **polytheistic**, including all of the primary Egyptian gods. There were, however, regional gods which were the principal gods in their regions. Derived from other African cultures, there was also a lion warrior god. This civilization was vital through the last half of the first millennium BC, but it suffered about 300 years of gradual decline until it was eventually conquered by the Nuba people.

The **Phoenicians** were sea traders well known for their manufacturing skills in glass and metals and the development of their famous purple dye. They became so very proficient in the skill of navigation, they were able to sail by the stars at night. Further, they devised an alphabet using symbols to represent single sounds, which was an improved extension of the Egyptian principle and writing system. The ancient **Assyrians** were warlike and aggressive due to a highly organized military and used horse drawn chariots.

The **Minoans** had a system of writing using symbols to represent syllables in words. They built palaces with multiple levels containing many rooms, water, and sewage systems with flush toilets, bathtubs, hot and cold running water, and bright paintings on the walls. The **Mycenaeans** later changed the Minoan writing system to aid their own language and used symbols to represent syllables.

The ancient **Persians** developed an alphabet, contributed the religions and/or philosophies of **Zoroastrianism**, **Mithraism**, and **Gnosticism**, and allowed conquered peoples to retain their own customs, laws, and religions. In **India**, the caste system was developed, the principle of **zero** in mathematics was discovered, and the major religion of Hinduism was begun.

China is considered by some historians to be the oldest, uninterrupted civilization in the world and was in existence around the same time as the ancient civilizations founded in Egypt, Mesopotamia, and the **Indus Valley**. The Chinese studied nature and weather; stressed the importance of education, family, and a strong central government; followed the religions of Buddhism, Confucianism, and Taoism; and invented such things as gunpowder, paper, printing, and the magnetic compass.

China began building the Great Wall, practiced crop rotation and terrace farming, increased the importance of the silk industry, and developed caravan routes across Central Asia for extensive trade all while many of the nations of Europe were still in their infancy. They also increased proficiency in rice cultivation and developed a written language based on drawings or pictographs. The Chinese language has no alphabet symbolizing sounds; instead, each word or character had a form different from all others.

Skill 7.3 Understand fundamental ideas and beliefs of Hinduism, Buddhism, and Confucianism

In **India**, **Vedic Hinduism** as practiced by the Aryans, evolved into its now recognizable form as Dravidian states south of the Indus River were conquered. Local deities and heroes such as Krishna, Naga, and Hanuman were incorporated into the Hindu belief system of multiple aspects of a single godhead. Industry and commerce developed along with extensive trading with the Near East. Outstanding advances in the fields of science and medicine were made along with its being one of the first in navigation and maritime enterprises during this time.

Buddhism is an offshoot of Brahmanical Hindu thought, which arose during the fifth century BCE. However, unlike traditional Hinduism, Buddhism was founded by Gautama Siddartha Shakyamuni, a crown prince who sought enlightenment and renounced the material world after observing suffering in the form of illness, old age, and death, much to the dismay of his father, the maharajah. After years of asceticism and austerities, the prince achieved enlightenment after meditating under a tree for forty-nine days. He was called the "**Buddha**" (a Sanskrit word meaning "Awakened One") after his enlightenment and told his followers that life was suffering, suffering was caused by desire, and desire was caused by delusion of the mind, which leads to death and rebirth, and leads to another cycle of suffering.

Buddhists believe that to avoid suffering, one must get rid of the delusions that cause desire and break the cycle of life, death, and rebirth, called "samsara" a concept from Hindu theology. Other concepts adapted from Hindu theology are "**karma**," which is the balance of action versus later effect that will trigger samsara, and "dharma," which can mean "fate", "destiny", or "unbreakable rules that govern all phenomena," depending on its context. Escape from the cycles of samsara was called "**nirvana**," or "extinguishment." Buddhism later split off into two main schools: Theravada ("Older Way") or Southern Buddhism and Mahayana ("Great Vehicle").

Theravada Buddhism teaches that individuals can gain enough merit over countless cycles of rebirth and eventually attain enlightenment. This branch of Buddhism is the original one as practiced shortly after the Buddha's death. It is this form that spread south to Sri Lanka and Southeast Asia.

Mahayana Buddhism is a later school that revises the Theravada and teaches that certain individuals who had achieved enlightenment declined and stayed behind to assist other, less enlightened individuals attain enlightenment rather than passing into Nirvana. They also believed that all beings pass completely into Nirvana. This is the form that spread to Tibet and eastward to China, Korea, and Japan.

One tremendous bit of legacy that we can trace to the Aryans was the **caste system**, which permeates nearly all aspects of Indian society today. The prohibitions might be less these days, but the castes are still there. The twin great religions of Hinduism and Buddhism had their genesis in India; both are still very much alive today, emphasizing their doctrines of rebirth, enlightenment, nirvana, and more. The Hindu doctrine of reincarnation especially went hand-in-hand with the caste system, making it nearly impossible for the disadvantaged to *ever* improve their fortunes.

Confucianism is a Chinese religion based on the teachings of the Chinese philosopher Confucius. There is no clergy, no organization, and no belief in a deity or in life after death. It emphasizes political and moral ideas with respect for authority and ancestors. Rulers were expected to govern according to high moral standards. In the aftermath of the fall of Qin, **Confucianism** became the official political philosophy of the Han. Scholarship and the criterion for appointment to the imperial bureaucracy were based on the Five Classics: Odes, History, Rites (Etiquette), Change (Yi Jing), and the Spring and Autumn Annals (a history of a portion of the Zhou Dynasty edited by Confucius).

Additionally, scholars were expected to have a thorough knowledge of the Analects of Confucius (a collection of his teachings) and Mencius (Meng Zi was a

Confucian scholar who expanded on the themes espoused by Confucius and his most esteemed students). The accomplishments of the Han Dynasty were so unprecedented and profound, that later Chinese referred to themselves as "People of the Han" and Chinese characters have been called "Han Words" (literal translation of the two characters that make up the word for "Chinese characters") ever since.

Skill 7.4   Examine origins, central teachings, and legacies of Judaism

The **Hebrews**, also known as the ancient **Israelites** instituted "**monotheism**," which is the worship of one God, Yahweh, and combined the sixty-six books of the Hebrew and Christian Greek scriptures into the Bible we have today. They also created a powerful legacy of political and philosophical traditions, much of which survives to this day. In law and religion, especially, we can draw a more or less straight line from then to now. Modern western societies owe a tremendous debt to both the legal and religious aspects of these ancient societies.

Israel was not the first ancient civilization to have a series of laws for its people to follow. However, thanks to the popularity of the **Ten Commandments**, we think of the Israelites in this way. This simple set of laws, some of which are not laws at all but societal instructions, maintains to this day a central role in societies the world over. Such commandments as the ones that prohibit stealing and killing were revolutionary in their day because they applied to everyone, not just the disadvantaged. In many ancient cultures, the rich and powerful were above the law because they could buy their way out of trouble and because it wasn't always clear what the laws were. Echoing the Code of Hammurabi and preceding Rome's Twelve Tables, the Ten Commandments provided a written record of laws, so all knew what was prohibited.

The civilization of Israel is also known as the first to assume a worship of just one god. The Christian communities built on this tradition, and both faiths exist and are expanding today, especially in western countries. Rather than a series of gods, each of which was in charge of a different aspect of nature or society, the ancient Israelites and Christians believed in just one god, called Yahweh or God, depending on which religion you look at. This divine being was, these peoples believed, the "one, true god," was lord over all. This worship of just one god had more of a personal nature to it, and the result was the believers thought themselves able to talk (or, more properly, pray) directly to their god, whereas the peoples of Mesopotamia and Egypt thought of the gods as distant and unapproachable.

Skill 7.5   Understand institutions, culture, and legacies of Greek civilization

Ancient Greece is often called the "**Cradle of Western Civilization**" because of the enormous influence it had not only on the time in which it flourished, but on western culture ever since. Early Greek institutions have survived for thousands of years, and have influenced the entire world.

The **Athenian form of democracy**, with each citizen having an equal vote in his own government, is a philosophy upon which all modern democracies are based. In the United States, the Greek tradition of democracy was honored in the choice of **Greek architectural** styles for the nation's government buildings. The modern **Olympic Games** are a revival of an ancient Greek tradition and many of the events are recreations of original contests.

The works of the Greek epic poet **Homer** are considered the earliest in western literature, and are still read and taught today. The tradition of the theater was born in Greece, with the plays of Aristophanes and others. In philosophy, **Aristotle** developed an approach to learning that emphasized observation and thought, and **Socrates** and **Plato** contemplated the nature of being and the origins and ideals of government and political relations. Greek mythology, centered around a pantheon of gods and the mortals they interact with, has been the source of inspiration for literature into the present day.

In the field of mathematics, **Pythagoras** and **Euclid** laid the foundation of geometry and **Archimedes** calculated the value of pi. Herodotus and Thucydides were the first to apply research and interpretation to written history.

In the arts, Greek sensibilities were held as perfect forms to which others might strive. In sculpture, the Greeks achieved an idealistic aesthetic that had not been perfected before that time.

The Greek civilization served as an inspiration to the Roman Republic, which followed in its tradition of democracy, and was directly influenced by its achievements in art and science. Later, during the Renaissance, European scholars and artists would rediscover ancient Greece's love for dedicated inquiry and artistic expression, leading to a surge in scientific discoveries and advancements in the arts.

Skill 7.6   Have knowledge of Alexander the Great and the spread of Greek culture

Alexander was a Macedonian who was tutored by the Greek philosopher Aristotle, and who became one of the greatest conquerors of history. Alexander lived in the fourth century BC.

Alexander was the son of Philip II of Macedon who had united the various city-states of Greece into one kingdom. Upon Philip's death, these states again sought independence, but were conquered and reunited by Alexander. From there, Alexander expanded his empire to the east and south, reaching as far as Egypt and India. He founded the city of **Alexandria** in Egypt, which became a major center of learning. At its peak, Alexander's empire covered most of the known world.

As Alexander conquered and moved through foreign regions, he increased his forces by absorbing foreign officers and soldiers into his own army. He also encouraged his own soldiers to marry into local populations. This policy of inclusion and expansion had the effect of bringing Greek culture to the east with its ideals of learning and inquiry. For example, Alexander was apparently very affected by Persian culture after conquering a part of that region, and for a time took to wearing Persian style clothing and adopting some of their customs. This exemplified the spread of eastern culture to the west.

Alexander died mysteriously after a sudden illness at the age of 33 in 323 BCE. Having left no heir, his empire was split into four kingdoms. His reputation did not die, however, and Greek culture in general and Alexander, in particular, served as the inspiration for the Roman leaders who would eventually recreate much of his empire in the following centuries.

Skill 7.7   Examine institutions, culture, and legacies of the Roman Republic and Empire

The ancient civilization of Rome owed much to the Greeks. Romans admired Greek architecture and arts, and built upon these traditions to create a distinct tradition of their own that would influence the western world for centuries.

In government, the Romans took the Athenian concept of democracy and built it into a complex system of **representative government** that included executive, legislative and judicial functions. In the arts, Romans created a realistic approach to portraiture, in contrast to the more idealized form of the Greeks. In architecture, Rome borrowed directly from the Greek tradition, but also developed the dome and the arch, allowing for larger and more dramatic forms. The Romans continued the Greek tradition of learning, often employing Greeks to educate their children.

The Roman Republic flourished in the centuries leading up to the advent of the Christian era. An organized bureaucracy and active political population provided elite Roman citizens with the means to ascend to positions of considerable authority. During the first century BCE, **Gaius Julius Caesar** ambitiously began to gather support among the ruling authorities of the Republic, eventually being named one of the two annually elected Consuls. Caesar was ultimately named dictator for life, and was the transitional leader between the Roman Republic and what would become the Roman Empire.

The Roman Empire extended through much of Europe and Roman culture extended with it. Everywhere the Romans went, they built roads, established cities, and left their mark on the local population. The Roman language, Latin, spread as well and was transformed into the Romance languages of French and Spanish. The Roman alphabet, which was based on the Greek transformation of Phoenician letters, was adopted throughout the empire and is still used today.

Like the Republic, the Roman Empire also looked to the east to Greece for inspiration. Now it was the Macedonian conqueror Alexander, who had unified Greece and introduced the culture throughout the eastern world, who provided Roman emperors with a role model. The empire itself has served as a model for modern government, especially in federal systems such as that found in the United States. The eventual decline and fall of the empire has been a subject that has occupied historians for centuries.

Skill 7.8   Understand origins, central teachings, and spread of Christianity

The rise of Christianity in early modern Europe was due as much to the iron hand of feudalism as it was to the Church itself. **Feudalism**, more than any other element, helped the Church get its grip on Europe. That grip, some would argue, has yet to be relinquished.

Like the caste system in India, feudalism kept people in strict control according to their social class. If you were a peasant, you had been born that way and you had an excellent chance of staying that way for your entire life. The rich and powerful were also the highest class in society, and the friends of the rich and powerful were the clergy.

The Church also, through its warnings of death and damnation without salvation, had rigid control of the belief systems of most of the people throughout Europe. In this way, the Church was able to assume more than just traditionally religious roles in people's lives. Clergy were respected and trusted members of society and people consulted them on secular matters as well as religious ones.

Also at this time, a desire to travel to the Holy Land, to Palestine, and what is now Israel, grew in a big way. The Church encouraged this, and pilgrimage routes sprang up.

In a way that governments never could, Christianity unified Europe. Especially with the pope at the head of the religion, the peoples of Europe could correctly be called Christendom because they all had the same beliefs, the same worries, and the same tasks to perform in order to achieve the salvation they so desperately sought. The Church was only too happy to capitalize on this power, which increased throughout the Middle Ages until it met a stalwart from Germany named **Martin Luther**.

Skill 7.9   Understand the decline and fall of the Roman Empire

The causes of the decline and fall of the Roman Empire are widely debated even today. What is referred to as the fall of the empire is more properly described as the fall of the Western Roman Empire, as the eastern empire based in Constantinople continued on for a thousand years after Rome fell. The Roman Empire had gained dominion over the largest number of people of any empire in history at that time, stretching from the Atlantic Ocean in the west to Persia in the east, and from North Africa to the island of Britain. This vast empire stood for centuries, ruled by a series of emperors beginning in the first decades CE.

In the third century, the empire began experiencing an increase in civil unrest as well as increased invasions from outside. Internally, civil war became an almost constant factor as there were no clear rules for accession to the position of Emperor. Military factions battled for the position with Diocletian ascending to the role in 285 CE.

Diocletian realized that the vast empire was spread too wide to be governed effectively by one person in Rome. He divided the empire in half along a north-south line east of Italy and named his friend, Maximian, emperor of the eastern portion. Each emperor, who held the title **Augustus**, also named a junior emperor, entitled Caesar. Thus, the empire now had four emperors.

This system worked well for some time, as the four men were able to cooperate effectively. When Diocletian and Maximian withdrew, Augustus elevated their Caesars to the posts, and conflict soon followed. Constantius, who was Maximian's Caesar, died while in office and the issue of succession was hotly contested by Constantius's military backers who installed his son, Constantine, as Augustus in opposition to Severus, who had been Constantius's Caesar.

Several years of conflict ensued, with many pretenders to the position of Augustus. In the end, it was **Constantine** who won out as the sole Augustus. In 330 CE, he proclaimed the empire unified again and moved the capital from Rome to Byzantium, which was subsequently known as **Constantinople**. Constantine eventually converted to Christianity, and the Roman Empire was thenceforth officially a Christian state. Constantine divided the rule of the empire among his sons but conflict over control of the empire continued for decades, with several emperors ascending the throne, all Christian.

The invasions by Germanic tribes continued to increase in their force and frequency. With power divided and the capital of the empire moved to the east, Rome became a prime target for these invading forces. The traditional "fall" of the Roman Empire is widely recognized as the defeat of Rome in 476 by Germanic invaders who deposed the western emperor and took control of the government. The eastern empire would continue to flourish for another thousand years, even regaining the Italian region from the Ostrogoths' various campaigns of conquest. It stood until it was conquered in 1453 by the Ottomans.

Skill 7.10   Identify the rise and achievements of Byzantine civilization

The **Byzantines** (Christians) made important contributions in art and the preservation of Greek and Roman achievements, including architecture especially in Eastern Europe and Russia, the Code of Justinian, and Roman law. Byzantium was known for its exquisite artwork, including the famous church Hagia Sophia.

Bordering the east of Europe was the **Byzantine Empire**, which was the Eastern Roman Empire after it was split into two by Emperor Diocletian. Diocletian's successor, Emperor Constantine, renamed the capital Byzantium to **Constantinople**, after himself. With the fall of Western Rome in 476 CE, the Byzantine emperors, starting with Justinian, attempted to regain the lost western territories. Due to ineffective rulers between the seventh and ninth centuries CE, any gains were completely lost, reverting the territorial limits to the eastern Balkans of Ancient Greece and Asia Minor. The late ninth through the eleventh centuries was considered the Golden Age of Byzantium.

Although Constantine had earlier made Christianity the official state religion of Rome, it left an unresolved conflict between Christian and Classical, i.e., Greek and Roman, ideals for the Byzantines. There were points of contention between the Pope in Rome and the Patriarch of Constantinople including celibacy of priests, language of the Liturgy (Latin in the west, Greek in the east), religious doctrine, and other un-reconciled issues. These issues led to the **Great Schism** which permanently split the church into the Roman Catholic and the Eastern Orthodox Churches.

Perhaps the most wide-ranging success of the Byzantine Empire was in the area of trade. Uniquely situated at the gateway to both West and East, Byzantium could control trade going in both directions. Indeed, the Eastern Empire was much more centralized and rigid in its enforcement of its policies than the feudal West.

Skill 7.11   Understand the relationship of Greek and Roman political concepts to modern government

Athenian democracy was a direct form of democracy, with every male citizen above the age of 20 able to vote in the legislative assembly. The assembly was made up of a minimum of 6,000 and voted on proposals made by a council of 500 citizens who were chosen by lot. Within the council of 500, one person was chosen each day to serve as the head of state. Trials were held by jury, without judges, with jurors being chosen from the pool of citizens. Athenian democracy differed from representative democracy in that each voter had the right to vote directly on public issues and no formal leaders were elected.

The concept of "**one person, one vote**," which was the basis of Greek democracy, is still the primary ideal behind all modern democracies. **Direct democracy** after the Greek method has not survived as a national form of government, although smaller groups such as town meetings still practice a form of direct democracy over some matters. The Greeks provided the philosophy of democracy, but the modern form of national democratic government owes much to the Romans.

Democracy in the Roman Republic was an indirect form. Citizens were classified into groups based on economic status or tribal affiliation and were allowed to vote within that group. The majority vote of the group then determined how the group would vote in an assembly. There were three voting assemblies: the Curiate Assembly, made up of elite Roman; the Centuriate Assembly, made up of elite and common citizens; and the Tribal Assembly, which represented all citizens and conducted most trials. The Roman Republic also had a **Senate** made up of appointees who served for life. The Senate had no direct legislative power, but was nonetheless influential in its ability to recommend or oppose action by the assemblies.

The highest elected office in the Roman Republic was **consul**. Two consuls were elected by the Centuriate Assembly annually, each with veto power over the other's actions. The consuls held considerable administrative power, and were also expected to act as military leaders in times of war.

Nearly all modern democracies are formed in some fashion after the Roman model, with the legislative, executive, and judicial functions placed in separate bodies. The framers of the U.S. Constitution were well versed in the Roman system, and created counterparts in the new American government. Like the Roman Republic, the U.S. system has an indirect form of democratic government with representative assemblies, including a Senate with six-year terms and the more "common" House of Representatives with two-year terms. Instead of consuls, the U.S. has a President who oversees the executive function of the country and represents the nation to the world. The president is elected in a national election; however, it is the Electoral College, overseen by the Senate, which formally elects the national leader.

Unlike the early Roman Republic, the U.S. has established a permanent independent court system. The complex Roman system also had conflicting powers among the various political bodies, making it difficult for one body to gain complete control over the others. This was also built into the American system as a series of "checks and balances" which ensure that no one branch of the government becomes too dominant.

COMPETENCY 8.0   THE MAJOR DEVELOPMENTS OF WORLD HISTORY DURING THE GROWTH OF AGRICULTURAL AND COMMERCIAL CIVILIZATIONS: 500 TO 1500

Skill 8.1   **Describe the important contributions of the institutions, religion, and culture of the Byzantine Empire**

(See Skill 7.10)

Skill 8.2   **Know origins and principles of Islam and the consequences of Islamic expansion**

A few years after the death of the Emperor Justinian, **Mohammed** was born (570 CE) in a small Arabian town near the Red Sea. Before this time, Arabians played only an occasional role in history. Arabia was a vast desert of rock and sand, except for the coastal areas on the Red Sea. It was populated by nomadic wanderers called **Bedouins**, who lived in scattered tribes near oases where they watered their herds. Tribal leaders engaged in frequent war with one another. The family or tribe was the social and political unit, under the authority of the head of the family, within which there was cruelty, infanticide, and suppression of women.

Their religion was a crude and superstitious paganism and idolatry. Although there was regular contact with Christians and Jews through trading interactions, the idea of monotheism was foreign. What vague unity there was within the religion was based upon common veneration of certain sanctuaries. The most important of these was a small square temple called **the Kaaba** (cube), located in the town of **Mecca**. Arabs came from all parts of the country in annual pilgrimages to Mecca during the sacred months when warfare was prohibited. For this reason, Mecca was considered the center of Arab religion.

In about 610, a prophet named **Mohammed** came to some prominence. He called his new religion **Islam** (submission [to the will of God]) and his followers were called **Moslems**—those who had surrendered themselves. His first converts were members of his family and his friends. As the new faith began to grow, it remained a secret society. But when they began to make their faith public, they met with opposition and persecution from the pagan Arabians who feared the new religion and the possible loss of the profitable trade with the pilgrims who came to the Kaaba every year.

Islam slowly gained ground, and the persecutions became more severe around Mecca. In 622, Mohammed and his close followers fled the city and found refuge in **Medina** to the north. His flight is called the **Hegira**. This event marks the beginning of the Moslem calendar. Mohammed took advantage of the ongoing feuds between Jews and Arabs in the city and became the ruler of Medina, making it the capital of a rapidly growing state.

In the years that followed, Islam changed significantly. It became a fighting religion and Mohammed became a political leader. The group survived by raiding caravans on the road to Mecca and plundering nearby Jewish tribes. This was a victorious religion that promised plunder and profit in this world and the blessings of paradise after death. It attracted many converts from the Bedouin tribes. By 630, Mohammed was strong enough to conquer Mecca and make it the religious center of Islam, toward which all Moslems turned to pray, and the *Kaaba* the most sacred **Mosque** or temple. Medina remained the political capital.

By taking over the pilgrimage, the sacred city, and the sanctuary from paganism, Mohammed made it easier for converts to join the religion. By the time of his death in 632, most of the people of Arabia had become at least nominal adherents of Islam.

Mohammed left behind a collection of divine revelations (**surahs***)* he believed were delivered by the angel Gabriel. These were collected and published in a book called the **Koran (**reading), which has since been the holy scripture of Islam. The revelations were never dated or kept in any kind of chronological order. After the prophet's death, they were organized by length (in diminishing order). The *Koran* contains Mohammed's teachings on moral and theological questions, his legislation on political matters, and his comments on current events.

Islam has five basic principles, known as the **Pillars of Islam**:

1. The oneness and omnipotence of God—**Allah**.
   - Mohammed is the prophet of Allah to whom all truth has been revealed by God.
   - To each of the previous prophets (Adam, Noah, Abraham, Moses and Jesus) a part of the truth was revealed.
2. One should **pray five times a day** at prescribed intervals, facing Mecca.
3. **Charity**—for the welfare of the community.
4. **Fasting** from sunrise to sunset every day during the holy month of Ramadan to cleanse the spirit.
5. **Pilgrimage to Mecca** should be made if possible and if no one suffers thereby.

The moral principles of Islam are:

- The practice of the virtues of charity, humility, and patience.
- Enemies are to be forgiven.
- Avarice, lying, and malice are condemned.
- Drinking (alcohol), eating pork, and gambling are prohibited.

Mohammed believed on the Day of Judgment all souls would be judged. The infidel would be condemned to a hell (**gehennem**) of perpetual fire; the good/faithful would go to Paradise, a beautiful place of cool waters, sensual delights, and ease. He emphasized a strong sense of predestination. The **Koran** elevated the level of women. A man could marry as many as four wives if he loved them equally. Divorce was easy, but the wife had to be given a dowry.

Mohammed drew freely upon Christianity, Judaism, and Arab paganism. His knowledge of the first two was limited to what he learned through casual conversation. The resulting doctrine was a mixture of ideas that is original when taken as a whole. It appealed to both the simple Arab of the prophet's day and to the faith of more civilized people.

Mohammed died without either a political or a religious succession plan. His cousin, Ali, who had married Mohammed's daughter Fatima, believed his kinship and his heroism as a warrior gave him a natural claim to leadership. But Muslims in Medina thought one of their own should succeed Mohammed. **Abu Bakr** was finally chosen. He took the title of **Caliph**. The title was retained throughout the duration of the Muslim Empire.

These Muslim Arabians immediately launched an amazing series of conquests that extended the empire from the Indus to Spain. It has often been said that these conquests were motivated by religious fanaticism, and the determination to force Islam upon the infidel. In fact, however, the motives were economic and political.

During the period of expansion there was a brief civil war that occurred because Ali was proclaimed Caliph at Medina. He was opposed by an aristocratic family of Mecca called the **Umayyad**. Ali was assassinated in 661, and the Umayyads emerged supreme, handing the caliphate down in their family for nearly a century. Because their strongest support was in Syria, they moved the capital from Medina to Damascus.

Despite political divisions, the Muslim world maintained strong economic, religious, and cultural unity throughout this period. Mohammed had taught that all Muslims are brothers, equal in the sight of God. Conversion to Islam erased the differences between peoples of different ethnic origin.

The converts to Islam, who brought their cultural traditions, probably contributed more to this emerging synthetic civilization than the Arabs. This blending of cultures, facilitated by a common language, a common religion, and a strong economy, created learning, literature, science, technology, and art which surpassed anything found in the Western Christian world during the Early Middle Ages. Interestingly, the most brilliant period of Muslim culture was from the eighth century through the eleventh, coinciding with the West's darkest cultural period.

Reading and writing in Arabic, the study of the Koran, arithmetic and other elementary subjects were taught to children in schools attached to the mosques. In larger and wealthier cities, the mosques offered more advanced education in literature, logic, philosophy, law, algebra, astronomy, medicine, science, theology, and the tradition of Islam. Books were produced for the large reading public. The wealthy collected private libraries and public libraries arose in large cities.

The most popular subjects were theology and the law. But the more important field of study was philosophy. The works of the Greek and Hellenistic philosophers were translated into Arabic and interpreted with commentaries. These were later passed on to the Western Christian societies and schools in the twelfth and thirteenth centuries. The basis of Muslim philosophy was Aristotelian and Neo-platonic ideas, which were essentially transmitted without creative modification.

The Muslims were also interested in natural science. They translated the works on Galen and Hippocrates into Arabic and added the results of their own experience in medicine. Avicenna was regarded in Western Europe as one of the great masters of medicine. They also adopted the work of the Greeks in the other sciences and modified and supplemented them with their own discoveries. Much of their work in chemistry was focused on alchemy (the attempt to transmute base metals into gold). The **Muslim** culture outdistanced the Western world in the field of medicine, primarily because the people weren't constrained by the sort of superstitious fervor which had so embraced the West at this time. The Muslim doctor, **Al-Razi,** was one of the most well-known physicians in the world and was the author of a medical encyclopedia, as well as a handbook for smallpox and measles

Adopting the heritage of Greek mathematics, the Muslims also borrowed a system of numerals from India. This laid the foundation for modern arithmetic, geometry, trigonometry, and algebra.

Muslim art and architecture tended to be mostly uniform in style, allowing for some regional modification. They borrowed from Byzantine, Persian, and other sources. The floor plan of the mosques was generally based on Mohammed's house at Medina. The notable unique elements were the tall **minarets** from which the faithful were called to prayer. Interior decoration was the style now called **arabesque**. Mohammed had banned paintings or other images of living creatures. These continued to be absent from mosques, although they occasionally appeared in book illustration and secular contexts. But their skilled craftsmen produced the finest art in jewelry, ceramics, carpets, and carved ivory.

The Muslims also produced sophisticated literature in both prose and poetry. Little, however, of their poetry or prose was carried down by Western culture.

The best-known works of this period are the short stories known as the **Arabian Nights** and the poems of **Omar Khayyam**.

Skill 8.3   Understand the beginning of international slave trade

The trans-African slave trade refers to the movement of black African slaves over trade routes through the deserts of northern Africa to slave trading posts on the eastern and northern coasts of the continent. From these posts, slaves were transported to markets in Muslim cities such as Morocco, Cairo, Algiers, and Tripoli. The practice began sometime in the ninth century, and continued into the early years of the twentieth century, predating and outlasting the trans-Atlantic slave trade by Europeans.

The slaves themselves were sometimes captured by Arab traders on raiding missions, or were enslaved by other black groups as a result of war and subsequently traded into the slave market. These people came largely from sub-Saharan Africa, and once captured were moved across the deserts by caravan routes. These routes stretched from oasis to oasis from the interior to the coastal trading posts.

Slaves were exchanged for a variety of goods, including gold, horses, dye, jewels, and cloth. They were sold mainly to become servants, or to join harems if they were female. Some male slaves were castrated and served as eunuchs who acted as guards for the harems of wealthy Muslims.

Arabs dominated the sea routes of the Red Sea and the Indian Ocean during the Middle Ages and the slave trade expanded to bring laborers from posts on the eastern coast of Africa to the agricultural areas of India.

Little primary evidence remains of the Arab slave trade in Africa, and exact figures on the number of Africans who were sold into slavery are unknown. The trade was significant, however, not only in the widespread area it affected but in the number of people upon which slavery was inflicted.

Skill 8.4   Show an understanding of the political, economic and social structure of European feudalism and manorialism

During the Middle Ages, the system of **feudalism** became a dominant feature of the economic and social system in Europe. Feudalism began as a way to ensure that a king or nobleman could raise an army when needed. In exchange for the promise of loyalty and military service, **lords** would grant a section of land, called a **fief** to a **vassal**, as those who took this oath of loyalty were called. The vassal was then entitled to work the land and benefit from its proceeds or to grant it in turn as a fief to another. At the bottom of this ladder were **peasants** who actually worked the land. At the top was the king to whom all lands might legally belong.

The king could ensure loyalty among his advisors by giving them use of large sections of land which they in turn could grant as fiefs.

Manorialism, which also arose during the Middle Ages is similar to feudalism in structure, but consisted of self-contained manors that were often owned outright by a nobleman. Some manors were granted conditionally to their lords, and some were linked to the military service and oaths of loyalty found in feudalism, meaning that the two terms overlap somewhat. Manors usually consisted of a large house for the lord and his family, surrounded by fields and a small village that supported the activities of the manor. The lord of the manor was expected to provide certain services for the villagers and laborers associated with the manor including the support of a church.

Also coming into importance at this time was the era of **knighthood** and its code of **chivalry** as well as the tremendous influence of the Roman Catholic Church. Until the period of the Renaissance, the Church was the only place where people could be educated. The **Bible** and other books were hand-copied by monks in the monasteries. Cathedrals were built and decorated with art depicting religious subjects.

Land is a finite resource, and as the population grew in the middle centuries of the Middle Ages, the manorial/feudal system became less and less effective as a system of economic organization. The end of the system was sealed by the outbreak and spread of the **Black Death**, which killed more than one-third of the total population of Europe. Those who survived and were skilled in any job or occupation were in demand and many serfs and peasants found freedom and, for that time, a decidedly improved standard of living.

With the increase in trade and travel, cities sprang up and began to grow. Craft workers in the cities developed their skills to a high degree, eventually organizing **guilds** to protect the quality of the work and to regulate the buying and selling of their products. City government developed and flourished, centered around strong town councils. Active in city government and the town councils were the wealthy businessmen who made up the rising middle class. Strong nation-states became powerful and people developed a renewed interest in life and learning.

Skill 8.5 Understand the significance of the Catholic Church, monasteries, and universities in European civilization during the Middle Ages

The Medieval Catholic Church was the single most unifying organization in the West, exercising influence at every level of society. Catholic bishops and archbishops were named from the ranks of noblemen and acted as advisors to royal leaders. Parish priests oversaw the indoctrination of peasants and the collection of church taxes, called tithes. The church was the central building of most medieval towns.

The Catholic Church was also the primary provider of formal education, establishing universities in Italy and France. The **university** tradition of higher learning was itself an extension of an interest in learning that grew out of the Catholic monasteries, which were isolated communities of religious monks devoted to service to the Church.

(See also Skill 8.6)

Skill 8.6   Understand the importance and accomplishments of the European government in the High Middle Ages

The **High Middle Ages** refers to the period in Europe between the Early and Late Middle Ages, spanning approximately the eleventh, twelfth, and thirteenth centuries. The period is noted for a rapid increase in population that contributed to dramatic changes in society, culture, and political organization.

During this period, the concept of the nation state took hold as populations became more stable and people began to think of themselves as belonging to a larger group of ethnically similar cultures. In Italy, the independent nation states such as Venice, Pisa, and Florence were established, providing a basis for the Renaissance. The concept of inherited nobility gained wide acceptance and knighthood and chivalry developed as virtuous codes of conduct.

The **Crusades** took place during the High Middle Ages, further strengthening the importance of these orders of knights, and solidifying the strength of the western Church throughout Europe. The routes, opened by Crusaders marching to Jerusalem, opened the way for an increase in trade and contributed to the growth of many cities based on this trade.

A merchant class developed and began to exert its influence on political and economic affairs. As the power and influence of the Church grew, it contributed to the growth of art and architecture, particularly in the development of the great Gothic cathedrals, most of which were constructed during this era.

Crucial advances in thinking and technology occurred during the High Middle Ages. Improvements in shipbuilding and clock-making led to advances in navigation and cartography, setting the stage for the Age of Exploration. The field of printing, while not yet to the stage that Gutenberg was to take it in the fifteenth century, expanded the availability of texts, serving a growing educated class of people. The philosophy of Scholasticism, which emphasized empiricism and opposed mysticism in Christian education, was espoused by **Thomas Aquinas**.

The population increase which had brought these significant developments to Europe in the High Middle Ages was suddenly reversed in the mid-fourteenth century by the **Black Plague**, which decimated the region. As the concept of the nation state arose, so did the idea of national borders and national sovereignty, leading to numerous wars, which in turn had deleterious effects on the economy. These events are now used to mark the period of transition between the High Middle Ages and the Late Middle Ages.

Skill 8.7   Identify origins, course, and consequences of the Crusades

The **Crusades** were a series of military campaigns beginning in the eleventh century against the encroaching Muslim Empire, particularly in the holy land of Palestine and the city of Jerusalem. They continued into the thirteenth century as Jerusalem and other holy cities changed hands between Christian and Muslim forces. Several crusades took place within Europe, as well, such as the efforts to re-conquer portions of the Muslim-occupied Iberian Peninsula.

The Christian Byzantine Empire was centered in Constantinople. The empire was under attack from Seljuk Turk forces who had taken Palestine. The eastern emperor, Alexius I, called on his western counterpart **Pope Urban II** for assistance. Urban saw the situation as an opportunity to reunite Christendom, which was still in the throes of schism between the Eastern Orthodox and the Western Catholic sects, and to invest the papacy with religious authority.

In 1095, Urban called on all Christians to rally behind the campaign to drive the Turks out of the Holy Land. Participation in the crusade, Urban said, would count as full penance for sin in the eyes of the Church. A force of crusaders marched to Jerusalem and captured it, massacring the inhabitants. Along the way, several small Crusader states were established. A second crusade was led against Damascus in 1145, but was unsuccessful.

In 1187, **Saladin**, the Sultan of Egypt recaptured Jerusalem, and a third Crusade was called for by Pope Gregory VIII. This Crusade was joined by the combined forces of France, England, and the Holy Roman Empire but fell short of its goal to recapture Jerusalem. The fourth Crusade took place in 1202, under Pope Innocent III. The intention of the fourth Crusade was to enter the Holy Land through Egypt. The plan was changed, however, and forces were diverted to Constantinople.

One result of the Crusades was to establish and reinforce the political and military authority of the Catholic Church and the Roman pope. The religious fervor spurred on by the Crusades would eventually culminate in such movements as the **Inquisition** in Spain and the expulsion of the **Moors** from Europe. The marches of the crusaders also opened new routes between Europe and the East along which culture, learning, and trade could travel.

Skill 8.8   Identify political, economic, and cultural developments in the major civilizations of Asia, Africa, and the Americas

The Mongol Empire was founded by Genghis Khan and during the height of the empire covered a majority of the territory from Southeast Asia to central Europe. One of the primary military tactics of conquest was to annihilate any cities that refused to surrender.

Government was by decree on the basis on a code of laws developed by Genghis Khan. It is interesting that one of the tenets of this code was that the nobility and the commoners shared the same hardship. The society, and the opportunity to advance within the society, was based on a system of **meritocracy**. The carefully structured and controlled society was efficient and safe for the people. Religious tolerance was guaranteed. Theft and vandalism were strictly forbidden. Trade routes and an extensive postal system were created linking the various parts of the empire. Taxes were quite onerous, but teachers, artists, and lawyers were exempted from the taxes. Mongol rule, however, was absolute. The response to all resistance was collective punishment in the form of destruction of cities and slaughter of the inhabitants.

The lasting achievements of the Mongol Empire include:

- Reunification of China and expansions of its borders
- Unification of the Central Asian Republics that later formed part of the USSR
- Expansion of Europe's knowledge of the world.

The Ming Dynasty in China followed the Mongol-led Yuan Dynasty. In addition to its expansion of trade and exploration of surrounding regions, the period is well known for its highly talented artists and craftsmen. The Hongwu emperor rose from peasant origins. He distributed land to small farmers in an effort to help them support their families. To further protect these family farms, he proclaimed title of the land non-transferable. He also issued an edict by which anyone who cultivated wasteland could keep the land as their property and would never be taxed. One of the major developments of the time was the development of systems of irrigation for farms throughout the empire. Hongwu maintained a strong army by creating military settlements. During peacetime, each soldier was given land to farm and if he could not afford to purchase equipment, it was provided by the government.

The legal code created during the period is generally considered one of the greatest achievements of the dynasty. The laws were written in understandable language and in enough detail to prevent misinterpretation. The law reversed previous policy toward slaves and promised them the same protection as free citizens. Great emphasis was placed on family relations. It was clearly based on Confucian ideas. The other major accomplishment of this dynasty was the decision to begin building the **Great Wall of China** to provide protection from northern horsemen.

The Mogul Empire reached its height during the reign of **Akbar**. In the administration of the empire, Akbar initiated two approaches that are notable. First, he studied local revenue statistics for the various provinces within the empire. He then developed a revenue plan that matched the revenue needs of the empire with the ability of the people to pay the taxes. Although the taxes were heavy, one-third to one half of the crop, it was possible to collect the taxes and meet the financial needs of the empire. Second, he created a rank and pay structure for the warrior aristocracy that was based on number of troops and obligations.

Akbar introduced a policy of acceptance and assimilation of Hindus, allowed temples to be built, and abolished the poll tax on non-Muslims. He devised a theory of "rulership as a divine illumination" and accepted all religions and sects. He encouraged widows to remarry, discouraged marriage of children, outlawed the practice of sati, and persuaded the merchants in Delhi to recognize special market days for women who were otherwise required to remain secluded at home. The empire supported a strong cultural and intellectual life. He sponsored regular debates among religious and scholarly individuals with different points of view.

The unique style of architecture of the Mogul Empire was its primary contribution to South Asia. The **Taj Mahal** was one of many monuments built during this period. The culture was a blend of Indian, Iranian, and Central Asian traditions. Other major accomplishments were:

- Centralized government
- Blending of traditions in art and culture
- Development of new trade routes to Arab and Turkish lands
- A unique style of architecture
- Landscape gardening
- A unique cuisine
- The creation of two languages (Urdu and Hindi) for the common people.

The conquest of **Ghana** by Muslim Berbers in 1076 permitted rule to devolve to a series of lesser successor states. By the thirteenth century, the successor state of Kangaba established the Kingdom of Mali. This vast trading state extended from the Atlantic coast of Africa to beyond Gao on the Niger River in the east. The government of the Mali kingdom was held together by military power and trade. The kingdom was organized into a series of feudal states that were ruled by a king. Most of the kings used the surname "Mansa" (meaning, "sultan"). The most powerful and effective of the kings was Mansa Musa.

Much of the history of **Mali** was preserved by Islamic scholars because the Mali rulers converted to Islam and were responsible for the spread of Islam throughout Africa. The expansion of the Mali kingdom began from the city of Timbuktu and gradually moved downstream along the Niger River. This provided increasing control of the river and the cities along its banks, which were critical for both travel and trade. The Niger River was a central link in trade for both west and North African trade routes.

The religion and culture of the kingdom of Mali was a blend of Islamic faith and traditional African belief. The influence of the Islamic Empire provided the basis of a large and very structured government which allowed the king to expand both territory and influence. The people, however, did not follow strict Islamic law. The king was thought of in traditional African fashion as a divine ruler removed from the people. A strong military and control of the Niger River, and the trade that flourished along the river, enabled Mali to build a strong feudal empire.

Farther to the east, the king of the **Songhai** people had earlier converted to Islam in the eleventh century. Songhai was at one time a province of Mali. By the fifteenth century, Songhai was stronger than Mali and it emerged as the next great power in western Africa. Songhai was situated on the great bend of the Niger River. From the early fifteenth to the late sixteenth centuries, the Songhai Empire stood, one of the largest empires in the history of Africa. The first king Sonni Ali conquered many neighboring states, including the Mali Empire. This gave him control of the trade routes and cities like Timbuktu. He was succeeded by Askia Mohammad who initiated political reform and revitalization. He also created religious schools, built mosques, and opened his court to scholars and poets from all parts of the Muslim world.

During the same period, the **Zimbabwe** kingdom was built. "Great Zimbabwe" was the largest of about 300 stone structures in the area. This capital city and trading center of the Kingdom of Makaranga was built between the twelfth and fifteenth centuries. It was believed to have housed as many as 20,000 people. The structures are built entirely of stone, without mortar. The scanty evidence that is available suggests that the kingdom was a trading center that was believed to be part of a trading network that reached as far as China.

The area known today as the Republic of **Benin** was the site of an early African kingdom known as Dahomey. By the seventeenth century, the kingdom included a large part of West Africa. The kingdom was economically prosperous because of slave trading relations with Europeans, primarily the Dutch and Portuguese, who arrived in the fifteenth century. The coastal part of the kingdom was known as "**the Slave Coast**." This kingdom was known for a very distinct culture and some very unusual traditions. In 1729, the kingdom started a female army system. A law was passed stating that females would be inspected at the age of 15. Those thought beautiful were sent to the palace to become wives of the king. Those who were sick or were considered unattractive were executed. The rest were trained as soldiers for two years. Human sacrifice was practiced on holidays and special occasions. Slaves and prisoners of war were sacrificed to gods and ancestors.

The slave trade provided economic stability for the kingdom for almost three hundred years. The continuing need for human sacrifices caused a decrease in the number of slaves available for export. As many colonial countries declared the trade of slaves illegal, demand for slaves subsided steadily until 1885 when the last Portuguese slave ship left the coast. With the decline of the slave trade, the kingdom began a slow disintegration. The French took over in 1892.

The North American and South American Native Americans could not have been more different, yet in some ways they were the same as well. Differences in geography, economic focus, and the preponderance of visitors from overseas produced differing patterns of occupation, survival, and success.

Those people who lived in North America had large concentrations of people and houses, but they didn't have the kind of large civilization centers like the cities of elsewhere in the world. These people didn't have an exact system of writing, either. These were two technological advances that were found in many other places in the world, including, to varying degrees, South America.

We know the most about the empires of South America, the Aztec, Inca, and Maya. People lived in South America before the advent of these empires, of course. One of the earliest people of record was the **Olmecs**, who left behind little to prove their existence except a series of huge carved figures.

The **Aztecs** dominated Mexico and Central America. They weren't the only people living in these areas, just the most powerful. The Aztecs had many enemies, some of whom were only too happy to help Hernando Cortes precipitate the downfall of the Aztec society. The Aztecs had access to large numbers of metals and jewels, and they used the metals to make weapons and the jewels to trade for items they didn't already possess. Though, in practice, the Aztecs didn't do a whole lot of trading; rather, they conquered neighboring tribes and demanded tribute from them. This is the source of so much of the Aztec riches. They also believed in a handful of gods and believed that these gods demanded human sacrifice in order to continue to smile on the Aztecs. The center of Aztec society was the great city of **Tenochtitlan**, which was built on an island so as to be easier to defend and boasted a population of 300,000 at the time of the arrival of the conquistadors. Tenochtitlan was known for its canals and its pyramids, none of which survive today.

The **Inca** Empire stretched across a vast period of territory down the western coast of South America and was connected by a series of roads. A series of messengers ran along these roads, carrying news and instructions from the capital, Cusco, another large city along the lines of but not as spectacular as

Tenochtitlan. The Incas are known for inventing the *quipu*, a string-based device that provided them with a method of keeping records. The Inca Empire, like the Aztec Empire, was very much a centralized state, with all income going to the state coffers and all trade going through the emperor as well. The Incas worshiped the dead, their ancestors, and nature and often took part in what we could consider strange rituals.

The most advanced Native American civilization was the **Maya**, who lived primarily in Central America. They were the only Native American civilization to develop writing, which consisted of a series of symbols that has still not been deciphered. The Mayans also built huge pyramids and other stone figures and sculptures, mostly of the gods they worshiped. The Mayans are most famous, however, for their **calendars** and for their mathematics. The Mayan calendars were the most accurate on the planet until the 16th century. The Mayans also invented the idea of zero, which might sound like a small thing except that no other culture had thought of such a thing. Mayan worship resembled the practices of the Aztec and Inca, although human sacrifices were rare. The Mayans also traded heavily with their neighbors.

(See also Skill 1.1)

COMPETENCY 9.0   **THE MAJOR DEVELOPMENTS OF WORLD HISTORY DURING THE GLOBAL AGE: 1450 TO 1750**

Skill 9.1   **Show an understanding of the origins, principal figures, and influence of the Renaissance**

The word "**Renaissance**" literally means "rebirth" and signaled the rekindling of interest in the glory of ancient classical Greece and Rome civilizations. It was the period in human history marking the start of many ideas and innovations leading to our modern age.

The **Renaissance** began in Italy with many of its ideas starting in Florence, controlled by the infamous Medici family. Education, especially for some of the merchants, required reading, writing, math, the study of law, and the writings of classical Greece and Rome. Contributions of the Italian Renaissance period occurred in many disciplines.

Art - The more important artists were Giotto and his development of perspective in paintings; Leonardo da Vinci who was not only an artist but also a scientist and inventor; Michelangelo who was a sculptor, painter, and architect; and others including Raphael, Donatello, Titian, and Tintoretto.

Political philosophy - specifically the writings of Machiavelli on the machinations of power.

Literature - the writings of Boccaccio and the poet Petrarch.

Science - Galileo's contributions to both astronomy and physics changed the way people viewed the world around them and the heavens above.

Medicine - the work of Brussels-born Andrea Vesalius earned him the title of "father of anatomy" and had a profound influence on the Spaniard Michael Servetus and the Englishman William Harvey.

In Germany, Gutenberg's invention of the **printing press** with movable type facilitated the rapid spread of Renaissance ideas, writings and innovations, thus ensuring the enlightenment of most of Western Europe. Contributions were also made by Durer and Holbein in art, and by Paracelsus in science and medicine.

The effects of the Renaissance in the Low Countries can be seen in the literature and philosophy of Erasmus and the art of van Eyck and Breughel the Elder. Rabelais and de Montaigne in France also contributed to literature and philosophy. In Spain, the art of El Greco and de Morales flourished, as did the writings of Cervantes and De Vega. In England, Sir Thomas More and Sir Francis Bacon wrote and taught philosophy and inspired by Vesalius.

William Harvey made important contributions in medicine. The greatest talent was found in literature and drama and given to mankind by **Chaucer, Spenser, Marlowe, Jonson,** and the incomparable **Shakespeare.**

Skill 9.2   Understand the significant ideas, leaders and events of the Reformation

The **Reformation** period consisted of two phases: the Protestant Revolution and the Catholic Reformation. The Protestant Revolution came about because of religious, political, and economic reasons. The religious reasons stemmed from abuses in the Catholic Church including fraudulent clergy with their scandalous immoral lifestyles; the sale of religious offices, indulgences, and dispensations; different theologies within the Church; and frauds involving sacred relics.

The political reasons for the **Protestant Revolution** involved the increase in the power of rulers who were considered "absolute monarchs" wanting all power and control, especially over the Church, and the growth of "nationalism" or patriotic pride in one's own country. Economic reasons included the greedy desire of ruling monarchs to possess and control all lands and wealth of the Church, deep animosity against the burdensome papal taxation, the rise of the affluent middle class and its clash with medieval Church ideals, and the increase of an active system of "intense" capitalism.

The Protestant Revolution began in Germany with the revolt of **Martin Luther** against Church abuses. It spread to Switzerland where it was led by Calvin. It began in England with the efforts of King Henry VIII to have his marriage to Catherine of Aragon annulled so he could wed another and have a male heir. The results were the increasing support given not only by the people but also by nobles and some rulers, and of course, the attempts of the Church to stop it.

The **Catholic Reformation** was undertaken by the Church to "clean up its act" and to slow or stop the Protestant Revolution. The major efforts to this end were supplied by the Council of Trent and the Jesuits. Six major results of the Reformation included:

- Religious freedom
- Religious tolerance
- More opportunities for education
- Power and control of rulers limited
- Increase in religious wars
- An increase in fanaticism and persecution

Skill 9.3   Understand the importance and results of the Age of Exploration

The **Age of Exploration** actually had its beginnings centuries before exploration actually took place. The rise and spread of Islam in the seventh century and its subsequent control over the holy city of Jerusalem led to the European holy wars and the Crusades to free Jerusalem and the Holy Land from this control. Even though the Crusades were not a success, those who survived and returned to their homes and countries in Western Europe brought back with them new products such as silks, spices, perfumes, and new and different foods, all of which were luxuries which were unheard of that gave new meaning to colorless, drab, dull lives.

New ideas, new inventions, and new methods also went to Western Europe with the returning Crusaders and from these new influences was the intellectual stimulation which led to the period known as the Renaissance. The revival of interest in classical Greek art, architecture, literature, science, astronomy, and medicine as well as the increased trade between Europe and Asia and the invention of the printing press helped to push the spread of knowledge and start of exploration.

The Renaissance had ushered in a time of curiosity, learning, and incredible energy sparking the desire for trade to procure these new, exotic products and to find better, faster, cheaper trade routes to get to them. The work of geographers, astronomers, and mapmakers made important contributions and many studied and applied the work of such men as **Hipparchus** of Greece, **Ptolemy** of Egypt, **Tycho Brahe** of Denmark, and **Fra Mauro** of Italy.

For many centuries, various mapmakers made many maps and charts, which in turn stimulated curiosity and the seeking of more knowledge. At the same time, the Chinese were using the magnetic compass in their ships. Pacific islanders were going from island to island, covering thousands of miles in open canoes while navigating by sun and stars. Arab traders were sailing all over the Indian Ocean in their **dhows**.

The trade routes between Europe and Asia were slow, difficult, dangerous, and very expensive. Between sea voyages on the Indian Ocean and Mediterranean Sea, and the camel caravans in central Asia and the Arabian Desert, trade was still controlled by the Italian merchants in **Genoa** and **Venice**. It would take months and even years for the exotic luxuries of Asia to reach the markets of Western Europe. A faster, cheaper way had to be found. A way which would bypass traditional routes and end the control of the Italian merchants.

Prince Henry of Portugal (also called the Navigator) encouraged, supported, and financed the Portuguese seamen who led in the search for an all-water route to Asia. A shipyard was built along with a school teaching navigation. New types of sailing ships were built which would carry the seamen safely through the ocean waters. Experiments were conducted with newer maps, newer navigational methods, and newer instruments. These included the astrolabe and the compass that enabled sailors to determine direction as well as latitude and longitude for exact location. Although Prince Henry died in 1460, the Portuguese continued sailing along and exploring Africa's west coastline.

In 1488, **Bartholomew Diaz** and his men sailed around Africa's southern tip and headed toward Asia. Diaz wanted to push on but turned back because his men were discouraged and weary from the long months at sea, extremely fearful of the unknown, and refusing to travel any further.

However, the Portuguese were finally successful ten years later in 1498 when **Vasco da Gama** and his men, continuing the route of Diaz, rounded Africa's Cape of Good Hope, sailing across the Indian Ocean, reaching India's port of Calicut (Calcutta). Six years earlier, Columbus had reached the New World and an entire hemisphere, but da Gama had proved Asia could be reached from Europe by sea.

With the increase in trade and travel, cities sprang up and began to grow. Craft workers in the cities developed their skills to a high degree, eventually organizing guilds to protect the quality of the work and to regulate the buying and selling of their products. City government developed and flourished centered on strong town councils. Active in city government and the town councils were the wealthy businessmen who made up the growing middle class.

In addition, there were a number of individuals and events during the time of exploration and discoveries. The **Vivaldo brothers** and **Marco Polo** wrote of their travels and experiences. From the Crusades, the survivors made their way home to different places in Europe bringing with them fascinating, new information about exotic lands, people, customs, and desired foods and goods, such as spices and silks.

The first Europeans in the New World were Norsemen led by **Eric the Red,** and later, his son Leif the Lucky. However, before any of these, the ancestors of today's Native Americans and Latin American Indians crossed a land bridge across the Bering Strait from Asia to Alaska, eventually settling in all parts of the Americas.

Christopher Columbus, sailing for Spain, is credited with the discovery of America although he never set foot on its soil. **Magellan** is credited with the first circumnavigation of the earth. Other Spanish explorers made their marks in parts of what are now the United States, Mexico, and South America.

For France, claims to various parts of North America were the result of the efforts of such men as **Champlain, Cartier, LaSalle, Father Marquette,** and **Joliet.**

Dutch claims were based on the work of one **Henry Hudson. John Cabot** gave England its stake in North America along with **John Hawkins, Sir Francis Drake,** and the half-brothers **Sir Walter Raleigh and Sir Humphrey Gilbert.**

Skill 9.4   Understand the significance of the rise of absolute monarchies and constitutional governments in Europe

The most familiar form of government throughout history was the **monarchy**. We can include dictatorships or authoritarian governments in this description because the basic idea—that one person was in charge of the government—applies to all. In this kind of government, the head of state was responsible for governing his or her subjects. In earlier times, this meant laws that weren't exactly written down, though written laws have increasingly been the standard as the centuries have progressed. Monarchies and one-person governments still exist today, although they are rare. In these states, the emphasis is on keeping the monarch in power, and many laws of the country have been written with that purpose in mind.

An **absolute monarchy** is a form of government where a king or queen rules with complete authority without any legal opposition. The absolute monarch arose out of the concept of the **divine right of kings**. This ideal held that monarchs received authority to rule from God. It arose during the late Middle Ages as feudalism increased the relative wealth and power of kings compared to other nobles. In theory, an absolute monarch has total power over his or her subjects. In practice, absolute monarchs were expected to act wisely and to seek counsel on important decisions from advisors and church leaders, and in some cases, were restricted by public agreements.

This increased power of monarchy combined with the relative weakness of the Church during the Reformation in the sixteenth century led to monarchs exercising influence over religious matters. This was the case of **Henry VIII of England**, who seized all Catholic Church property in his dominion, claiming responsibility only to God. **Louis XIV** of France was another absolute monarch who believed that the monarch was the embodiment of the state. In Russia, **Peter the Great** and his successors ruled as absolute monarchs until the early twentieth century.

Peter the Great of Russia was named **Czar** (sometimes spelled **Tsar**) in 1682, when he was ten years old, with his mother, Sophia, as regent. During his reign, Peter suppressed revolt and dissent with violence, eventually being named Emperor of Russia. Peter was a reformer who brought Western culture to Russia and traveled to Europe to learn about the newest military technology. Peter also laid the foundations of a legislative body by creating a Governing Senate made up of his appointees, and introduced a system of ranking based on merit and service rather than heredity.

In the 1640s, England saw a series of civil wars between the Royalist supporters of the **King Charles I** and the Parliamentarian army led by Oliver Cromwell. Prior to the civil wars, Parliament was called only at the king's will, and then mainly to levy taxes. Dispute over Charles' autocratic rule, his taking of a Catholic wife, his desire to engage in war in Europe, and what some took to be illegal attempts at taxation led to armed conflict. After extended fighting, the forces of Parliament succeeded, naming Cromwell "Protector." Charles I was tried for treason and beheaded. Cromwell's rule was short-lived, however, and after his death in 1658 the regime collapsed. By 1660 the monarchy had been restored.

In contrast to absolute monarchy based on religious right, constitutional governments derive their authority from written documents that lay out a form of government and define its powers and limitations. Beginning with the Magna Carta in England, the practice in many European countries has been to mix the two forms into a "**constitutional monarchy**." This form of government recognizes a monarch as leader, but invests most of the legal authority in a legislative body such as a Parliament. Great Britain still operates as a constitutional monarchy, as do many other European countries. European monarchs have been reduced to mainly ceremonial figures in modern government, however.

Skill 9.5   Understand the rise and decline of the Ottoman Empire

The Ottoman Empire began in 1299, when Osman I declared independence for the Turkish principalities that he had gathered under his name. The Ottoman state followed a policy of steady expansion, and was soon encroaching on the borders of the Byzantine Empire. In 1453, under the leader **Mehmed II**, the Ottomans captured Istanbul, which was to become the capital of the growing empire.

The Ottoman Empire continued its remarkable expansion in the early sixteenth century under the Sultan **Selim I**. Selim expanded his borders to the east and south, taking control of Persia and Egypt and establishing a naval foothold in the Red Sea. This naval strength was built upon by Selim's successors until the empire controlled not only the Red Sea, but the Black Sea, the Persian Gulf, and a large section of the Mediterranean.

By the late sixteenth century, the empire had also expanded inland to control all of southeast Europe, and took advantage of its location between Europe and the Orient to control access to the spice and silk trade routes.

Maintaining such a large frontier far from its capital proved to be difficult, and beginning in the early seventeenth century, Europeans made successful inroads along the western Ottoman borders. The technological advantages that the Ottomans had once held over Europe disappeared as the West made significant advances of its own, and gained access to ancient learning from China and other regions to which the Ottomans had restricted access. In the early nineteenth century, under Mahmud II, the Ottoman Empire adopted a policy of modernization based on European customs, architecture, and legislation. The rise of nationalism throughout Europe affected the empire, as well, as former sovereign states which had been conquered began to express nationalistic goals. These developments marked the beginning of the end for the empire. Despite several attempts to reform the government, economic depression and political unrest plagued the declining state.

The Ottomans fought in WWI in alliance with Germany, and were defeated in 1918, when the army was disbanded. The harsh peace terms led to an upsurge in Turkish nationalism and revolution. The Ottoman sultanate was abolished by Turkish revolutionaries in 1922, and members of the family were expelled from Turkey.

COMPETENCY 10.0   **THE MAJOR DEVELOPMENTS OF WORLD HISTORY DURING THE AGE OF REVOLUTIONARY CHANGE: 1700 TO 1914**

Skill 10.1   **Be able to explain the contributions of the scientific revolution**

The **Scientific Revolution** and the **Enlightenment** were two of the most important movements in the history of civilization, resulting in a new sense of self-examination and a wider view of the world than ever before.

The Scientific Revolution was, above all, a shift in focus from **belief to evidence**. Scientists and philosophers wanted to see proof not just believe what other people told them. It was an exciting time, if you were a forward-looking thinker.

A Polish astronomer, **Nicolaus Copernicus**, began the Scientific Revolution. He crystallized a lifetime of observations into a book that was published about the time of his death. In this book, Copernicus argued that the Sun, not the Earth, was the center of a solar system and that other planets revolved around the Sun, not the Earth. This flew in the face of established, i.e., Church-mandated, doctrine. The Church still wielded tremendous power at this time, including the power to banish people or sentence them to prison or even death.

The Danish astronomer **Tycho Brahe** was the first to catalog his observations of the night sky, of which he made thousands. Building on Brahe's data, German scientist **Johannes Kepler** instituted his theory of planetary movement, embodied in his famous Laws of Planetary Movement. Using Brahe's data, Kepler also confirmed Copernicus's observations and argument that the Earth revolved around the Sun.

The most famous defender of this idea was **Galileo Galilei**, an Italian scientist who conducted many famous experiments in the pursuit of science. He is most well-known, however, for his defense of the **heliocentric** (sun-centered) idea. He wrote a book comparing the two theories, but most readers could easily tell he favored the new one. He was convinced of this mainly because of what he had seen with his own eyes. He had used the relatively new invention of the telescope to see four moons of Jupiter. They certainly did not revolve around the Earth, so why should everything else? His ideas were not at all favored with the Church, which continued to assert its authority in this and many other matters. The Church was still powerful enough at this time, especially in Italy, to order Galileo to be placed under house arrest. Galileo died under house arrest, but his ideas did not die with him.

Picking up the baton was an English scientist named **Isaac Newton**, who became perhaps the most famous scientist of all. He is known as the discoverer of gravity and a pioneering voice in the study of optics (light), calculus, and physics. More than any other scientist, Newton argued for (and proved) the idea of a mechanistic view of the world: You can see how the world works and prove how the world works through observation. Up to this time, people believed what other people told them. Newton, following in the footsteps of Copernicus and Galileo, changed all that.

Skill 10.2   Discuss the influence of Enlightenment thinkers on political and economic development

This naturally led to the **Enlightenment**, a period of intense self-study that focused on ethics and logic. More so than at any time before, scientists and philosophers questioned cherished truths, widely held beliefs, and their own sanity in an attempt to discover why the world worked—from within. "I think, therefore I am" was one of the famous sayings of that or any day, uttered by **Rene Descartes**, a French scientist-philosopher whose dedication to logic and the rigid rules of observation were a blueprint for the thinkers who came after him.

One of the giants of the era was England's **David Hume**, a pioneer of the doctrine of empiricism: believing things only when you've seen the proof for yourself. Hume was a prime believer in the value of skepticism; in other words, he was naturally suspicious of things that other people told him to be true and constantly set out to discover the truth for himself. These two related ideas influenced many great thinkers after Hume, and his writings, of which there are many, continue to inspire philosophers to this day.

Perhaps the most famous Enlightenment thinker is **Immanuel Kant** of Germany. Both a philosopher and a scientist, he took a definitely scientific view of the world. He wrote the movement's most famous essay, "Answering the Question: What Is Enlightenment?" and he answered his famous question with the motto "Dare to Know." For Kant, the human being was a rational being capable of hugely creative thought and intense self-evaluation. He encouraged all to examine themselves and the world around them. He believed that the source of morality lay not in nature of in the grace of God but in the human soul itself. He believed that man believed in God for practical, not religious or mystical, reasons.

During the Enlightenment, the idea of the "**social contract**" confirmed the belief that government existed because people wanted it to, the people had an agreement with the government they would submit to it as long as it protected them and didn't encroach on their basic human rights. This idea was first made famous by the Frenchman **Jean-Jacques Rousseau** but was also adopted by England's John Locke and America's Thomas Jefferson.

Thomas Hobbes (1588–1679) was the author of the book *Leviathan* (l651) which was actually written as a reaction to the disorders caused by the English civil wars that had culminated with the execution of King Charles I. Hobbes perceived people as rational beings, but unlike Locke and Jefferson, he had no faith in their abilities to live in harmony with one another without a government. The trouble was, as Hobbes saw it, people were selfish and the strong would take from the weak. However, the weak being rational would in turn band together against the strong. For Hobbes, the state of nature became a chaotic state in which every person becomes the enemy of every other. It became a war of all against all, with terrible consequences for all.

John Locke (1632–1704) was an important thinker on the nature of democracy. He regarded the mind of man at birth as a tabula rasa, a blank slate upon which experience imprints knowledge and behavior. He did not believe in the idea of intuition or theories of innate knowledge. Locke also believed all men are born good, independent and equal, and it is their actions which will determine their fate. Locke's views, espoused in his most important work, *Two Treatises of Civil Government* (1690) attacked the theory of the divine right of kings and the nature of the state as conceived by Thomas Hobbes. Locke argued sovereignty did not reside in the state, but with the people. The state is supreme, but only if it is bound by civil and what he called "**natural**" law.

Many of Locke's political ideas, such as those relating to natural rights, property rights, the duty of the government to protect these rights, and the rule of the majority, were embodied in the Constitution of the United States. He further held that revolution was not only a right, but also often an obligation and advocated a system of checks and balances in government. A government comprised of three branches of which the legislative is more powerful than either the executive or the judicial. He also believed in the separation of the church and state. All of these ideas were to be incorporated in the Constitution of the United States. As such, Locke is considered in many ways the true founding father of our Constitution and government system. He remains one of history's most influential political thinkers to this day.

Jean-Jacques Rousseau (1712–1778) was one of the most famous and influential political theorists before the French Revolution. His most important and most studied work is **The Social Contract** (1762). He was concerned with what should be the proper form of society and government. However, unlike Hobbes, Rousseau did not view the state of nature as one of absolute chaos.

The problem as Rousseau saw it was that the natural harmony of the state of nature was due to people's intuitive goodness not to their actual reason. Reason only developed once a civilized society was established. The intuitive goodness was easily overwhelmed however by arguments for institutions of social control, which likened rulers to father figures and extolled the virtues of obedience to such figures. To a remarkable extent, strong leaders have, in Rousseau's judgment, already succeeded not only in extracting obedience from the citizens that they ruled, but also more importantly, have managed to justify such obedience as necessary.

Rousseau's most direct influence was upon the **French Revolution** (1789–1815*)*. In the ***Declaration of the Rights of Man and The Citizen*** (1789), he explicitly recognized the sovereignty of the general will as expressed in the law. In contrast to the American **Declaration of Independence**, it contains explicit mention of the obligations and duties of the citizen, such as assenting to taxes in support of the military or police forces for the common good. In modern times, ideas such as Rousseau's have often been used to justify the ideas of authoritarian and totalitarian systems.

Karl Marx (1818–1883), was perhaps the most influential theorist of the 19th century and his influence has continued in various forms until this day. Contrary to popular belief, he was not the first to believe in socialist ideas, many of which had been around for some time and in various forms. Nevertheless, he was the first to call his system truly "scientific" or "**Scientific Socialism**". (Also called Marxian Socialism or as it is more widely known Marxism). It was opposed to other forms of socialism that had been called, (with some derision), "**Utopian Socialism**." These were socialist ideas which though they sounded good would never really work in the real world. In fact, it is the very idea of Marxism being "scientific" that has appealed to so many thinkers in modern history. This and the underlying aspect of prophecy and redemption that is inherent, though seldom acknowledged, in Marxist ideology, have made it that much more attractive to those looking for something to believe in. Marx expounded his ideas in two major theoretical works, ***The Communist Manifesto*** (1848*)* and ***Das Capital***, (Volume 1, 1867*)*.

Skill 10.3   Understand the origins and consequences of the American and French Revolutions

The period from the 1700s to the 1800s was characterized in Western countries by opposing political ideas of democracy and nationalism. This resulted in strong nationalistic feelings and people of common cultures asserting their belief in the right to have a part in their government.

The **American Revolution** resulted in the successful efforts of the English colonists in America to win their freedom from Great Britain. After more than one hundred years of mostly self-government, the colonists resented the increased British meddling and control, declared their freedom, won the Revolutionary War with aid from France, and formed a new independent nation.

The **French Revolution** was the revolt of the middle and lower classes against the gross political and economic excesses of the rulers and the supporting nobility. It ended with the establishment of the first in a series of French Republics. Conditions leading to revolt included extreme taxation, inflation, lack of food, and the total disregard for the impossible, degrading, and unacceptable condition of the people on the part of the rulers, nobility, and the Church.

The American Revolution and the French Revolution were similar yet different, liberating their people from unwanted government interference and installing a different kind of government. They were both fought for the liberty of the common people, and they both were built on writings and ideas that embraced such an outcome; yet, there is where the similarities end. Both Revolutions proved people could expect more from their government and such rights as self-determination were worth fighting— and dying—for.

Several important differences need to be emphasized:

- The British colonists were striking back against unwanted taxation and other sorts of "government interference." The French people were starving and, in many cases, destitute and were striking back against an autocratic regime that cared more for high fashion and courtly love than bread and circuses.
- The American Revolution involved a years'-long campaign, of often bloody battles, skirmishes, and stalemates. The French Revolution was bloody to a degree but mainly an overthrow of society and its outdated traditions.
- The American Revolution resulted in a representative government, which marketed itself as a beacon of democracy for the rest of the world. The French Revolution resulted in a consulship, a generalship, and then an emperor—probably not what the perpetrators of the Revolution had in mind when they first struck back at the king and queen.

Still, both Revolutions are looked back on as turning points in history, as times when the governed stood up to the governors and said, "Enough."

Skill 10.4   Describe the spread of democratic ideas beyond Europe and the United States

The major turning point for Latin America, already unhappy with Spanish restrictions on trade, agriculture, and the manufacture of goods, was Napoleon's move into Spain and Portugal. Napoleon's imprisonment of King Ferdinand VII, made the local agents of the Spanish authorities feel they were, in fact, agents of the French. Conservative and liberal locals joined forces, declared their loyalty to King Ferdinand, and formed committees (*juntas*). Between May 1810 and July 1811, the *juntas* in Argentina, Chile, Paraguay, Venezuela, Bolivia, and Colombia all declared independence. Fighting erupted between Spanish authorities in Latin America and the members and followers of the *juntas*. In Mexico City, another *junta* declared loyalty to Ferdinand and independence.

Society in Latin America was sharply distinguished according to race and the purity of Spanish blood. **Miguel Hidalgo**, a 60-year-old priest and enlightened intellectual, disregarded the racial distinctions of the society. He had been fighting for the interests of the Indians and the part Indian/part white citizens of

Mexico, including a call for the return of land stolen from the Indians. He called for an uprising in 1810.

Simon Bolivar had been born into Venezuela's wealthy society and educated in Europe. With Francisco de Miranda, he declared Venezuela and Columbia to be republics and removed all Spanish trading restrictions. They removed taxes on the sale of food, ended payment of tribute to the government by the local Indians, and prohibited slavery. In March 1812 Caracas was devastated by an earthquake. When the Spanish clergy in Caracas proclaimed the earthquake God's act of vengeance against the rebel government, they provided support for the Spanish government officials, who quickly regained control.

When Ferdinand was returned to power in 1814, it was no longer possible for the rebel groups to claim to act in his name. Bolivar was driven to Colombia, where he gathered a small army that returned to Venezuela in 1817. As his army grew, Spain became concerned and the military moved into the interior of Venezuela. This action aroused the local people to active rebellion. As he freed slaves, he gained support and strength. Realizing he did not have the strength to take Caracas, Bolivar moved his people to Colombia. Bolivar's forces defeated the Spanish and organized "Gran Colombia" (which included present-day Ecuador, Colombia and Panama), and became president in 1819. When Ferdinand encountered difficulties in Spain, soldiers assembled to be transported to the Americas revolted. Several groups in Spain joined the revolt and, together, drove Ferdinand from power. Bolivar took advantage of the opportunity and took his army back into Venezuela. In 1821, Bolivar defeated the Spanish, took Caracas, and established Venezuelan freedom from Spanish rule.

In Peru, **San Martin** took his force into Lima amid celebration. Bolivar provided assistance in winning Peru's independence in 1822. Bolivar now controlled Peru. By 1824, Bolivar had combined forces with local groups and rid South America of Spanish control.

In 1807, Queen Maria of Portugal fled to escape Napoleon. The royal family sailed to Brazil, where they were welcomed by the local people. Rio de Janeiro became the temporary capital of Portugal's empire. Maria's son **Joao** ruled as regent. He opened Brazil's trade with other nations, gave the British favorable tax rates in gratitude for their assistance against Napoleon, and opened Brazil to foreign scholars, visitors, and immigrants. In 1815, he made Brazil a kingdom that was united with Portugal. By 1817 there was economic trouble in Brazil and some unrest over repression (such as censorship). This discontent became a rebellion that was repressed by Joao's military.

When Napoleon's forces withdrew from Portugal, the British asked Joao to return. Liberals took power in Portugal and in Spain and both drafted liberal constitutions. By 1821, Joao decided to return to Portugal as a constitutional monarch. He left his oldest son **Pedro** on the throne in Brazil. When Portugal tried to reinstate economic advantages for Portugal and restrict Brazil, resistance began to grow. Pedro did not want to be controlled by Portugal and was labeled a rebel. When he learned that Portuguese troops had been sent to arrest him, he prohibited the landing of the ship, sent them back to Portugal and declared independence in 1822. In a little more than a month, he was declared Emperor of Brazil.

Skill 10.5   Explain the causes and consequences of the agricultural and industrial revolutions

The **Agricultural Revolution** occurred first in England. It was marked by experimentation that resulted in increased production of crops from the land and a new and more technical approach to the management of agriculture. The revolution in agricultural management and production was hugely enhanced by the Industrial Revolution and the invention of the steam engine. The introduction of steam-powered tractors greatly increased crop production and significantly decreased labor costs. Developments in agriculture were also enhanced by the Scientific Revolution and the learning from experimentation that led to philosophies of crop rotation and soil enrichment. Improved system of irrigation and harvesting also contributed to the growth of agricultural production.

The **Industrial Revolution**, which began in Great Britain and spread elsewhere, was the development of power-driven machinery, fueled by coal and steam, leading to the accelerated growth of industry with large factories replacing homes and small workshops as work centers. The lives of people changed drastically and a largely agricultural society changed to an industrial one. In Western Europe, the period of empire and colonialism began. The industrialized nations seized and claimed parts of Africa and Asia in an effort to control and provide the raw materials needed to feed the industries and machines in the "mother country." Later developments included power based on electricity and internal combustion, replacing coal and steam.

(See Skill 4.2 for additional information)

Skill 10.6   Understand the major developments in the arts and literature of the period 1700–1914

Baroque painters of the seventeenth and eighteenth centuries across Europe shared similar traits in their works. Italy's Caravaggio, Flanders' **Rubens,** and **Rembrandt van Rijn** used dramatic chiaroscuro (strong lighting) and strong diagonals to illustrate the climax of well-known myths and stories, while their portraiture often gave insight in to the minds of their sitters.

Baroque architecture was often ornamental, with emphasis on light and dark, movement, emotion and affluence. The large scale of Baroque buildings lent a feeling of drama to the architecture, as evidenced by Louis XIV's **Palace of Versailles.**

Some of the most spectacular Baroque achievements were in the field of music. Opera incorporated the Baroque characteristics of dramatic storytelling and sensational shifts from soft to loud, joy to suffering. **Bach**'s cantatas powerfully express the profound religious faith of the Reformation, usually in a contrapuntal mode for four voices. His music for keyboard, in the form of **fugues**, also reflects the Baroque penchant for ornamentation, dramatic shifts, and large-scale performance. Oratorios and sonatas also tended toward the dramatic, with an emphasis on contrasting passages and tempos, as well as instrumental experimentation.

The reign of England's Elizabeth I ushered in an era of splendor for English literature. **Shakespeare**'s plays focused on the drama of human psychology, dealing with the turbulent and often contradictory emotions experienced in life. In the process, he vastly enriched the English language with original vocabulary and eloquent phrasing. Elsewhere in Europe, lyric poetry and sonnets took on new, more dramatic characteristics, while the novel developed into a more popular, easy-to-read format, as exemplified by **Cervantes'** *Don Quixote.*

The eighteenth century spawned several artistic styles, the first of which was an offshoot of Baroque, known as **Rococo** (rocks and shells) which utilized decorative motifs. In architecture, it referred generally to a style of interior design featuring a light, delicate feeling, enhanced with curvilinear furniture and gilt tracery, often based on a shell motif. In exterior design, it featured undulating walls, reliance on light and shadow for dramatic effect, and caryatid ornamentation. In painting, Rococo exuded sentimentality, love of pleasure, and delight in love. Rococo musicians improvised pretty "ornaments", or additions to the musical scores, and composers included delicate and artificial passages in their works.

The classical **symphony** grew out of the eighteenth century Italian overture, which usually had three separate movements and was played as a prelude to an operatic or vocal concert. Early symphonies were short and were included on musical programs with other works, mainly vocal. In the early years of the nineteenth century, **Ludwig von Beethoven** began to experiment with the form of the symphony, expanding it into an extended orchestral work that is usually the main piece in a program.

Simultaneously with rococo, a style known as Expressive developed in music. This style was original and uncomplicated, yet well-proportioned and logical as evidenced in many works by C.P.E. Bach. The classical style also rose which was based on classical ideals. A highly defined structure, a predominant melody, and an increase in contrasts of rhythm marked the classical style, as evidenced by many of the works by **Mozart**. Many musical forms such as opera and sonata changed to accommodate these classical requirements. Haydn, Mozart, and Beethoven all composed in their own manner within the classical constraints.

Other painting styles of the eighteenth century included Humanitarianism, the chief characteristic of which was social commentary, and **Neo-classicism**, the works of which not only detailed historical subject matter, but strived to embrace the classical ideals of proportion, harmony, and rationalism. Neo-classicism in architecture reflected the idea that while ancient architectural styles enhance present buildings, architects are free to mix elements from various periods with their own creative expressions to produce unique architecture, thus producing a kind of eclecticism.

The Industrial Age brought with it a myriad of changes as Europe dealt with the every-quickening pace of modern life. This was mirrored by the multiplicity of styles that surfaced during the century.

Romanticism in the visual arts implied a variety of sub-styles, most of which were characterized by a sense of melancholy, love of nature, emotionalism, and a sense of the exotic. Romanticism was often regarded as a reaction against the cool restraint of neo-classicism. Romantic music was an extension of classical music. Romantic authors emphasized love of nature, emotionalism, and the exotic and bizarre in their works, as evidenced by **Wordsworth**, **Byron,** and **Shelley**. **Realism** in the visual arts emerged during the second half of the century. Realistic authors such as **Balzac** wrote novels which depicted human beings caught in an uncompromising society.

The painting style known as **Impressionism** was inspired by scientific studies of light and the philosophy that the universe is constantly changing. Artists attempted to capture the transitory aspect of the world by recording a particular moment or "impression", usually working out-of-doors, and fairly quickly. Many of the impressionist paintings have a candid quality to them, probably a direct influence of the new medium of photography. Post-impressionism in art refers to a collection of personal styles, all inspired in some way by impressionism. The styles were as diverse as the artists, ranging from the emotional intensity of **Van Gogh**, to the precision of **Seurat**, to the allegory of **Gaugin**.

Literature also underwent a profound change in the period between the 18th and early 20th centuries. The idea of the "popular" novel came into its own as ordinary citizens began to have the time and interest in reading poems, stories, and books. American authors such as **James Fenimore Cooper,** and later **Mark Twain,** embraced both a "frontier spirit" and, especially in Twain's case, reflected the life of the common man. **Charles Dickens** became one of the first modern novelists, with best-sellers and serial installments of his stories that took a harsh look at real life. Others turned inwards, resulting in the works of **Sigmund Freud** and **Henry David Thoreau**, as well as the novels of **Joseph Conrad**. Melville,

Dickenson, **Poe**, **Bronte**, and a host of other writers helped literature become a major art form that remained accessible to the masses.

Skill 10.7   Causes, key events, and consequences of the new imperialism

In Europe, Italy and Germany were each totally united into one nation from many smaller states. Other key events were revolutions in Austria and Hungary, the Franco-Prussian War, the dividing of Africa among the strong European nations, interference and intervention of Western nations in Asia, and the breakup of Turkish dominance in the Balkans.

Africa was divided among France, Great Britain, Italy, Portugal, Spain, Germany, and Belgium who controlled the entire continent except for the nations of Liberia and Ethiopia. In Asia and the Pacific Islands, only China, Japan, and present-day Thailand (Siam) kept their independence. The others were controlled by the strong European nations.

An additional reason for **European imperialism** was the harsh, urgent demand for the raw materials needed to fuel and feed the great Industrial Revolution. These resources were not available in the huge quantity so desperately needed which both necessitated and rationalized the partitioning of the continent of Africa and parts of Asia. In turn, these colonial areas would purchase the finished manufactured goods. Europe in the 19th century was a crowded place. Populations were growing but resources were not. The peoples of many European countries were also agitating for rights as never before. To address these concerns, European powers began to look elsewhere for relief.

One of the main places for European imperialist expansion was Africa. Britain, France, Germany, and Belgium took over countries in Africa and claimed them as their own. The resources (including people) were then shipped back to the mainland and claimed as colonial gains. The Europeans made a big deal about "civilizing the savages," reasoning that their technological superiority gave them the right to rule and "educate" the peoples of Africa.

Southeast Asia was another area of European expansion at this time, mainly by France. So, too, was India, colonized by Great Britain. These two nations combined with Spain to occupy countries in Latin America. Spain also seized the rich lands of the Philippines.

As a result of all this activity, a whole new flood of goods, people, and ideas began to come back to Europe and a whole group of people began to travel to these colonies, to oversee the colonization and to "help bring the people up" to the European level. European leaders could also assert their authority in these colonies as they could not back home.

In the United States, **territorial expansion** occurred in the expansion westward under the banner of **"Manifest Destiny."** In addition, the U.S. was involved in the War with Mexico, the Spanish-American War, and supported the Latin American colonies of Spain in their revolts for independence. In Latin America, the Spanish colonies were successful in their fight for independence and self-government.

The time from 1830 to 1914 is characterized by the extraordinary growth and spread of patriotic pride in a nation along with intense, widespread imperialism. Loyalty to one's nation included national pride; extension and maintenance of sovereign political boundaries; unification of smaller states with common language, history, and culture into more powerful nations or smaller national groups who, as part of a larger multi-cultural empire, wished to separate into smaller, political, cultural nations.

COMPETENCY 11.0   THE MAJOR DEVELOPMENTS OF WORLD HISTORY DURING THE ERA OF THE GREAT WARS: 1900 TO 1945

Skill 11.1   Understand the causes and results of the World War I

World War I: 1914 to 1918
Emotions ran high in early 20th century Europe, and minor disputes magnified into major ones and sometimes quickly led to threats of war. Especially sensitive to these conditions was the area of the states on the Balkan Peninsula. Along with the imperialistic colonization for industrial raw materials, military build-up (especially by Germany), and diplomatic and military alliances, the conditions for one tiny spark to set off the explosion were in place. In July 1914, a Serbian national assassinated **Archduke Ferdinand**, the Austrian heir to the throne, and his wife as they visited Sarajevo. War began a few weeks later. There were a few attempts to keep war from starting, but these efforts were futile. Eventually nearly 30 nations were involved, and the war didn't end until 1918.

One of the major causes of the war was the tremendous surge of **nationalism** during the 1800s and early 1900s. People of the same nationality or ethnic group sharing a common history, language or culture began uniting or demanding the right of unification, especially in the empires of Eastern Europe, such as Russian Ottoman and Austrian-Hungarian Empires. Getting stronger and more intense were the beliefs of these peoples in loyalty to common political, social, and economic goals considered to be before any loyalty to the controlling nation or empire. Other causes were the increasing strength of military capabilities, massive colonization for raw materials needed for industrialization and manufacturing, and military and diplomatic alliances.

World War I saw the introduction of such warfare as use of tanks, airplanes, machine guns, submarines, poison gas, and flame throwers. Fighting on the Western front was characterized by a series of **trenches** which were used throughout the war until 1918. The atrocities of war took everyone by surprise and led to much of the animosity that marked the terms of the end of the war. It would lead to a ban on certain weapons, particularly poison gas, and leave the nations of Europe unwilling to go to war again.

When Germany agreed in 1918 to an armistice, it assumed the peace settlement would be drawn up on the basis of U.S. President Woodrow Wilson's Fourteen Points, which it considered equitable and made no attempt at recriminations. Instead, at the Paris Peace Conference, Germany was subjected to harsh reparations, being asked to pay the other countries for damages caused during the war. Heavy restrictions were placed on Germany as well, taking away arms and territories, losses that weighed heavily on the German psyche. The European powers even went so far as the force Germany to assume responsibility for causing the war.

Pre-war empires lost tremendous amounts of territories as well as the wealth of natural resources in them. New, independent nations were formed and some predominately ethnic areas came under control of nations of different cultural backgrounds. Some national boundary changes overlapped and created tensions and hard feelings as well as political and economic confusion. The wishes and desires of every national or cultural group could not possibly be realized and satisfied, resulting in disappointments for both; those who were victorious and those who were defeated. Germany received harsher terms than expected from the treaty which weakened its post-war government and, along with the world-wide depression of the 1930s, set the stage for the rise of Adolf Hitler and his Nationalist Socialist Party and World War II.

(See Skill 5.2 for additional information)

Skill 11.2   Understand the importance of Lenin, the Russian Revolution, and emergence of Communist totalitarianism

Until the early years of the twentieth century, Russia was ruled by a succession of **Czars**. The Czars ruled as autocrats or, sometimes, despots. Society was essentially feudalistic and was structured in three levels. The top level was held by the Czar. The second level was composed of the rich nobles who held government positions and owned vast tracts of land. The third level of the society was composed of the remaining people who lived in poverty as peasants or serfs. There were several unsuccessful attempts to revolt during the nineteenth century, caused largely by discontent among these three levels, especially the peasant, but they were quickly suppressed. The two revolutions of the early 20th century, in 1905 and 1917, however, were quite different.

Discontent with the social structure, with the living conditions of the peasants, and with working conditions despite industrialization were among the causes of the **1905 Revolution**. This general discontent was aggravated by the **Russo-Japanese War** (1904–1905) with inflation, rising prices, etc. Peasants who had been able to eke out a living began to starve. Many of the fighting troops were killed in battles. Russia lost to Japan because of poor leadership, lack of training, and inferior weaponry. Czar Nicholas II refused to end the war despite setbacks, and in January 1905, Port Arthur fell.

A trade union leader (Father Gapon) organized a protest to demand an end to the war, initiate industrial reform, obtain more civil liberties, and organize a constituent assembly. More than 150,000 peasants joined a demonstration outside the Czar's **Winter Palace**. Before the demonstrators even spoke, the palace guard opened fire on the crowd. This destroyed the people's trust in the Czar. Illegal trade unions and political parties formed and organized strikes to gain power.

The strikes eventually brought the Russian economy to a halt. This led Czar Nicholas II to sign the **October Manifesto** which created a constitutional monarchy, extended some civil rights, and gave the parliament limited legislative power. In a very short period of time, the Czar disbanded the parliament and violated the promised civil liberties.

The violation of the October Manifesto would help foment the **1917 Revolution**. There were other factors as well. Defeats on the battlefields during WWI caused discontent, loss of life, and a popular desire to withdraw from the war. The war had also caused another surge in prices and scarcity of many items. Most of the peasants could not afford to buy bread. In addition, the Czar's behavior triggered more unrest. The Czar continued to appoint unqualified people to government posts and handle the situation with general incompetence. The Czar also listened to his wife, Alexandra's, advice. She was strongly influenced by Rasputin. This caused increased discontent among all levels of the social structure.

Workers in Petrograd (now called St. Petersburg) went on strike in 1917 over the need for food. The Czar again ordered troops to suppress the strike. This time, however, the troops sided with the workers. The revolution then took a unique direction. The parliament created a provisional government to rule the country. The military and the workers also created their own governments called **soviets** (popularly elected local councils). The parliament was composed of nobles who soon lost control of the country when they failed to comply with the wishes of the populace. The result was chaos.

The most significant differences between the 1905 and 1917 revolutions were the formation of political parties and their use of propaganda and the support of the military and some of the nobles in 1917. The political leaders who had previously been driven into exile returned. **Lenin**, Stalin, and Trotsky won the support of the peasants with the promise of "Peace, Land, and Bread." The parliament, on the other hand, continued the country's involvement in the war. Lenin and the Bolshevik party gained the support of the **Red Guard** and together overthrew the provisional government. In short order, they had complete control of Russia and established a new communist state.

Skill 11.3   Describe the political, social and economic consequences of the Great Depression

(See Skill 6.2 and other references throughout this study guide)

Skill 11.4   Understand the impact of events, issues, and effects of Mussolini and the emergence of Fascism

The effects of the Depression were very strong throughout Europe, which was still rebuilding after the devastation of World War I. Germany was especially hard hit, as U.S. reconstruction loans dried up. Unemployment skyrocketed in

Germany, leaving millions out of work.

During the Depression in Germany, large numbers of urban workers found themselves unemployed and dissatisfied with the government. Communist and Fascist paramilitary organizations arose, promising dramatic action and economic restructuring. These organizations found a receptive audience among the disgruntled German workers. It was out of this climate that the **Nazi Party** emerged.

After a failed attempt at a coup, many of the Nazi leaders, including **Adolf Hitler**, were jailed. Upon his release, Hitler was able to take leadership again and build the fascist Nazi party into a political organization with seats in the German parliament. Hitler was eventually named Chancellor of Germany, from which position he implemented his policies of military expansion and aggression that culminated in the Second World War.

Fascist movements often had socialists' origins. For example, in Italy, where fascism first arose in place of socialism, **Benito Mussolini**, sought to impose what he called **corporativism**. A fascist "corporate" state would, in theory, run the economy for the benefit of the whole country like a corporation. It would be centrally controlled and managed by an elite who would see that its benefits would go to everyone.

Fascism has always declared itself the uncompromising enemy of communism, with which, however, fascist actions have much in common. (In fact, many of the methods of organization and propaganda used by fascists were taken from the experience of the early Russian communists, along with the belief in a single strong political party, secret police, etc.) The propertied interests and the upper classes, fearful of revolution, often gave their support to fascism on the basis of promises by the fascist leaders to maintain the status quo and safeguard property, in effect, accomplishing a revolution from above with their help as opposed to from below, against them. However, fascism did consider itself a revolutionary movement of a different type.

Once established, a fascist regime ruthlessly crushed communist and socialist parties as well as all democratic opposition. It regimented the propertied interests to its national goals and won the potentially revolutionary masses to fascist programs by substituting a rabid nationalism for class conflict. Thus, fascism may be regarded as an extreme defensive expedient adopted by a nation faced with the, sometimes illusionary, threat of communist subversion or revolution. Under fascism, capital is regulated, as labor and fascist contempt for legal or constitutional guarantees effectively destroyed whatever security the capitalistic system had enjoyed under pre-fascist governments.

In addition, fascist or similar regimes are at times anti-Communist. This is evidenced by the Soviet-German treaty of 1939. During the period of alliance created by the treaty, Italy and Germany and their satellite countries ceased their anti-Communist propaganda. They emphasized their own revolutionary and proletarian origins and attacked the so-called plutocratic western democracies.

The fact that fascist countries sought to control national life by methods identical to those of communist governments make such nations vulnerable to communism after the fascist regime is destroyed.

Skill 11.5   Understand the origins of World War II

The war had seriously damaged the economies of the European countries, both the victors and the defeated, leaving them deeply in debt. There was difficulty on both sides paying off war debts and loans. It was difficult to find jobs and some countries, such as Japan and Italy, found themselves without enough resources and more than enough people. Solving these problems by expanding the territory merely set up conditions for war later. Germany suffered horribly with runaway inflation ruining the value of its money and wiping out the savings of millions. Even though the U.S. made loans to Germany, which helped the government to restore some order and provide a short existence of some economic stability in Europe, the Great Depression only served to undo any good that had been done. Mass unemployment, poverty, and despair greatly weakened the democratic governments that had been formed and greatly strengthened the increasing power and influence of extreme political movements, such as communism, fascism, and national-socialism. These ideologies promised to put an end to the economic problems faced by Europeans.

The extreme form of patriotism called nationalism that had been the chief cause of World War I grew even stronger after the war ended in 1918. The political, social, and economic unrest fueled nationalism and became an effective tool enabling dictators to gain and maintain power from the 1930s to the end of World War II in 1945. In the Soviet Union, **Joseph Stalin** succeeded in gaining political control and establishing a strong harsh dictatorship. **Benito Mussolini** and the Fascist party, promising prosperity and order in Italy, gained national support and set up a strong government. In Japan, although the ruler was considered Emperor **Hirohito,** actual control and administration of government came under military officers. In Germany, the results of war, harsh treaty terms, loss of territory, great economic chaos, and collapse, all enabled **Adolf Hitler** and his National Socialist, or **Nazi,** party to gain complete power and control.

Germany, Italy, and Japan initiated a policy of aggressive territorial expansion with Japan being the first to conquer. In 1931, Japanese forces seized control of **Manchuria**, a part of China containing rich natural resources, and in 1937 began an attack on the rest of China, occupying most of its eastern part by 1938. Italy invaded **Ethiopia** in Africa in 1935, having complete control by 1936. The Soviet Union did not invade or take over any territory but along with Italy and Germany, actively participated in the **Spanish Civil War**, using it as a proving ground to test tactics and weapons, setting the stage for World War II.

In March 1933, Adolph Hitler became the dictator of Germany. The Nazis began boycotting Jewish shops and dismissing them from civil servant positions. Jews, political opponents, and individuals of cultural minorities were interned in forced work camps such as Dachau. Other camps were built and by the end of the war the Germans had built numerous concentration camps / death camps throughout Germany and the Third Reich, in which they killed hundreds of thousands of people, including men, women, and children.

November 9, 1938, is known as Kristallnacht. On that night, thousands of Jewish homes were ruined, hundreds of synagogues were destroyed, and many Jews were killed. The time period from 1941 to 1945 the Nazi regime was involved with the intentional destruction of the Jews and political dissidents as well as gypsies and others the regime considered undesirable. The period if known as the **Holocaust.** During this time, nearly six million Jews were killed in addition to approximately five million non-Jews. The term "holocaust" means sacrifice by burning, massacre, and calamity.

In Germany, almost immediately after taking power, in direct violation of the World War I peace treaty, Hitler began the buildup of the armed forces. He sent troops into the Rhineland in 1936, then invaded Austria in 1938, and united it with Germany. In 1938, he seized control of the Sudetenland, part of western Czechoslovakia where mostly Germans lived, followed by the rest of Czechoslovakia in March 1939. Despite his territorial designs, the other nations of Europe made no moves to stop Hitler.

Preferring not to embark on another costly war, the European powers opted for a policy of **appeasement**, believing that once Hitler had satisfied his desire for land he would be satisfied, and war could be averted. Then, on September 1, 1939, Hitler began World War II in Europe by invading **Poland**.

(See Skill 5.3 for additional information)

Skill 11.6   Understand key events and issues pertaining to the outcome of World War II

By 1940, Germany had invaded and controlled Norway, Denmark, Belgium, Luxembourg, the Netherlands, and France. German military forces struck in what came to be known as the **blitzkrieg**, or "lightning war." A shock attack, it relied on the use of surprise, speed, and superiority in firepower. The German blitzkrieg coordinated land and air attacks to paralyze the enemy by disabling its communications and coordination capacities.

When France fell in June 1940, the Franco-German armistice divided France into two zones: one under German military occupation and one under nominal French control (the southeastern two-fifths of the country). The National Assembly, summoned at Vichy, France, ratified the armistice and granted **Philippe Pétain** control of the French State. The **Vichy** government then collaborated with the Germans, eventually becoming little more than a rubber stamp for German policies. Germany would occupy the whole of France in 1942, and by early 1944 a **resistance** movement created a period of civil war in France. The Vichy regime was abolished after the liberation of Paris.

With Europe safely conquered, Hitler turned his sights to England. The **Battle of Britain** (June 1940–April 1941) was a series of intense raids directed against Britain by the **Luftwaffe**, Germany's air force. Intended to prepare the way for invasion, the air raids were directed against British ports and Royal Air Force (**RAF**) bases. In September 1940, London and other cities were attacked in the "**blitz**," a series of bombings that lasted for 57 consecutive nights. Sporadic raids until April 1941. The RAF was outnumbered but succeeded in blocking the German air force, and eventually Hitler was forced to abandon his plans for invasion, Germany's first major setback in the war.

After successes in North Africa and Italy, and following the D-Day Invasion, the Allied forces faced a protracted campaign across Europe. Each gain was hard won, and both the weather and local terrain, at times worked against them. The **Battle of the Bulge**, also known as Battle of the Ardennes (December 16, 1944–January 28, 1945) was the largest World War II land battle on the Western Front, and the last major German counteroffensive of the war. Launched by Adolf Hitler himself, the German army's goal was to cut Allied forces in half and to retake the crucial port of Antwerp. Secretly massed Panzer tank-led units launched their assault into the thinnest part of the Allied forces.

Though surprised and suffering tremendous losses, Allied forces still managed to slow the Germans. American tanks moved swiftly to counterattack and cut German supply lines. The attack resulted in a bulge seventy miles deep into Allied lines, but all forward momentum for the Germans was essentially stopped by Christmas. It took another month before the Allies could push back to the original line. Both sides suffered great casualties, but the Germans' losses were a crushing blow, as the troops and equipment lost were irreplaceable.

During the war, Allied forces flew extensive bombing raids deep into German territory. Launched from bases in England, both American and RAF bomber squadrons proceeded to massively bomb German factories and cities. Although the raids were dangerous, with many planes and lives lost both to the Luftwaffe and ant-aircraft artillery, the raids continued throughout the war. German cities were reduced to virtually rubble by war's end, and the impact on Germany's production capacity and transportation lines helped swing the tide of war.

Before war in Europe had ended, the Allies had agreed on a military occupation of Germany that divided the country into four zones each being administered by one of the Allies—Great Britain, France, the Soviet Union, and the United States, with the four powers jointly administering Berlin. After the war, the Allies agreed Germany's armed forces would be abolished, the Nazi Party outlawed, and the territory east of the Oder and Neisse Rivers taken away from Germany. Nazi leaders were accused of war crimes and brought to trial at **Nuremburg**.

Major consequences of the war included horrendous death and destruction, millions of displaced persons, the gaining of strength and spread of Communism, and Cold War tensions as a result of the beginning of the nuclear age. World War II ended more lives and caused more devastation than any other war. Besides the losses of millions of military personnel, the devastation and destruction directly affected civilians and reduced cities, houses, and factories to ruin and rubble and totally wrecked communication and transportation systems. Millions of civilian deaths, especially in China and the Soviet Union, were the results of famine. More than 12 million people were uprooted by the war's end and the people had no place to live. Included in those numbers were prisoners of war, those who survived Nazi concentration camps and slave labor camps, orphans, and people who escaped war-torn areas and invading armies. Changing national boundary lines also caused the mass movement of displaced persons.

Germany and Japan were completely defeated; Great Britain and France were seriously weakened; and the Soviet Union and the United States became the world's leading powers. Although allied during the war, the alliance fell apart as the Soviets pushed Communism in Europe and Asia. In spite of the tremendous destruction it suffered, the Soviet Union was stronger than ever. During the war, it took control of Lithuania, Estonia, and Latvia and by mid-1945 parts of Poland, Czechoslovakia, Finland, and Romania. It helped Communist governments gain power in Bulgaria, Romania, Hungary, Czechoslovakia, Poland, and North Korea. China fell to Mao Zedong's Communist forces in 1949. Until the fall of the Berlin Wall in 1989 and the dissolution of Communist governments in Eastern Europe and the Soviet Union, the United States and the Soviet Union faced off in what was called a Cold War. The possibility of the terrifying destruction by nuclear weapons loomed over both nations.

Decolonization refers to the period after World War II when many African and Asian colonies and protectorates gained independence from the powers that had colonized them. The independence of India and Pakistan from Britain in 1945 marked the beginning of an especially important period of decolonization that lasted through 1960. Several British colonies in eastern Africa and French colonies in western Africa and Asia, also formed as independent countries during this period.

Colonial powers had found it efficient to draw political boundaries across traditional ethnic and national lines, thereby dividing local populations and making them easier to control. With the yoke of colonialism removed, many new nations found themselves trying to reorganize into politically stable and economically viable units. The role of nationalism was important in this reorganization, as formerly divided peoples had opportunity to reunite.

(See Skill 5.3 for additional information)

**COMPETENCY 12.0   THE MAJOR DEVELOPMENTS OF WORLD
                      HISTORY FROM 1945 TO THE PRESENT**

**Skill 12.1   Know the causes, key events, and consequences of the Cold
                 War**

The major thrust of U.S. foreign policy from the end of World War II to 1990 was
the post-war struggle between non-Communist nations, led by the United States,
and the Soviet Union and the Communist nations who were its allies. It was
referred to as a **Cold War** because its conflicts did not lead to a major war of
fighting, or a "hot war." Both the Soviet Union and the United States embarked
on an arsenal buildup of atomic and hydrogen bombs as well as other nuclear
weapons. Both nations had the capability of destroying each other but because
of the continuous threat of nuclear war and accidents, extreme caution was
practiced on both sides. The efforts of both sides to serve and protect their
political philosophies and to support and assist their allies resulted in a number of
events during this 45-year period.

After 1945, social and economic chaos continued in Western Europe, especially
in Germany. Secretary of State George C. Marshall came to realize that Europe's
problems were serious and could affect the U.S. To aid in the recovery, he
proposed a program known as the European Recovery Program or the **Marshall
Plan**. Although the Soviet Union withdrew from any participation, the U.S.
continued the work of assisting Europe in regaining its economic stability. In
Germany, in particular, the situation was critical, with the American Army
shouldering the staggering burden of relieving the serious problems of the
German economy. In February 1948, Britain and the U.S. combined their two
German zones, with France joining in June.

In 1946, Josef Stalin stated publicly that the presence of capitalism and its
development of the world's economy made international peace impossible. This
led an American diplomat in Moscow named **George F. Kennan** to propose the
idea of **containment**, as a response to Stalin and as a statement of U.S. foreign
policy. The goal of the U.S. would be to limit the extension or expansion of Soviet
Communist policies and activities. After Soviet efforts to make trouble in Iran,
Greece, and Turkey, U.S. President Harry Truman stated what is known as the
Truman Doctrine which committed the U.S. to a policy of intervention in order to
contain or stop the spread of communism throughout the world.

The Soviets were opposed to German unification and, in April 1948, took serious
action to either stop it or to force the Allies to give up control of West Berlin to the
Soviets. The Soviets blocked all road traffic access from West Germany to West
Berlin, which lay wholly within Soviet-controlled East Germany. To avoid any
armed conflict, it was decided to airlift into West Berlin the needed food and
supplies. During the **Berlin Airlift**, from June 1948 to mid-May 1949, Allied air

forces flew in all that was needed for the West Berliners, forcing the Soviets to lift the blockade and permit vehicular traffic access to the city.

The Cold War was, more than anything else, an ideological struggle between proponents of democracy and those of communism. The two major players were the United States and the Soviet Union, but other countries were involved as well. It was a "cold" war because no large-scale fighting took place directly between the two big protagonists. It wasn't just differing forms of government that was driving this war, either. Economics were a main concern as well. A concern in both countries was that the precious resources (such as oil and food) from other like-minded countries wouldn't be allowed to flow to "the other side." These resources didn't much flow between the U.S. and Soviet Union, either.

The Soviet Union kept much more of a tight leash on its supporting countries, including all of Eastern Europe, which made up a military organization called the Warsaw Pact. The Western nations responded with a military organization of their own, **NATO or North Atlantic Treaty Organization**. Another prime battleground was Asia, where the Soviet Union had allies in China, North Korea, and North Vietnam, and the U.S. had allies in Japan, South Korea, Taiwan, and South Vietnam. The Korean War and Vietnam War were major conflicts in which both big protagonists played big roles but didn't directly fight each other.

The main symbol of the Cold War was the **arms race**, a continual buildup of missiles, tanks, and other weapons that became ever more technologically advanced and increasingly more deadly. The ultimate weapon, which both sides had in abundance, was the nuclear bomb. Spending on weapons and defensive systems eventually occupied great percentages of the budgets of the U.S. and the USSR, and some historians argue this high level of spending played a large part in the end of the latter.

The war was a cultural struggle as well. Adults brought up their children to hate "the Americans" or "the Communists." Cold War tensions spilled over into many parts of life in countries around the world. The ways of life in countries on either side of the divide were so different that they served entirely foreign to outside observers.

Skill 12.2   Understand the origins, course, and consequences of the Korean and Vietnam Wars

Korean War: 1950 to 1953

Korea was under control of Japan from 1895 to the end of the Second World War in 1945. At war's end, the Soviet and U.S. military troops moved into Korea with the U.S. troops in the southern half and the Soviet troops in the northern half. The 38-degree North Latitude line (38th parallel) served as the boundary.

The General Assembly of the UN in 1947 ordered elections throughout all of Korea to select one government for the entire country. The Soviet Union would not allow the North Koreans to vote, so they set up a Communist government there. The South Koreans set up a democratic government but both claimed the entire country. At times, there were clashes between the troops from 1948 to 1950. After the U.S. removed its remaining troops in 1949 and announced in early 1950 that Korea was not part of its defense line in Asia, the Communists decided to act and invaded the south.

Participants were: North and South Korea, United States of America, Australia, New Zealand, China, Canada, France, Great Britain, Turkey, Belgium, Ethiopia, Colombia, Greece, South Africa, Luxembourg, Thailand, the Netherlands, and the Philippines. It was the first war in which a world organization played a major military role and it presented quite a challenge to the UN, which had only been in existence five years.

The war began June 25, 1950, and ended July 27, 1953. A truce was drawn up and an armistice agreement was signed ending the fighting. A permanent treaty of peace has never been signed and the country remains divided between the Communist North and the Democratic South. It was a very costly and bloody war destroying villages and homes, displacing and killing millions of people.

The Vietnam War

Though ostensibly an American war, conflict in the region began with what is often called the French Indochina War, which waged from 1946 to 1954. This conflict involved France, which had ruled Vietnam as its colony (French Indochina), and the newly independent Democratic Republic of Vietnam under **Ho Chi Minh**. On May 7, 1954, at a French military base known as **Dien Bien Phu**, Vietminh troops emerged victorious after a 56-day siege, leading to the end of France's involvement in Indochina. The war ended in Vietnamese victory and the country was then divided into the communist-dominated north and the U.S.-supported south. Almost inevitably, war soon broke out between the two.

In the fighting that ensued, fighters trained in the north (the **Viet Cong**) fought a guerrilla war against U.S.-supported South Vietnamese forces. North Vietnamese forces would later join the fight, supported by Soviet advisors and equipment. At the height of U.S. involvement, there were more than half a million U.S. military personnel in Vietnam. The **Tet Offensive** of 1968, in which the Viet Cong and North Vietnamese attacked thirty-six major South Vietnamese cities and towns, marked a turning point in the war. Many in the U.S. had come to oppose the war on moral and practical grounds, and President Lyndon B. Johnson decided to shift to a policy of "de-escalation."

Peace talks began in Paris. Between 1969 and 1973, U.S. troops were withdrawn from Vietnam, although by 1970 the war had expanded to Cambodia and Laos. Peace talks, which had reached a stalemate in 1971, started again in 1973, producing a cease-fire agreement. Fighting continued, and there were numerous truce violations. In 1975 the North Vietnamese launched a full-scale invasion of the south. The south surrendered later that year, and in 1976 the country was reunited as the Socialist Republic of Vietnam. More than two million people (including 58,000 Americans) died over the course of the war, about half of them civilians.

In related conflict, Cambodia experienced its own civil war between communists and non-communists during that period, which was won by the communist **Khmer Rouge** in 1975. After several years of horrifying atrocities under **Pol Pot**, the Vietnamese invaded in 1979 and installed a puppet government. Fighting between the Khmer Rouge and the Vietnamese continued throughout the 1980s; Vietnam withdrew its troops by 1989. In 1993 UN-mediated elections established an interim government and Cambodia's monarchy was reestablished. In Laos, North Vietnam's victory over South Vietnam brought the communist Pathet Lao into complete control.

(See Skill 5.5 for additional information)

Skill 12.3   Discuss revolution, reaction, modernization, and democratic movements in Latin America

(See Skill 10.4)

Skill 12.4   Recognize and be able to discuss major developments of the 20th Century in the arts, music, literature, religion, and philosophy

The twentieth century experienced a revolution in music. In keeping with the exceptionally high value of individuality and unique personal expression, there was a quest for new and unique forms of musical expression.

The major forms inspired by classical music have continued, though with certain modifications. The symphony has continued in form, but with greater dissonance and great experimentation in rhythm. Major symphonic composers of the century include: Gustav Mahler, Jean Sibelius, Dmitry Shostakovich, Serge Prokofiev, and Sergey Rachmaninov, as well as Leonard Bernstein. Opera began to change after WWII as composers began to incorporate other musical forms that were emerging during the century. Notable operatic composers include Benjamin Britten, Karlheinz Stockhausen, Virgil Thomson, Douglas Moore, Philip Glass, and John Adams. Ballet tended to focus on music written specifically for its needs. This trend included such composers as Claude Debussy, Maurice Ravel, and R. Strauss. **Igor Stravinsky**'s *The Rite of Spring*, however was internationally recognized for its violent rhythms and dissonance. The second half of the century was marked by the tendency to re-stage ballets with existing music. The exceptions were Aaron Copland Hans Werner Henze, and Benjamin Britten.

Musical theater was an evolution from the operettas of the Romantic Period and the traditions of the European music hall and American vaudeville. Most notable in this form are **Leonard Bernstein** and **Steven Sondheim**. Film music also developed during this century. The soundtracks for films were either adaptations of classical music or new compositions from composers such as Elmer Bernstein, Bernard Herrman, Max Steiner, and Dmitri Tiomkin.

American popular music evolved from folk music. This was the music of the first half of the century, characterized by a consistent structure of two verses, a chorus, and a repetition of the chorus. The songs were written to be sung by average persons, and the tunes were usually harmonized. Much of this music originated in New York's **Tin Pan Alley**. Particularly notable during this period were **Irving Berlin, George and Ira Gershwin**, and a host of others. After WWII, teen music began to dominate. New forms emerged from various ethnic and regional groups including Blues, Rhythm and Blues, and Rap from the African American community; Country music from the South and Southwest; and folk music, jazz, rock and roll, and rock.

In art, the primary expression of the first half of the century was **Modernism**. The Avant Garde perspective encouraged all types of innovation and experimentation. Key elements of this movement have been abstraction, cubism, surrealism, realism, and abstract expressionism. Notable among the artists of this period for the birth or perfection of particular styles are Henri Matisse, **Pablo Picasso**, George Rouault, Gustav Klimt, George Braque, **Salvador Dali**, Hans Arp, Rene Magrite, and Marcel Duchamp.

In the U.S., realism tended to find regional expressions, including the Ashcan School and Robert Henri, Midwestern Regionalism, and Grant Wood. Other particularly notable painters are **Edward Hopper** and **Georgia O'Keeffe**. The New York School came to be known for a style known as Abstract Expressionism and included such artists as **Jackson Pollock, Willem de Kooning**, and Larry Rivers. Other painters of the period were Mark Rothko, Clement Greenberg, Ellsworth Kelly, and painters in the Op Art Movement.

In sculpture, many of the same patterns and trends were applied. Innovations included the exploration of empty space (Henry Moore), the effort to incorporate cubism in three dimensions (Marcel Duchamp), and the use of welded metal to create kinetic sculpture (Alexander Calder).

Postmodernism has been the description of the expansion of forms and the valuing of innovation since 1950. This has included Minimalism, Figurative Styles, Pop Art, Conceptual Art, and Installation Art. Photography developed as an art form, as well, during the twentieth century.

The literature of this period had been an attempt to come to terms with the nature and the cost of war, of the meaning of the human struggle for freedom, and the ability to enjoy basic human and civil rights. Literature cried out against and embraced change. By the beginning of the twentieth century, literature was reflecting the struggle of the modern individual to find a place and a meaning in a new world which seemed like a jungle. Literature reflected the observation that not only does the modern human not know how to find meaning, he/she does not actually know what he/she is seeking. It is this crisis of identity that has been the subject of most modern literature. This can be seen is the writings of **James Joyce**, Eugene O'Neill, Luigi Pirandello, Samuel Beckett, George Bernard Shaw, T.S. Eliot, **Kafka**, Camus, Pasternak, Graham Greene, Tennessee Williams, and a host of others.

Religion can be closely tied to ethnicity, as it is frequently one of the common social institutions shared by an ethnic group. Like ethnicity, religion varies in practices and beliefs even within the large major religions. Some religions and religious sects link their beliefs closely to their ancestry, and so are closely linked to the concept of race.

Variations in race, ethnicity, and religion—both real and perceived—are primary ways in which cultures and cultural groups are defined. They are useful in understanding cultures, but can also be the source of cultural biases and prejudices.

Eight common religions are practiced today. Interestingly, all of these religions have divisions or smaller sects within them. Not one of them is totally completely unified.

Judaism is the oldest of the eight and was the first to teach and practice the belief in one God, Yahweh.

Christianity came from Judaism, grew and spread in the first century throughout the Roman Empire, despite persecution. A later schism resulted in the Western (Roman Catholic) and Eastern (Orthodox) parts. Protestant sects developed as part of the Protestant Revolution. The name "Christian" means one who is a follower of Jesus Christ who started Christianity. Christians follow his teachings and examples, living by the laws and principles of the Bible.

Islam was founded in Arabia by Mohammed who preached about God, Allah. Islam spread through trade, travel, and conquest and followers of it fought in the Crusades. In addition, there have been other wars against Christians and today against the Jewish nation of Israel. Followers of Islam, called Muslims, live by the teachings of the Koran, their holy book, and of their prophets.

Hinduism was begun by people called Aryans around 1500 BCE and spread into India. The Aryans blended their culture with that of the Dravidians, the natives they conquered. Today it has many sects, promotes worship of hundreds of gods and goddesses, and has the belief of reincarnation. Though forbidden today by law, a prominent feature of Hinduism in the past was a rigid adherence to and practice of the caste system.

Buddhism developed in India from the teachings of Prince Gautama and spread to most of Asia. Its beliefs opposed the worship of numerous deities, the Hindu caste system, and the supernatural. Worshippers must be free of attachment to all things worldly and devote themselves to finding release from life's suffering.

Confucianism is a Chinese philosophy based on the teachings of the Chinese philosopher, Confucius. Although ostensibly considered a religion, there is no formal priesthood nor belief in deities or any sort of after-life. Instead, it focuses on social relationships, placing an emphasis on proper behavior and ideas including a sense of respect for authority and ancestors. Achievement was governed by a series of examinations, and those who passed them were expected to govern according to high moral standards.

Daoism is a native Chinese belief system with veneration for many deities and natural phenomena. It teaches all followers to make the effort to achieve the two goals of happiness and immortality. Practices and rituals include meditation, prayer, magic, reciting scriptures, special diets, breath control, beliefs in geomancy, fortune telling, astrology, and communicating with the spirits of the dead.

Shinto is the native religion of Japan which was developed from native folk beliefs of worshipping spirits and demons in animals, trees, and mountains. According to its mythology, deities created Japan and its people, which resulted in worshipping the emperor as a god. Shinto never had strong doctrines on salvation or life after death.

(See also Skill 7.3)

Skill 12.5   Know and understand the causes of the collapse of the Soviet Empire

The Cold War continued in varying degrees from 1947 to 1991, when the Soviet Union collapsed. The "**Iron Curtain**" referred to the ideological, symbolic, and physical separation of Europe between East and West. The **Berlin Wall** fell in 1989, and this set into motion the collapse of the Soviet system of government in Eastern Europe. By 1991, communist regimes in Eastern European countries had been largely overthrown, marking the shredding of the "Iron Curtain." None of this would have been possible without the presence of change in the Soviet Union itself.

Mikhail Gorbachev was elected leader by the Politburo in 1984, bringing with him a program of reform intended to bolster the flagging Soviet economy. As part of his plan, Gorbachev instituted a policy of economic freedoms called **perestroika**, which allowed private ownership of some businesses. He relaxed the government's control over the media in a policy of openness, called **glasnost** and instituted free, multi-party elections.

Gorbachev felt these new policies were required to apply pressure to more conservative members of the government, thereby increasing his support. The media seized upon their new freedom, however, and began reporting on the corruption and economic problems of the Soviet Union, which had been largely hidden from the public by the previous state-controlled news services. Meanwhile, the United States, under President Ronald Reagan, had rapidly increased its military spending, outpacing the Soviet Union and increasing economic pressure.

Faced with growing independence movements in many of the Eastern Bloc countries, the government under Gorbachev reversed Brezhnev's policies of tight control via the Communist Party. Unlike previous efforts, protestors and advocates for democracy were not met with tanks and repression, but rather allowed democracy to take hold. As the countries of Eastern Europe and the Soviet states began pulling away from Russia, there were certain hardline factions who opposed the new policy. A coup was launched in 1991 to overthrow Gorbachev. Ironically, the defeat of the coup through peaceful means proved the final nail in the old Soviet coffin.

When the Soviet Union finally collapsed, it was replaced by a Russian Federation led by **Boris Yeltsin**. The fifteen republics of the former USSR became independent nations with varying degrees of freedom and democracy in government and together formed the Commonwealth of Independent States (CIS). The former Communist nations of Eastern Europe also emphasized their independence with democratic forms of government.

Skill 12.6   Explain the persistence of nationalism and conflict in the post–Cold War world

Nationalism is most simply defined as the belief that the nation is the basic unit of human association and is a well-defined group of people sharing a common identity. This process of organizing new nations out of the remains of former colonies was called **nation building**.

Nation building in this fashion did not always result in the desired stability. Pakistan, for example, eventually split into Bangladesh and Pakistan along geographic and religious lines. Ethnic conflicts in newly formed African nations arose, and are still flaring in some areas. As the United States and the Soviet Union emerged as the dominant world powers, these countries encouraged dissent in post-colonial nations such as Cuba, Vietnam, and Korea, which became arenas for Cold War conflict.

With the emergence of so many new independent nations, the role of **international organizations** such as the newly formed United Nations grew in importance. The **United Nations** was formed after World War II to establish peaceful ties between countries. Dismayed by the failure of the former League of Nations to prevent war, the organizers of the United Nations provided for the ability to deploy peacekeeping troops and to impose sanctions and restrictions on member states. Other international organizations arose to take the place of former colonial connections. The British Commonwealth and the French Union, for example, maintained connections between Britain and France and their former colonies.

Global migration saw an increase in the years during, and following, World War II. During the war years, many Jews left the hostile climate under Nazi Germany for the United States and Palestine and the newly established state of **Israel**. Following the war, the Allied countries agreed to force German people living in Eastern Europe to return to Germany, affecting more than 16 million people. In other parts of the world, instability in post-colonial areas often led to migration. Colonial settlers who had enjoyed the protection of a colonial power sometimes found themselves in hostile situations as native peoples gained independence and ascended to power, spurring migration to more friendly nations. Economic instability in newly formed countries created an incentive for people to seek opportunity elsewhere.

Individuals and societies have divided the earth's surface through conflict for a number of reasons:

- The domination of peoples or societies, e.g., nationalism, religion, or colonialism
- The control of valuable resources, e.g., oil
- The control of strategic routes, e.g., the Panama Canal

Religion, political ideology, national origin, language, and race can spur conflicts. Conflicts can result from disagreement over how land, oceans, or natural resources will be developed, shared, and used. Conflicts have resulted from trade, migration, and settlement rights. Conflicts can occur between small groups of people, between cities, between nations, between religious groups, and between multi-national alliances.

Today, the world is primarily divided by political/administrative interests into state sovereignties. A particular region is recognized to be controlled by a particular government, including its territory, population, and natural resources. The only area of the earth's surface today which is not defined by state or national sovereignty, is Antarctica.

Alliances are developed among nations on the basis of political philosophy, economic concerns, cultural similarities, religious interests, and military defense. Some of the most notable alliances today are:

- The United Nations
- The North Atlantic Treaty Organization
- The Caribbean Community
- The Common Market
- The Council of Arab Economic Unity
- The European Union

Throughout human history there have been conflicts on virtually every scale over the right to divide the Earth according to differing perceptions, needs, and values. These conflicts have ranged from tribal conflicts to urban riots, to civil wars, to regional wars, and to world wars. While these conflicts have traditionally centered on control of land, new disputes are beginning to arise over the resources of the oceans and space. International organizations such as the UN and the World Bank have programs to assist developing nations with loans and education so they might join the international economy. Many countries are taking steps to regulate immigration.

Ethnic cleansing in Yugoslavia occurred in Kosovo in the 1990s when the Serbian government expelled ethnic Albanians from the province. The Serbian officials also confiscated all identity documentation from those who were expelled so that any attempt to return could be refused by claiming that, without documents to prove Serbian citizenship, the people must be native Albanians. The effort even went so far as to destroy archival documents that proved citizenship.

In 1989 the Serbian president, **Slobodan Milosevic**, abrogated the constitutional autonomy of Kosovo. He and the minority of Serbs in Kosovo had long bristled at the fact that Muslim Albanians were in control of an area considered sacred to Serbs. In 1998, growing tensions led to armed clashes between Serbs and the Kosovo Liberation Army (**KLA**), which had begun killing Serbian police and politicians. The Serbs responded with a ruthless counteroffensive, inducing the UN Security Council to condemn the Serbs' excessive use of force, including ethnic cleansing (killing and expulsion), and the imposition of an arms embargo, but the violence continued. After diplomatic efforts broke down, **NATO** responded with an 11-week bombing campaign which extended to Belgrade and significantly damaged Serbia's infrastructure. NATO and Serbia signed an accord in June 1999 outlining Serbian troop withdrawal and the return of nearly one million ethnic Albanian refugees as well as 500,000 displaced within the province.

Rwandan Genocide was the 1994 mass extermination of hundreds of thousands of ethnic **Tutsis** and moderate **Hutu** sympathizers in Rwanda and was the largest atrocity during the Rwandan Civil War. This genocide was mostly carried out by two extremist Hutu militia groups between April and mid-July 1994. Hundreds of thousands of people were slaughtered.

In the wake of the Rwandan Genocide, the United Nations and the international community drew severe criticism for its inaction. Despite international news media coverage of the violence as it unfolded, most countries, including France, Belgium, and the United States, declined to intervene or speak out against the massacres. Canada continued to lead the UN peacekeeping force in Rwanda. However, the UN Security Council did not authorize direct intervention or the use force to prevent or halt the killing.

The genocide ended when a Tutsi-dominated expatriate rebel overthrew the Hutu government and seized power. Fearing reprisals, hundreds of thousands of Hutu and other refugees fled into eastern Zaire (now the Democratic Republic of the Congo). People who had actively participated in the genocide hid among the refugees, fueling the First and Second Congo Wars. Rivalry between Hutu and Tutsi tribal factions is also a major factor in the Burundi Civil War.

In early 1990s **South Africa**, the system of racial segregation called **apartheid** was abolished. Apartheid was an institutionalized discriminatory system of restricted contact between races. The population was separated and defined by law into 'whites', 'blacks', 'colored', and 'mixed racial'. The long-term aim of this policy was to restrict the majority African population to small 'homelands', which were to be governed and developed separately from white South Africa. With the election of South Africa's first democratic government in 1994, the last vestiges of apartheid were officially removed, but the policy continues to have consequences on the South African landscape and its society.

The **Iranian Revolution** in 1979 transformed a constitutional monarchy, led by the Shah, into an Islamic populist theocratic republic. The new ruler was Ayatollah Ruhollah Khomeini. This revolution occurred in two essential stages. In the first, religious, liberal, and leftist groups cooperated to oust the **Shah** (king). In the second stage, the Ayatollah rose to power and created an Islamic state.

The Shah had faced intermittent opposition from the middle classes in the cities and from Islamic figures. These groups sought a limitation of the Shah's power and a constitutional democracy. The Shah enforced censorship laws and imprisoned political enemies. At the same time, living conditions of the people improved greatly and several important democratic rights were given to the people. Islamic **Mullahs** fiercely opposed giving women the right to vote.

The Shah was said to be a puppet of the U.S. government. A series of protests in 1978 escalated until December of that year when more than two million people gathered in Tehran in protest against the Shah. In a very short period of time, the Ayatollah Khomeini had gathered his revolutionaries and completed the overthrow of the monarchy.

The revolution accomplished certain goals, including reduction of foreign influence and a more even distribution of the nation's wealth. It did not change repressive policies or levels of government brutality. It reversed policies toward women, restoring ancient policies of repression. Religious repression became rife, particularly against members of the Baha'i Faith. The revolution has also isolated Iran from the rest of the world, being rejected by both capitalist and communist nations. This isolation, however, allowed the country to develop its own internal political system rather than having a system imposed by foreign powers.

The countries of the Middle East, despite their economic similarities, have important differences in their governments, belief systems, and global outlooks. Iran and Iraq fought a devastating war in the 1980s. **Iraq** invaded **Kuwait** in the late 1990s. It is not outside the realm of possibility other conflicts will arise in the future.

Another large factor of the instability in the Middle East is ethnic strife. It's not just Muslims who occupy these countries. Each country has its own ethnic mix. A good example of this is Iraq, which has a huge minority of **Kurdish** people. Saddam Hussein, the former dictator of Iraq, made a habit of persecuting Kurds just because of who they were. Iraq also provides an example of religious conflict, with the minority Shiites now in power and Hussein's Sunnis out of power. These two groups of people agree on very little outside the basics of Islamic faith. The prospect of a civil war in Iraq looms large, as it does in other neighboring countries that have their own ethnic problems.

Religious conflict is the status quo in Israel as well, as **Israelis** and **Palestinians** continue a centuries-old fight over religion and geography. This conflict goes back to the beginnings of Islam, during the seventh century. Muslims claimed Jerusalem, capital of the ancient civilization of Israel, as a holy city, in the same way that Jews and Christians did. Muslims seized control of Palestine and Jerusalem and held it for a great many years, prompting Christian armies from Europe to muster for the Crusades in a series of attempts to "regain the Holy Land." For hundreds of years after Christendom's failure to secure the area, these lands were ruled by Muslim leaders and armies. In recent centuries, Palestine was made a British colony and then eliminated in favor of the modern state of Israel. Since that last event in 1948, the conflict has escalated to varying degrees.

The addition of Israel to the Middle East equation presents a religious conflict not only with the Palestinians but also with the Arab peoples of neighboring Egypt and Syria. The armed forces of all of these countries have many advanced weapons that would seem to be a deterrent to further bloodshed, yet the attacks continue. In the last 40 years, Israel has won two major wars with its neighbors. Nearly daily conflict continues, much as it has for thousands of years. This conflict is not so much an economic one, but a full-blown war in this region would certainly involve Israel's neighbors and, by extension, other large countries in the world, most notably the United States.

Skill 12.7   Know global economic developments since 1945

Globalism is defined as the principle of the interdependence of all the world's nations and their peoples. Within this global community, every nation, in some way and to a certain degree, is dependent on other nations. Since no one nation has all of the resources needed for production, trade with other nations is required to obtain what is needed for production, to sell what is produced or to buy finished products, and to earn money to maintain and strengthen the nation's economic system.

Developing nations receive technical assistance and financial aid from developed nations. Many international organizations have been set up to promote and encourage cooperation and economic progress among member nations. Through the elimination of such barriers to trade as tariffs, trade is stimulated resulting in increased productivity, economic progress, increased cooperation, and understanding on diplomatic levels.

Those nations that are not part of an international trade organization not only must make economic decisions concerning what to produce, how and for whom, but must also deal with the problem of tariffs and quotas on imports. Regardless of international trade memberships, economic growth and development are vital and affect all trading nations. Businesses, labor, and governments share common interests and goals in a nation's economic status. International systems of banking and finance have been devised to assist governments and businesses in setting the policy and guidelines for the exchange of currencies.

Globalization refers to the complex of social, political, technological, and economic changes that result from increasing contact, communication, interaction, integration, and interdependence of peoples of disparate parts of the world. The term is generally used to refer to the process of change or as the cause of turbulent change. Globalization may be understood in terms of positive social and economic change, as in the case of a broadening of trade resulting in an increase in the standard of living for developing countries. It may also be understood negatively in terms of the abusive treatment of developing countries in the interest of cultural or economic imperialism. These negative understandings generally point to cultural assimilation, plundering and profiteering, the destruction of the local culture and economy, and ecological indifference.

The period of European peace after the defeat of Napoleon and the reliance upon the gold standard during that time is often referred to as "**The First Era of Globalization**." It began to disintegrate with the crisis over the gold standard in the late 1920s and early 1930s and included Europe, several European-influenced areas in the Americas, and Oceania. The exchange of goods based upon the common gold standard resulted in prosperity for all countries involved. Communication and the exchange of ideas between these countries also prospered. Since WWII, globalization of trade has been accomplished primarily through trade negotiations and treaties.

Globalization also involves exchange of money, commodities, information, ideas, and people. Much of this has been facilitated by the great advances in technology in the last 150 years. The effects of globalization can be seen across all areas of social and cultural interaction. Economically, globalization brings about broader and faster trade and flow of capital, increased outsourcing of labor, the development of global financial systems (such as the introduction of the **Euro**), the creation of trade agreements, and the birth of international organizations to moderate the agreements. From a social and cultural point of view, globalization results in greater exchange of all segments of the various cultures, including ideas, technology, food, clothing, fads, etc. Travel and migration create multicultural societies. The media facilitates the exchange of cultural and social values. As values interact, a new set of shared values begins to emerge.

The global economy had its origins in the early twentieth century with the advent of the airplane, which made travel and trade easier and less time-consuming than ever. Trucks, trains, and ships carry cargo all over the world. Trains travel faster than ever, as do ships. Roads are more prevalent and usually in better repair than they have ever been, making truck and even car travel not the dead-end option it once was. With the recent advent of the Internet, the world might be better termed a global neighborhood.

With all of this capability has come increasing demand. People had traditionally gotten their goods using their own means or from traders who lived nearby. As technology improved, trade routes got longer and demand for things from overseas grew. This demand fed the economic imperative of creating more supply, and vice versa. As more people discovered goods from overseas, the demand for those foreign goods increased. Because people could get goods from overseas with relative ease, they continued to get them and demand more. Suppliers were only too happy to supply the goods.

Globalization has also brought about welcome and unwelcome developments in the field of **epidemiology**. Vaccines and other cures for diseases can be shipped relatively quickly all around the world. For example, this has made it possible for HIV vaccines to reach the most remote areas of the world. Unfortunately, the preponderance of global travel has also meant that the threat of spreading a disease to the world by an infected person traveling on an international flight is quite real.

The most recent example of technology contributing to globalization is the development of the **Internet**. Instant communication between people millions of miles apart is possible by plugging in a computer and connecting to the Net. The Internet is an extension of the telephone and cell phone revolutions; all three are developments that have brought faraway places closer together. All three allow people to communicate regardless of distance. This communication can facilitate friendly chatter and, of course, trade. A huge number of businesses use cell phones and the Internet to do business these days, and use computers to track goods and receipts quickly and efficiently.

Globalization has also brought financial and cultural exchange on a worldwide scale. A large number of businesses have investments in countries around the world. Financial transactions are conducted using a variety of currencies. The cultures of the countries of the world are increasingly viewed by people elsewhere through the wonders of television and the Internet. Not only in terms of goods, but also belief systems, customs, and practices being exchanged.

With this exchange of money, goods, and culture, has come an increase in immigration. Many people who live in less-developed nations see what is available in other places and want to move there in order to fully take advantage of all those more-developed nations have to offer. This can conceivably create an increase in immigration. Depending on the numbers of people who want to immigrate and the resources available, this could become a problem. The technological advances in transportation and communication have made such immigration easier than ever.

In theory, globalization is creating a new international society. Globalization is occurring at a rapid pace and is changing the composition of individual societies as it is creating a new international society. Trade and economic interests will undoubtedly continue to impel society forward on this course.

COMPETENCY 13.0   THE IMPACT OF SCIENCE AND TECHNOLOGY ON THE DEVELOPMENT OF CIVILIZATION

Skill 13.1   Discuss the scientific revolutions of the seventeenth through the twentieth centuries

The religious beliefs and institutions of a culture can greatly influence scientific research and technological innovation. During the Renaissance in Italy, for example, science was interpreted and dictated by Catholic religious doctrine, and theories that contradicted this doctrine were dismissed and their proponents sometimes punished.

Political factors have affected scientific advancement, as well, especially in cultures that partially support scientific research with public money. **Warfare** has traditionally driven technological advancement as cultures strive to outpace their neighbors with better weapons and defenses. Technologies developed for military purposes often find their way into the mainstream. Significant advances in flight technology, for example, were made during the two World Wars.

Socially, many cultures have come to value innovation and welcome new products as well as improvements to older products. This desire to continually advance and obtain the latest, newest technology creates economic incentive for innovation.

New technologies have made production faster, easier, and more efficient. People found their skills and abilities replaced by machines that were faster and more accurate. To some degree, machines and humans have entered an age of competition. Yet these advances have facilitated greater control over nature, lightened the burden of labor, and extended human life span. These advances in science, knowledge, and technology have also called into question for many the assumptions and beliefs that have provided meaning for human existence. Without the traditional belief structures that have given meaning to life, an emptiness and aimlessness has arisen for some that is a new by-product of technology and modern life.

The extraordinary advances in science and technology opened new frontiers and pushed back an ever-growing number of boundaries. These influences have had a profound effect in shaping modern civilization. Each discovery, machine, or insight built upon other new discoveries, machines, or insights. By the twentieth century, the rate of discovery and invention became nearly uncontrollable. In many cases, the results have been beneficial; others have been horrifying.

Advances in biology and medicine have **decreased infant mortality** and **increased life expectancy** dramatically. Antibiotics and new surgical techniques have saved countless lives. Inoculations have essentially erased many dreadful diseases. Yet new diseases have resulted from the careless disposal of by-products and the effects of industrialization on the environment and the individual.

Tremendous progress in communication and transportation has tied all parts of the earth and drawn them closer. There are still vast areas of unproductive land, extreme poverty, food shortages, rampant diseases, violent friction between cultures, the ever-present nuclear threat, environmental pollution, rapid reduction of natural resources, urban over-crowding, acceleration in global terrorism and violent crimes, and a diminishing middle class.

New technologies have changed the way of life for many. This is the computer age, and in many places, computers are even in elementary schools. Technology makes the world seem a much smaller place. Even young children have cell phones today. The existence of television and modern technology has us watching a war while it is in progress. **Outsourcing** is now popular because of technological advances. Call centers for European, American, and other large countries are now located in India, Pakistan, etc. Multinational corporations have relocated plants to foreign countries to lower costs.

In many places, technology has resulted in a mobile population. Popular culture has been shaped by mass production and the mass media. Mass production and technology have made electronic goods affordable to most. This is the day of the **cell phones and tablets**. The **Internet** and email allow people anywhere in the world to be in touch and allow people to learn about world events. In the industrial countries and many others, the popular culture is oriented toward the electronic era.

Some of the specific inventions and advancements of modern science include:

The **microscope,** which first appeared about 1590 and was steadily improved upon. The microscope revealed an entire world of invisible activity by bacteria and fungus and laid bare the cell structure of complex organisms. Advancements in microscopy led directly to important discoveries concerning germs, viruses, and the cause of disease, greatly aiding the field of medicine.

Electrical power is a phenomenon that has been known about for centuries, but not until the late nineteenth century had understanding and technology advanced to the point where it could be reliably produced and transmitted. The ability to transmit power by wire over distances changed the nature of industry, which previously had relied on sources such as steam plants or waterpower to move machinery.

The **Theory of Relativity** was proposed by Albert Einstein and revolutionized physics. Einstein proposed that the measurement of time and space changed relative to the position of the observer, implying that time and space were not fixed, but could warp and change. This had radical implications for Newtonian physics, particularly as it related to gravity, and opened new fields of scientific study.

Penicillin was developed in the mid twentieth century, and rapidly became an important drug, saving countless lives. Penicillin is derived from a mold which inhibited and even killed many kinds of germs. In drug form, it could be used to fight infections of various kinds in humans. Penicillin and similarly derived drugs are called antibiotics.

The **microchip** was developed in the 1950s as a way to reduce the size of transistor-based electronic equipment. By replacing individual transistors with a single chip of semiconductor material, more capability could be included in less space. This development led directly to the microprocessor, which is at the heart of every modern computer and most modern electronic products.

Skill 13.2   Causes and consequences of the agricultural, industrial, and information revolutions

(See Skill 10.5)

Skill 13.3   Contributions of major scientific thinkers

Science advanced considerably during the Renaissance, especially in the area of physics and astronomy. Copernicus, Kepler, and Galileo led a Scientific Revolution in proving that the earth was round and certainly not perfect, an earth-shattering revelation to those who clung to medieval ideals of a geocentric, church-centered existence. Sir Isaac Newton, aside from being considered a key figure in science, was also a mathematician, philosopher, astronomer, and alchemist who described the universal gravitation and the three laws of motion.

The effects of the Renaissance in the Low Countries can be seen in the literature and philosophy of **Erasmus** and the art of **van Eyck** and **Breughel the Elder**. **Rabelais** and **de Montaigne** in France also contributed to literature and philosophy. In Spain, the art of **El Greco** and **de Morales** flourished, as did the writings of **Cervantes** and **De Vega**. In England, **Sir Thomas More** and **Sir Francis Bacon** wrote and taught philosophy and were inspired by **Vesalius**. **William Harvey** made important contributions to medicine. The greatest talent was found in literature and drama and given to mankind by **Chaucer, Spenser, Marlowe, Jonson**, and the incomparable **Shakespeare**.

Rene Descartes was a French scientist-philosopher whose dedication to logic and the rigid rules of observation were a blueprint for the thinkers who came after him.

Madame Marie Curie was a noted contributor in the early field of radioactivity. Until 2006, she was the only woman to have won two Nobel prizes in two different fields (Science and Chemistry).

Skill 13.4 Know the scientific method and the evolution of a philosophy of science

The scientific method is the process by which researchers over time endeavor to construct an accurate (that is, reliable, consistent, and non-arbitrary) representation of the world. Recognizing that personal and cultural beliefs influence both our perceptions and our interpretations of natural phenomena, standard procedures, and criteria minimize those influences when developing a theory.

The scientific method has four steps:

1. **Observation** and description of a phenomenon or group of phenomena.
2. Formulation of a **hypothesis** to explain the phenomena.
3. Use of the hypothesis to **predict** the existence of other phenomena or to predict quantitatively the results of new observations.
4. Performance of **experimental tests** of the predictions by several independent experimenters and properly performed experiments.

While the researcher may bring certain biases to the study, it's important that bias not be permitted to enter into the interpretation. It's also important that data that doesn't fit the hypothesis not be ruled out. This is unlikely to happen if the researcher is open to the possibility that the hypothesis might turn out to be null. Another important caution is to be certain that the methods for analyzing and interpreting are flawless. Abiding by these mandates is important if the discovery is to make a contribution to human understanding.

Skill 13.5 Discuss contemporary issues in scientific and technological advances

Nuclear energy was once hailed as a cheap and relatively clean alternative to fossil fuels but fell largely out of favor in the U.S. owing to some high-profile accidents at nuclear plants. Nuclear technology has continued to advance, and is gaining attention once again as a potential resource. One of the crucial considerations in the use of nuclear energy is safety. Nuclear fuels are highly radioactive and very dangerous should they enter the environment. The nuclear waste from creating nuclear energy is another important issue, as the dangerous by-product must be carefully and safely stored. Internationally, there is concern that nuclear power plants may be outfitted to produce material for nuclear weapons, creating another level of controversy over the spread of nuclear technology.

Biotechnology is another area that shows promise, but also brings controversy. Advances in biotechnology have opened the possibility of cloning and genetically altering organisms. Serious ethical issues have been raised about proceeding with this type of research, especially where it relates to human beings or human tissues.

Skill 13.6   Explain how science and technology are addressing ecological issues and problems

Since the dawn of agriculture, humans have modified their environment to suit their needs and to provide food and shelter. These changes always impact the environment, sometimes adversely from a human perspective.

Agriculture, for instance, often involves loosening topsoil by plowing before planting. This in turn affects how water and wind act on the soil, and can lead to erosion. In extreme cases, erosion can leave a plot of agricultural land unsuitable for use. Technological advances have led to a modern method of farming that relies less on plowing the soil before planting, but more on chemical fertilizers, pesticides, and herbicides. These chemicals can find their way into groundwater, affecting the environment.

Cities are large examples of how technological change has allowed humans to modify their environment to suit their needs. Further advances in transportation and building methods allow for larger and denser communities, which themselves impact the environment in many ways. Concentrated consumption of fuels by automobiles and home heating systems affect the quality of the air in and around cities. The lack of exposed ground means that rainwater runs off of roads and rooftops into sewer systems instead of seeping into the ground, and often makes its way into nearby streams or rivers, carrying urban debris with it.

In the area of **ecology**, scientific research is focused primarily on finding efficient fuel alternatives. Advances in solar and wind power technology have made these options feasible in some areas. Hybrid technology that uses electricity and fuel cells to supplement fossil fuels has found a market niche that is expanding every year.

SUBAREA III.   GEOGRAPHY, GOVERNMENT, AND ECONOMICS

COMPETENCY 14.0   THE MAJOR PHYSICAL FEATURES OF THE WORLD AND THE EFFECTS OF GEOGRAPHIC FACTORS ON THE DEVELOPMENT OF HUMAN SOCIETIES

Skill 14.1   Discuss the shape, location, and relationship among major land masses, significant landforms, and bodies of water

The earth's surface is made up of 70% water and 30% land. Physical features of the land surface include mountains, hills, plateaus, plains, and valleys. Other minor landforms include deserts, deltas, canyons, mesas, basins, foothills, marshes, and swamps. Earth's water features include oceans, seas, lakes, rivers, and canals.

Mountains are landforms with rather steep slopes at least 2,000 feet or more above sea level. Mountains are found in groups called mountain chains or mountain ranges. At least one range can be found on six of the earth's seven continents. North America has the Appalachian and Rocky Mountains; South America has the Andes; the Himalayas are in Asia; Australia has the Great Dividing Range; the Alps are in Europe; and Africa has the Atlas, Ahaggar, and Drakensburg Mountains.

Hills are elevated landforms rising to an elevation of about 500 to 2000 feet. They are found everywhere on earth including Antarctica where they are covered by ice.

Plateaus are elevated landforms that are usually level on top. Depending on location, they range from being very cold to cool and healthful. Some plateaus are dry because they are surrounded by mountains that keep out any moisture. Some examples include the Kenya Plateau in East Africa, which is very cool. The plateau extending north from the Himalayas is extremely dry while those in Antarctica and Greenland are covered with ice and snow.

Plains are described as areas of flat or slightly rolling land, usually lower than the landforms next to them. Sometimes called lowlands (and sometimes located along **seacoasts),** they support the majority of the world's people. Some are found inland and many have been formed by large rivers. Those formed by rivers result in extremely fertile soil for successful cultivation of crops and numerous large settlements of people. In North America, the vast plains areas extend from the Gulf of Mexico north to the Arctic Ocean and between the Appalachian and Rocky Mountains. In Europe, rich plains extend east from Great Britain into central Europe on into the Siberian region of Russia. Plains in river valleys are found in China (the Yangtze River valley), India (the Ganges River valley), and Southeast Asia (the Mekong River valley).

Valleys are land areas that are found between hills and mountains. Some have gentle slopes containing trees and plants; others have very steep walls and are referred to as **canyons**. One famous example is Arizona's Grand Canyon of the Colorado River.

Deserts are large dry areas of land that receive ten inches or less of rainfall each year. Among the better-known deserts are Africa's large Sahara Desert, the Arabian Desert on the Arabian Peninsula, and the Outback desert covering roughly one-third of Australia.

Deltas are areas of lowlands formed by soil and sediment deposited at the mouths of rivers. The soil is generally very fertile and most fertile river deltas are important crop-growing areas. One well-known example is the delta of Egypt's Nile River, known for its production of cotton.

Mesas are the flat tops of hills or mountains usually with steep sides. Sometimes plateaus are also called mesas. **Basins** are considered to be low areas drained by rivers or low spots in mountains. **Foothills** are generally considered a low series of hills found between a plain and a mountain range. **Marshes** and **swamps** are wet lowlands providing growth of such plants as rushes and reeds.

Oceans are the largest bodies of water on the planet. The four oceans of the earth are the **Atlantic Ocean**, one-half the size of the Pacific and separating North and South America from Africa and Europe; the **Pacific Ocean**, covering almost one-third of the entire surface of the earth and separating North and South America from Asia and Australia; the **Indian Ocean**, touching Africa, Asia, and Australia; and the ice-filled **Arctic Ocean**, extending from North America and Europe to the North Pole. The waters of the Atlantic, Pacific, and Indian Oceans also touch the shores of Antarctica.

Seas are an expanse of salt water that covers most of the earth's surface and surrounds its land masses. Some examples include the Mediterranean Sea found between Europe, Asia, and Africa and the Caribbean Sea, touching the West Indies, South and Central America. A **lake** is a body of water surrounded by land. The Great Lakes in North America are a good example.

Rivers, considered a nation's lifeblood, usually begin as very small streams, formed by melting snow and rainfall, flowing from higher to lower land, emptying into a larger body of water, usually a sea or an ocean. Examples of important rivers for the people and countries affected by and/or dependent on them include the Nile, Niger, and Zaire Rivers of Africa; the Rhine, Danube, and Thames Rivers of Europe; the Yangtze, Ganges, Mekong, Hwang He, and Irrawaddy Rivers of Asia; the Murray-Darling in Australia; and the Orinoco in South America. River systems are made up of large rivers and numerous smaller rivers or tributaries flowing into them. Examples include the vast Amazon Rivers system in South America and the Mississippi River system in the United States.

Canals are man-made water passages constructed to connect two larger bodies of water. Famous examples include the **Panama Canal** across Panama's isthmus connecting the Atlantic and Pacific Oceans and the **Suez Canal** in the Middle East between Africa and the Arabian Peninsula connecting the Red and Mediterranean Seas.

Physical **locations** of the earth's surface features include the four major hemispheres and the parts of the earth's continents in them. Political **locations** are the political divisions, if any, within each continent. Both physical and political locations are precisely determined in two *ways:* (1) Surveying that is done to determine boundary lines and distance from other features. (2) Exact locations that are precisely determined by imaginary lines of **latitude** (parallels) and **longitude** (meridians). The intersection of these lines at right angles forms a grid, making it possible to pinpoint an exact location of any place using any two grid coordinates.

The **Eastern Hemisphere,** located between the North and South Poles and between the Prime Meridian (0 degrees longitude) east to the International Date Line at 180 degrees longitude, and consists of most of Europe, all of Australia, most of Africa, and all of Asia, except for a tiny piece of the easternmost part of Russia that extends east of 180 degrees longitude.

The **Western Hemisphere,** located between the North and South Poles and between the Prime Meridian (0 degrees longitude) west to the International Date Line at 180 degrees longitude, and consists of all of North and South America, a tiny part of the easternmost part of Russia that extends east of 180 degrees longitude, and a part of Europe that extends west of the Prime Meridian (0 degrees longitude).

The **Northern Hemisphere,** located between the North Pole and the Equator, contains all of the continents of Europe and North America and parts of South America, Africa, and most of Asia.

The **Southern Hemisphere,** located between the South Pole and the Equator, contains all of Australia, a small part of Asia, about one-third of Africa, most of South America, and all of Antarctica.

Of the **seven continents,** only one contains just one entire country and is the only island continent, **Australia.** Its political divisions consist of six states and one territory: Western Australia, South Australia, Tasmania, Victoria, New South Wales, Queensland, and Northern Territory.

Africa is made up of 54 separate countries, the major ones being Egypt, Nigeria, South Africa, Democratic Republic of the Congo, Kenya, Algeria, Morocco, and the large island of Madagascar.

Asia consists of 49 separate countries, some of which include China, Japan, India, Turkey, Israel, Iraq, Iran, Indonesia, Jordan, Vietnam, Thailand, and the Philippines.

Europe's 43 separate nations include France, Russia, Malta, Denmark, Hungary, Greece, Bosnia, and Herzegovina.

North America consists of Canada, the United States of America, the island nations of the West Indies, and the "land bridge" of Middle America, including Cuba, Jamaica, Mexico, Panama, and others.

Thirteen separate nations together occupy the continent of **South America,** among them such nations as Brazil, Paraguay, Ecuador, and Suriname.

The continent of **Antarctica** has no political boundaries or divisions but is the location of a number of science and research stations managed by nations such as Russia, Japan, France, Australia, and India.

A **landform** comprises a geomorphological unit. Landforms are categorized by characteristics such as elevation, slope, orientation, stratification, rock exposure, and soil type. Landforms by name include berms, mounds, hills, cliffs, valleys, and others. Oceans and continents exemplify highest-order landforms. Landform elements are parts of a landform that can be further identified. The generic landform elements are: pits, peaks, channels, ridges, passes, pools, planes, etc., and can be often extracted from a digital elevation model using some automated or semi-automated techniques.

Elementary landforms (segments, facets, relief units) are the smallest homogeneous divisions of the land surface, at the given scale/resolution. A plateau or a hill can be observed at various scales ranging from few hundred meters to hundreds of kilometers. Hence, the spatial distribution of landforms is often fuzzy and scale-dependent as is the case for soils and geological strata. A number of factors, ranging from plate tectonics to erosion and deposition can generate and affect landforms. Biological factors can also influence landforms— see, for example, the role of plants in the development of dune systems and salt marshes, and the work of corals and algae in the formation of coral reefs.

Weather is the condition of the air that surrounds the day-to-day atmospheric conditions, including temperature, air pressure, wind, and moisture or precipitation that includes rain, snow, hail, or sleet.

Climate is the average weather or daily weather conditions for a specific region or location over a long or extended period of time. Studying the climate of an area includes information gathered on the area's monthly and yearly temperatures and its monthly and yearly amounts of precipitation. In addition, a characteristic of an area's climate is the length of its growing season.

In northern and central United States, northern China, south central and southeastern Canada, and the western and southeastern parts of the former Soviet Union is found the **climate of four seasons**, the humid continental climate—spring, summer, fall, and winter. Cold winters, hot summers, and enough rainfall to grow a variety of crops are the major characteristics of this climate. In areas where the humid continental climate is found are some of the world's best farmlands as well as important activities such as trading and mining. Differences in temperatures throughout the year are determined by the distance a place is inland, away from the coasts.

The **steppe** or prairie climate is located in the interiors of the large continents like Asia and North America. These dry flatlands are far from ocean breezes and are called prairies or the Great Plains in Canada and the United States and steppes in Asia. Although the summers are hot and the winters are cold, the big difference is rainfall. In the steppe climate, rainfall is light and uncertain, 10 to 20 inches a year. Where rain is more plentiful, grass grows; in areas of less rain, the steppes or prairies gradually become deserts. These are found in the Gobi Desert of Asia, central and Western Australia, southwestern United States, and in the smaller deserts found in Pakistan, Argentina, and Africa south of the Equator.

The two major climates found in the high latitudes are tundra and taiga. The word **tundra,** which means marshy plain, is a Russian word and aptly describes the climatic conditions in the northern areas of Russia, Europe, and Canada. Winters are extremely cold and very long. Surprisingly, less snow falls in the area of the tundra than in the eastern part of the United States. However, due to the harshness of the extreme cold, very few people live there and no crops can be raised. Despite having a small human population, many plants and animals are found there.

The **taiga** is the northern forest region and is located south of the tundra. The world's largest forestlands are found here along with vast mineral wealth and fur bearing animals. The climate is so extreme that very few people live here because of an extremely short growing season in which to raise crops. The winter temperatures are colder and the summer temperatures are hotter than those in the tundra because the taiga climate region is farther from the waters of the Arctic Ocean. The taiga is found in the northern parts of Russia, Sweden, Norway, Finland, Canada, and Alaska with most of their lands covered with marshes and swamps.

The humid **subtropical climate** is found north and south of the tropics and is moist. The areas having this type of climate are found on the eastern side of their continents and include Japan, mainland China, Australia, Africa, South America, and the United States—the southeastern coasts of these areas. One feature of their locations is that warm ocean currents are found there. The winds that blow across these currents bring in warm moist air all year round. Long, warm summers; short, mild winters; and a long growing season allow for different crops to be grown several times a year. All of these contribute to the productivity of this climate type that supports more people than any of the other climates.

The **marine climate** is found in Western Europe, the British Isles, the U.S. Pacific Northwest, the western coast of Canada and southern Chile, southern New Zealand, and southeastern Australia. A common characteristic of these lands is that they are either near water or surrounded by it. The ocean winds are wet and warm, bringing a mild rainy climate to these areas. In the summer, the daily temperatures average at or below 70 degrees F. During the winter, because of the warming effect of the ocean waters, the temperatures rarely fall below freezing.

In northern and central United States, northern China, south central and southeastern Canada, and the western and southeastern parts of the former Soviet Union is found the **"climate of four seasons,"** the **humid continental climate**—spring, summer, fall, and winter. Cold winters, hot summers, and enough rainfall to grow a variety of crops are the major characteristics of this climate. In areas where the humid continental climate is found are some of the world's best farmlands as well as important activities such as trading and mining. Differences in temperatures throughout the year are determined by the distance a place is inland.

In certain areas of the earth there exists a type of climate unique to areas with high mountains, usually different from their surroundings. This type of climate is called a "**vertical climate**" because the temperatures, crops, vegetation, and human activities change and become different as one ascends the different levels of elevation. At the foot of the mountain, a hot and rainy climate is found with the cultivation of many lowland crops. As one climbs higher, the air becomes cooler. The climate changes sharply and economic activities change to grazing sheep and growing corn, for example. At the top of many mountains, snow is found all year.

Natural resources are naturally occurring substances that are considered valuable in their natural form. A **commodity** is generally considered a natural resource when the primary activities associated with it are extraction and purification, as opposed to creation. Natural resources include soil, timber, oil, minerals, and other goods taken more or less as they are from the Earth. Thus, mining, petroleum extraction, fishing, and forestry are generally considered natural-resource industries, while agriculture is not.

Natural resources are often classified into renewable and non-renewable resources. **Renewable** resources are generally living resources (fish, coffee, and forests, for example), which can restock (renew) themselves if they are not over-harvested. Renewable resources can restock themselves and be used indefinitely if they are sustained. Once renewable resources are consumed at a rate that exceeds their natural rate of replacement, the standing stock will diminish and eventually run out. The rate of sustainable use of a renewable resource is determined by the replacement rate and amount of standing stock of that particular resource. Non-living renewable natural resources include soil, as well as water, wind, tides, and solar radiation.

In recent years, the depletion of natural capital and attempts to move to sustainable development have been a major focus of development agencies. This is of particular concern in rainforest regions, which hold most of the Earth's natural biodiversity—irreplaceable genetic natural capital. Conservation of natural resources is the major focus of Natural Capitalism, environmentalism, the ecology movement, and Green Parties. Some view this depletion as a major source of social unrest and conflicts in developing nations.

Skill 14.2   Basic geographic terms and concepts

Geography involves studying location and how living things and earth's features are distributed throughout the earth. It includes where animals, people, and plants live and the effects of their relationship with earth's physical features. Geographers also explore the locations of earth's features, how they got there, and why it is so important.

What geographers study can be broken down into four areas:

1. **Location**: Being able to find the exact site of anything on the earth
2. **Spatial relations**: The relationships of earth's features, places, and groups of people with one another due to their location
3. **Regional characteristics**: Characteristics of a place such as landforms and climate, types of plants and animals, kinds of people who live there, and how the people use the land
4. **Forces that change the earth**: Human activities and natural forces.

Geographical studies are also divided into four categories:

1. **Regional**: Elements and characteristics of a place or region
2. **Topical**: One earth feature or one human activity occurring throughout the entire world
3. **Physical**: Earth's physical features and factors that create and change them, as well as their relationships to each other and human activities
4. **Human**: Human activity patterns and how they relate to the environment, including political, cultural, historical, urban, and social geographical fields of study

Special research methods used by geographers include mapping, interviewing, field studies, mathematics, statistics, and scientific instruments.

Eratosthenes was an ancient Greek mathematician who calculated the circumference of the earth.

Strabo wrote a geographical depiction of the known ancient world in 17 volumes.

Ptolemy contributed his skills in mapping and theories from studies in astronomy to geographic knowledge.

The **National Geographic Society** is publisher of the National Geographic magazine and funds expeditions and other activities furthering geographic education.

Geography is the study of the earth, its people, and how people adapt to life on earth and how they use its resources. It is undeniably connected to history, economics, political science, sociology, anthropology, and even a bit of archaeology. Geography not only deals with people and the earth today but also with:

- How the earth began?
- What is the background of the people of an area?
- What kind of government or political system do the people have?
- How does their political system affect their ways of producing goods and the distribution of the goods?
- What kind of relationships do these people have with other groups?
- How is the way they live their lives affected by their physical environment?
- In what ways do the people effect change in their way of living?

All of this is tied in with their physical environment, the earth, and its people.

Another way to describe where people live is by the **geography** and **topography** around them. The vast majority of people on the planet live in areas that are very hospitable. People live in the Himalayas and in the Sahara, but the populations in those areas are small indeed when compared to the plains of China, India, Europe, and the United States. People naturally want to live where they won't have to work hard just to survive, and world population patterns reflect this.

We can examine the spatial organization of the places where people live. For example, in a city, where are the factories and heavy industry buildings? Are they near airports or train stations? Are they on the edge of town, near major roads? What about housing developments? Are they near these industries, or are they far away? Where are the other industry buildings? Where are the schools and hospitals and parks? What about the police and fire stations? How close are homes to each of these things? Towns and especially cities are routinely organized into neighborhoods, so that each house or home is near to most things that its residents might need on a regular basis. This means that large cities have multiple schools, hospitals, grocery stores, fire stations, etc.

Related to this is the distance between cities, towns, villages, or settlements. In certain parts of the United States, and definitely in many countries in Europe, the population settlement patterns achieve megalopolis standards with no clear boundaries from one town to the next. Other, more sparsely populated areas have towns that are few and far between and have relatively few people in them. Some exceptions to this exist, of course, like oases in the deserts; for the most part, however, population centers tend to be relatively near one another or at least near smaller towns.

Most places in the world are in some manner close to agricultural land, as well. Food makes "the world go round" and some cities are more agriculturally inclined than others. Rare is the city, however, that grows absolutely no crops. The kind of food grown is almost entirely dependent on the kind of land available and the climate surrounding that land. Rice doesn't grow well in the desert, for instance, nor do bananas grow well in snowy lands. Certain crops are easier to transport than others and those are the crops that are usually grown near ports or other areas of export.

The one thing that changed all of these things, of course, is the **airplane**. Flight has made possible global commerce and goods exchange on a level never before seen. Foods from all around the world can be flown around the world and, with the aid of refrigeration techniques, be kept fresh enough to sell in markets nearly everywhere. The same is true of medicine and weapons.

Skill 14.3   Characteristics and uses of basic geographic sources

Information can be gained looking at a map that might take hundreds of words to explain, otherwise. Maps reflect the great variety of knowledge covered by social sciences. To show such a variety of information, maps are made in many different ways. Because of this variety, maps must be understood in order to make the best sense of them. Once they are understood, maps provide a solid foundation for social science studies.

To apply information obtained from **graphs,** one must understand the two major reasons why graphs are used:

1. To visually present a **model or theory** in order to show how two or more variables interrelate
2. To visually present **real world** data in order to show how two or more variables interrelate.

Most often used are those known as **bar graphs** and **line graphs**. (Charts are often used for similar reasons and are explained in the next section).

Graphs themselves are most useful when one wishes to demonstrate the sequential increase or decrease of a variable or to show specific correlations between two or more variables in a given circumstance.

Most common is the **bar graph**, because it is easy to see and is an understandable way of visually showing the difference in a given set of variables. However, it is limited in that it cannot really show the actual proportional increase or decrease of each given variable to each other. (In order to show a decrease, a bar graph must show the "bar" under the starting line, thus removing the ability to show how the various different variables would relate to each other).

Thus, in order to accomplish this one must use a **line graph**. Line graphs can be of two types: **linear** or **non-linear**. A linear line graph uses a series of straight lines; a non-linear line graph uses a curved line. Though the lines can be either straight or curved, all of the lines are called **curves**. A line graph uses a number line or **axis.** The numbers are generally placed in order, equal distances from one another. The number line is used to represent a number, degree, or some such other variable at an appropriate point on the line. Two lines are used, intersecting at a specific point. They are referred to as the X-axis and the Y-axis.

The Y-axis is a vertical line the X-axis is a horizontal line. Together they form a **coordinate system**. The difference between a point on the line of the X-axis and the Y-axis is called the **slope** of the line, or the change in the value on the vertical axis divided by the change in the value on the horizontal axis. The Y-axis number is called the **rise** and the X-axis number is called the **run**, thus the equation for slope is:

$$\text{SLOPE} = \frac{\text{RISE}}{\text{RUN}} - \text{(Change in value on the vertical axis)} \atop - \text{(Change in value on the horizontal axis)}$$

The slope tells the amount of increase or decrease of a given **specific** variable. When using two or more variables one can plot the amount of difference between them in any given situation. This makes presenting information on a line graph more involved. It also makes it more informative and accurate than a simple bar graph. Knowledge of the term slope, what it is, and how it is measured helps us to describe verbally the pictures we are seeing visually. For example, if a curve is said to have a slope of "zero", you should picture a flat line. If a curve has a slope of "one", you should picture a rising line that makes a 45-degree angle with the horizontal and vertical axis lines.

The preceding examples are for **linear** (straight line) curves. With **non-linear** curves (the ones that really do curve), the slope of the curve is constantly changing, so as a result, we must understand that the slope of the non-linear curved line will be at a specific point. How is this done? The slope of a non-linear curve is determined by the slope of a straight line that intersects the curve at that specific point.

In all graphs, an upward sloping line represents a direct relationship between the two variables. A downward slope represents an inverse relationship between the two variables. In reading any graph, one must always be very careful to understand what is being measured, what can be deduced, and what cannot be deduced from the given graph.

To use **charts** correctly, it is necessary to remember the reasons one uses graphs. The general ideas are similar. It is usually a question as to which is more capable of adequately portraying the information one wants to illustrate: a graph or chart. One can see the difference between bars and graphs and realize that in many ways graphs and charts are interrelated. One of the most common types, because it is easiest to read and understand, even for the layperson, is the **pie-chart**.

Pie-charts are used when one is trying to illustrate the differences in percentages among various items or when one is demonstrating the divisions of a whole.

Skill 14.4   Describe the uses of maps to obtain data for solving location problems and to answer questions, infer relationships, and analyze spatial change

We use **illustrations** of various sorts because it is often easier to demonstrate a given idea visually instead of orally. Sometimes it is even easier to do so with an illustration than a description. This is especially true in education and research because humans are visually stimulated. It is a fact that any idea presented visually in some manner is easier to understand and comprehend than simply getting an idea across verbally, by hearing it, or by reading it. Throughout this document, there are several illustrations that have been presented to explain an idea in a more precise way. Sometimes these will demonstrate the types of illustrations available for use in the arena of political science. The more common illustrations used in political science are illustrated by various types of **maps, graphs, and charts**.

Photographs and globes are useful, as well, but as they are limited in what kind of information that they can show, they are rarely used, unless, as in the case of a photograph, it is of a particular political figure or of a time that one wishes to visualize.

Although maps have advantages over globes and photographs, they do have a major disadvantage. This problem with all maps comes about because most maps are flat and the Earth is a sphere. It is impossible to reproduce exactly on a flat surface an object shaped like a sphere. In order to put the earth's features onto a map they must be stretched in some way. This stretching is called **distortion**.

Distortion does not mean that maps are wrong; it simply means that they are not perfect representations of the Earth or its parts. **Cartographers**, also called mapmakers, understand the problems of distortion. They try to design maps so that there is as little distortion as possible.

The process of putting the features of the Earth onto a flat surface is called **projection**. All maps are really map projections. There are many different types. Each one deals in a different way with the problem of distortion. Map projections are made in a number of ways, including the use of complicated mathematics. However, the basic ideas behind map projections can be understood by looking at the three most common types:

(1) **Cylindrical Projections**: These are done by taking a cylinder of paper and wrapping it around a globe. A light is used to project the globe's features onto the paper. Distortion is least where the paper touches the globe. For example, suppose that the paper was wrapped so that it touched the globe at the equator, the map from this projection would have just a little distortion near the equator. However, in moving north or south of the equator, the distortion would increase the place the paper touches if further away from the equator. The best known and most widely used cylindrical projection is the **Mercator Projection.** It was first developed in 1569 by Gerardus Mercator, a Flemish mapmaker.

(2). **Conical Projections**: The name comes from the fact that the projection is made onto a cone of paper. The cone is made so that it touches a globe at the base of the cone only. It can also be made so that it cuts through part of the globe in two different places. Again, there is the least distortion where the paper touches the globe. If the cone touches at two different points, there is some distortion at both of the points. Conical projections are most often used to map areas in the **middle latitudes**. Maps of the United States are most often conical projections. This is because most of the country lies within these latitudes.

(3). **Flat-Plane Projections**: These are made with a flat piece of paper that touches the globe at one point only. Areas near this point show little distortion. Flat-plane projections are often used to show the areas of the north and south poles. One such flat projection is called a **Gnomonic Projection**. On this kind of map, all meridians appear as straight lines. Gnomonic projections are useful because any straight line drawn between points on the projection forms a **Great-Circle Route**.

Great-Circle Routes can best be described by thinking of a globe and when using the globe the shortest route between two points on it can be found by simply stretching a string from one point to the other. However, in reality, if the string was extended so that it took into effect the globe's curvature, it would then make a great-circle. A great-circle is any circle that cuts a sphere, such as the globe, into two equal parts. Because of distortion, most maps do not show great-circle routes as straight lines. Gnomonic projections, however, do show the shortest distance between the two places as a straight line, and because of this, gnomonic projections are valuable for navigation. They are called Great-Circle Sailing Maps.

To properly analyze a given map one must be familiar with the various parts and symbols that most modern maps use. For the most part this is standardized, with different maps using similar parts and symbols. The similar parts and symbols can include:

The Title: All maps should have a title, just as all books should. The title tells you what information is to be found on the map.

The Legend: Most maps have a legend. A legend tells the reader about the various symbols that are used on that particular map and what the symbols represent (also called a *map key*).

The Grid: A grid is a series of lines that are used to find exact places and locations on the map. There are several different kinds of grid systems in use but most maps use the longitude and latitude system, known as the **Geographic Grid System**.

Directions: Most maps have some directional system to show which way the map is being presented. Often on a map, a small compass will be present, with arrows showing the four basic directions—north, south, east, and west.

The Scale: This is used to show the relationship between a unit of measurement on the map versus the real-world measure on the Earth. Maps are drawn to many different scales. Some maps show a lot of detail for a small area. Others show a greater span of distance. Whichever measure is being used, one should always be aware of what scale is being used. For instance, the scale might be something such as 1 inch = 10 miles for a small area. A map showing the whole world might have a scale in which 1 inch = 1,000 miles. The point is that one must look at the map key in order to see what units of measurements the map is using.

Maps have four main properties. They are: first, the size of the areas shown on the map; second, the shapes of the areas; third, consistent scales; and fourth, straight-line directions. A map can be drawn so that it is correct in one or more of these properties. No map can be correct in all of them.

Equal areas: One property that maps can have is that of equal areas. In an equal-area map, the meridians and parallels are drawn so that the areas shown have the same proportions as they do on the Earth. For example, Greenland, which is about 118th the size of South America, will be show as 118th the size on an equal area map. Meridians are also useful to determine time around the world. The **Mercator projection** is an example of a map that does not have equal areas. On it, Greenland appears to be about the same size of South America. This is because the distortion is very bad at the poles and Greenland lies near the North Pole.

Conformality: A second map property is conformality, or correct shapes. There are no maps that can show very large areas of the earth in their exact shapes. Only globes can really do that. However, conformal maps are as close as possible to true shapes. The United States is often shown by a Lambert Conformal Conic Projection Map.

Consistent Scales: Many maps attempt to use the same scale on all parts of the map. Generally, this is easier when maps show a relatively small part of the earth's surface. For example, a map of Florida might be a consistent-scale Map. Generally, because of distortion, maps showing large areas are not consistent-scale maps. Often, such maps will have two scales noted in the key. One scale, for example, might be accurate to measure distances between points along the Equator. Another might be then used to measure distances between the North Pole and the South Pole.

Maps showing physical features often try to show information about the elevation or **relief** of the land. **Elevation** is the distance above or below the sea level. The elevation is usually shown with colors, for instance, and all areas on a map at a certain level will be shown in the same color.

Relief Maps: These show the shape of the land surface—flat, rugged, or steep. Relief maps usually give more detail than simply showing the overall elevation of the land's surface. Relief is also sometimes shown with colors, but another way to show relief is by using **contour lines**. These lines connect all points of a land surface that are the same height surrounding the particular area of land.

Thematic Maps: These are used to show more specific information, often on a single **theme**, or topic. Thematic maps show the distribution or amount of something over a certain given area, such as population density, climate, economic information, cultural, political information, etc.

Political science would be almost impossible without maps. Information can be gained by looking at a map when it might take hundreds of words to explain the same information. Maps reflect the great variety of knowledge covered by political science. To show such a variety of information, maps are made in many ways. Because of this variety, maps must be understood in order to make the best sense of them. Once they are understood, maps provide a solid foundation for political science studies.

Two of the most important terms in the study of geography are absolute and relative location. Both technically describe the same thing, but both are also, in many respects, as different as day and night.

First, what is **location**? We want to know this in order to determine where something is and where we can find it. We want to point to a spot on a map and indicate "that is where we are" or "that is where we want to be." In another way, we want to know where something is as compared to other things. It is very difficult for many people to describe something without referring to something else. Associative reasoning is a powerful way to think.

Absolute location is the exact whereabouts of a person, place, or thing, according to any kind of geographical indicators you want to name. You could be talking about latitude and longitude, GPS, or any other kind of indicator. For example, Paris is at 48 degrees north longitude and 2 degrees east latitude. You can't get much more exact than that. If you had a map that showed every degree of latitude and longitude, you could pinpoint exactly where Paris is and have absolutely no doubt that your geographical depiction is accurate.

Many geographers prefer to use absolute location because of its precision. If you have access to maps, compasses, and GPS indicators, why not describe the absolute location of something? It's much more accurate than other means of describing where something is. An absolute location can also be much simpler. Someone might ask you where the nearest post office is and you might say, "It's at the southeast corner of First Avenue and Main Street." That's about as absolute as you can get.

Relative location, on the other hand, is *always* a description that involves more than one thing. When you describe a relative location, you tell where something is by describing what is around it. The same description of where the nearest post office is in terms of absolute location might be this: "It's down the street from the supermarket, on the right side of the street, next to the dentist's office."

We use relative location not to be less precise, but to be more in tune with the real world. Very few people carry exact maps or GPS locators around with them. Nearly everyone, though, can find a location if they have it described to them in terms of what is nearby.

Absolute location can be a bit more map-like and direction-oriented, as well. You might say that Chicago is east of Seattle or that St. Louis is north of New Orleans. This is not nearly as involved as the post office location description. In the same way, you might say that Chicago is on Lake Michigan.

Spatial organization is a description of how things are grouped in a given space. In geographical terms, this can describe people, places, and environments anywhere on Earth.

The most basic form of spatial organization for people is where they live. The vast majority of people live near other people in villages, towns, cities, and settlements. These people live near others in order to take advantage of the goods and services that naturally arise from cooperation. These villages, towns, cities, and settlements are, to varying degrees, near bodies of water. Water is a staple of survival for every person on the planet and is also a source of energy for factories and other industries, as well as a form of transportation for people and goods.

Skill 14.5   Explain the influence of geographic factors on patterns of human settlement, major historical events, and political, economic, social, and cultural developments

Human communities subsisted initially as gatherers—gathering berries, leaves, etc. With the invention of tools it became possible to dig for roots, hunt small animals, and catch fish from rivers and oceans. Humans observed their environments and soon learned to plant seeds and harvest crops. As people migrated to areas in which game and fertile soil were abundant, communities began to develop. When people had the knowledge to grow crops and the skills to hunt game, they began to understand division of labor. Some of the people in the community tended to agricultural needs while others hunted game.

As habitats attracted larger numbers of people, environments became crowded and created competition. The concept of division of labor and sharing of food soon came in more heavily populated areas and needed to be managed. Groups of people focused on growing crops while others concentrated on hunting. Experience led to the development of skills and of knowledge that made the work easier. Farmers began to develop new plant species and hunters began to protect animal species from other predators and used them for their own benefit. This ability to manage the environment led people to settle down and to guard and manage their resources.

Camps soon became villages. Villages became year-round settlements. Animals were domesticated and gathered into herds that met the needs of the village. With the settled life, it was no longer necessary to "travel light." Pottery was developed for storing and cooking food.

By 8000 BCE, culture was beginning to evolve in these villages. Agriculture was developed for the production of grain crops, which led to a decreased reliance on wild plants. Domesticating animals for various purposes decreased the need to hunt wild game. As farming and animal husbandry skills increased, the dependence upon wild game and food gathering declined. With this change came the realization that a larger number of people could be supported on the produce of farming and animal husbandry.

Life became more settled. It was then possible to turn attention to such matters as managing water supplies, producing tools, making cloth, etc. There was both the social interaction and the opportunity to reflect upon existence. Mythologies arose and various kinds of belief systems developed. Rituals arose that re-enacted the mythologies that gave meaning to life.

Two things seem to have come together to produce cultures and civilizations: a society and culture based on agriculture and the development of centers of the community with literate social and religious structures. The members of these hierarchies then managed water supply and irrigation, ritual and religious life, and exerted their own right to use a portion of the goods produced by the community for their own subsistence in return for their management. Further division of labor and community development were the result of sharpened skills, invention of more sophisticated tools, development of commerce with other communities, increased knowledge of the environment, the resources available to people, and responses to the needs to share goods, order community life, and protect their possessions from outsiders.

As trade routes developed and travel between **cities** became easier, trade led to specialization. Trade enables a people to obtain the goods they desire in exchange for the goods they are able to produce. This, in turn, leads to increased attention to refinements of technique and the sharing of ideas. The knowledge of a new discovery or invention provides knowledge and technology that increases the ability to produce goods for trade. As each community learns the value of the goods it produces and improves its ability to produce the goods in greater quantity, **industry** is born.

By nature, people are social creatures. They generally live in communities or settlements of some kind and of some size. Settlements are the cradles of culture, political structure, education, and the management of resources. The relative placement of these settlements or communities is shaped by the proximity to natural resources, the movement of raw materials, the production of finished products, the availability of a work force, and the delivery of finished products. Shared values, language, culture, religion, and subsistence will to some extent, determine the composition of communities.

Settlements begin in areas that offer the natural resources to support life—food and water. With the ability to manage the environment one finds a concentration of populations. With the ability to transport raw materials and finished products, comes mobility. With increasing technology and the rise of industrial centers, comes a migration of the workforce. From the time of ancient civilizations onward, systems of government were established to develop, regulate, and direct various types of activities as the people worked together in groups.

Cities are the major hubs of human settlement. Almost half of the population of the world now lives in cities. These percentages are much higher in developed regions. Established cities continue to grow. The fastest growth, however, is occurring in developing areas. In some regions, there are "metropolitan areas" made up of urban and suburban areas. In some places cities and urban areas have become interconnected into "**megalopoli**" (e.g., Tokyo-Kawasaki-Yokohama).

The concentrations of populations and the divisions of these areas among various groups that constitute the cities can differ significantly. North American cities are different from European cities in terms of shape, size, population density, and modes of transportation. While in North America, the wealthiest economic groups tend to live outside the cities, the opposite is true in Latin American cities.

There are significant differences among the cities of the world in terms of connectedness to other cities. While European and North American cities tend to be well linked both by transportation and communication connections, there are other places in the world in which communication between the cities of the country may be inferior to communication with the rest of the world.

Rural areas tend to be less densely populated due to the needs of agriculture. More land is needed to produce crops or for animal husbandry than for manufacturing, especially in a city in which the buildings tend to be taller. Rural areas, however, must be connected via communication and transportation in order to provide food and raw materials to urban areas. **Social policy** addresses basic human needs for the sustainability of the individual and the society. The concerns of social policy, then, include food, clean water, shelter, clothing, education, health, and social security. Social policy is part of public policy that is determined by the city, the state, and the nation, all of which are responsible for human welfare in a particular region.

Many factors affect and influence politics. **Geography**, **economics,** and **culture** are among the most important. Looking at geography, we should realize that the geographic location of a particular country can greatly affect the country's politics. Both domestic and foreign policies are determined by a given country's location. We can see historically how conflicts have arisen throughout history whenever two or more countries that are in close proximity to each other engage in warfare. It is a fact of human experience that a majority of wars throughout history have begun for the most part over the issue of land, later spreading to other lands in a continuing competition.

For instance, in an area such as Europe where there are many independent countries in close proximity to each other, the development of rivalries and conflicts is bound to arise. The main struggle is often over boundaries and control of the limited amount of land that is available for each national group. In fact, if we examine the history of European colonialism, we see that the struggle for empires and overseas lands was a direct result and outgrowth of the desire to become stronger economically.

In a nation such as the United States, for instance, separated for the most part from other nations by the wide oceans, the chances for conflict are much more diminished. The United States started small as colonies established along a wide coast. With its independence, it had the ability to expand throughout a large land area straight across to the other side of the continent. This has been the most important factor in America's growth from small, lightly populated former colonies, to the strongest major power in the world. The fact that this massive expansion was able to occur with limited conflict helped it in the extent and speed by which it occurred.

The ability of America to expand was directly related to its having few enemies or rivals for power on the continent. The native Indian populations were too unorganized and too weak to be able to stop expansion. The other European powers that had established control of parts of the North American continent were forced off the continent through wars and territorial acquisitions, a process that accelerated with the defeat of Great Britain in the American Revolution. With America's growing power, the leadership of the United States was able to proclaim the **Monroe Doctrine** that told the Europeans that they should stay out of this area of the world.

The only other countries that could possibly compete with the United States for hegemony on this continent were Mexico and Canada, both being less strong than the United States. Canada, after gaining independence, has remained part of the British Commonwealth of Nations. It has remained sparsely populated in parts of the country and has a culture and economy that are similar to the United States' culture and economy. Mexico has posed no real problem for the United States. Though there was a conflict with Mexico in the middle of the 1800s over land issues resulting from America's expansionist policy, those issues were resolved. Today, America continues to remain a stronger nation than Mexico.

The history of warfare in Europe can be directly traced to this basic conflict over land, especially among the great European powers of Germany, France, Russia, and Italy. Great Britain is also considered a great European power although it has no land borders within continental Europe. In fact, because of its close proximity to the European continent and its vulnerability to invasion, the one constant in British foreign policy has been the ability to keep any one power from gaining hegemony in Europe. That is a reason Britain went to war against Napoleon and why it became involved in World Wars I and II.

Throughout history, we see geographic location has been of supreme importance in the development of nations. It has been a major factor in a nation's ability to advance its interests, even in the modern era. In looking at continuing world events this fact is not likely to change.

The **Middle East** is another region defined by its geographic location and is in a position that enables it to exert tremendous influence on not only the trade that passes through its realm of influence, but also on the political relations between its countries and those of different parts of the world. From the beginnings of civilization, the Middle East has been a destination—for attackers, for adventure-seekers, for those starving for food, and those involved in resources from iron to oil. Now, as then, the countries of the Middle East play an important role in the economics of the world.

First and foremost is the importance of oil. Saudi Arabia, most notably, and also Iran, Iraq, Kuwait, Qatar, Dubai, and the United Arab Emirates are huge exporters of oil. In some cases, the amount of oil that one of these countries exports exceeds 90 percent of the country's total economic outflow. Most of the world requires oil in huge numbers, as it is needed to run machines and is especially needed in the area of transportation vehicles—cars, trucks, airplanes, and buses. The vast majority of the world's developed nations would be helpless without this oil, since the consumption for even a small, developed nation is in the billions of gallons every month. The Middle East is not the only place to obtain oil. Russia, for example, is another excellent source of oil. The appeal of the Middle East countries as sources of oil is that it is much easier to obtain and put on tankers than it is to procure from the wilds of central Russia. Hence, it's the geography of the Middle East that provides its economic importance to the world.

When looking at **economics**, we must consider what is known as **political economy**, which is the interrelationship between politics and economics. Politics and economics are closely tied together. In fact, it has been stated by many different theorists that politics itself is just the particular method that people have adapted in order to solve their economic problems.

One prominent theorist was Karl Marx. Other important theorists on how politics and economics interact are **Adam Smith** and his most famous work, *The Wealth of Nations* (1776). In it, he promoted the idea of **laissez faire**, or letting an economy run itself with little or no government interference. Also important was **Thomas Malthus**, who wrote about population problems relating to available food, land, and resources. **John Maynard Keynes** studied the business cycle and gave rise to an economic theory that bears his name.

Probably, the most important fact in economics is the question of the ordering of the economy, meaning how the economy is organized politically. Two of the most prominent methods are the **market economy** and **central planning**. The market is most closely associated with democratic free enterprise as is practiced in the United States. Central planning is an important feature of socialist, communist, and, to an extent, fascist systems. Whatever system is in place, all economies have to answer the basic questions of what to produce, how to produce it, and for whom to produce it. Calvin Coolidge once said, "the business of America is business." He may have been overstating it but this can be said to be true not only for the United States but also for more and more nations.

The third major component we will examine in politics is **culture**. Though it is being examined third, it is by no means third in importance. In fact, all three things we are examining can at times be of equal importance. The first two, **geography** and **economics**, are more or less external forces. People choose (usually) the types of government and economic policies they will follow.

In addition, a country can try to *lessen geographic pressure*. This can be done by staying neutral, like Switzerland, or by maintaining superior and powerful armed forces capable of repelling aggression directed against it, like Israel, whose survival has been a matter of sheer superior capabilities. Alternatively, a nation can simply be fortunate to live with large oceans for borders, like the United States.

However, a nation's culture is something that is immutable and intrinsically a part of a people. Thus, all of its politics will be naturally defined by it. The fact is that all peoples are different from each other. This is not a value judgment; it is not a question of superiority or inferiority. Terms such as "**Social Darwinism**" (the struggle among peoples in which only the strong survive) or "**White Man's Burden**" (the presumed justification for colonial expansion) have historically been used to justify ideas of national or cultural superiority because the white Europeans felt they had a burden or obligation to "civilize" the world.

However, culture simply means those attitudes and beliefs that a nation holds that affect their political and economic decisions. It is a fact of history that at certain times specific peoples and cultures have found themselves in positions of importance or power that gave them an advantage over others. Usually this is because those cultures found themselves better able to adapt to changing circumstances and times.

Examples of cultures that maximized their advantages have been the Roman Empire, Great Britain, Germany, Japan, and the United States. Each one of these arose from simple beginnings to positions of immense power in the world. This is directly traceable to their cultures, which proved them to be up to the challenges they were presented with. Thus, the keyword for success is **adaptability**.

COMPETENCY 15.0   BASIC POLITICAL SCIENCE TERMS, CONCEPTS, AND THEORIES, AND THE CHARACTERISTICS, ORGANIZATION, AND DEVELOPMENT OF VARIOUS POLITICAL SYSTEMS

Skill 15.1   Know definitions and application of basic terms and concepts of political science

Amendment - An amendment is a change or addition to the United States Constitution. Two-thirds of both houses of Congress must propose and then pass one. Or, two-thirds of the state legislatures must call a convention to propose one that then must be ratified by three-fourths of the state legislatures. To date, there are only 26 amendments to the Constitution that have passed. An amendment may be used to cancel out a previous one such as the 18th Amendment (1919), known as Prohibition, being canceled by the 21st Amendment (1933).

Articles of Confederation - The first American document that attempted to unite the newly independent colonies after the Revolution. It proved to be unworkable. It was superseded by the Constitution in 1787.

Australian Ballot - A device originated in Australia for choosing candidates for public office. Distinct features include that it is prepared and handled by public officials, paid for with public funds, is secret, and uniform in color and composition. It was used in the United States before the introduction of voting machines in 1892.

Bill of Rights - The first ten amendments to the United States Constitution that deal with civil liberties and civil rights. They were written mostly by James Madison and are, in brief:

1. Freedom of speech, the press, assembly, and religion.
2. Right to bear arms.
3. Security from the quartering of troops in homes.
4. Right against unreasonable search and seizures.
5. Right against self-incrimination.
6. Right to trial by jury, right to legal counsel.
7. Right to jury trial for civil actions.
8. Prohibition against cruel or unusual punishment.
9. Rights not granted in the Constitution shall not necessarily be denied to the people
10. Powers not mentioned in the Constitution shall be retained by the states or the people.

Checks and Balances - System set up by the Constitution in which each branch of the federal government has the power to check, or limit the actions of other branches.

Confederate States of America - The nation formed by the states that seceded from the federal Union around 1860 and 1861. It ceased to exist after its loss in the American Civil War in 1865.

Congress - In the United States, it is the supreme legislative assembly. It is a bicameral body, (one that consists of two parts), the **House of Representatives** and the **Senate**.

Constitution - The written document that describes and defines the system and structure of the United States government. Ratification of the Constitution by the required number of states, (nine of the original thirteen), was completed on June 21, 1788, when the Constitution officially became the supreme law of the land.

Constitutional Convention - Meeting of delegates from 12 states who wrote a new constitution for the United States in 1787.

County - A unit of local government formerly known in Great Britain as "shire." All states now have county governments except for Louisiana, (which prefers the term "parish"), Alaska, and Connecticut.

Declaration of Independence - The document that stated that the British colonies in America had become a free and independent nation, adopted July 4, 1776.

Democracy - A form of government in which the people rule. The word "democrat" comes from the ancient Greek "demo"-people and "kratia" -to rule.

Democracy (Direct) - A form of government in which the people assemble at a specific period and times to perform the functions usually delegated to a representative legislature. Sometimes the term "pure" democracy is used. It was prevalent in ancient Greece.

Democracy (Indirect) - A form of government in which the people rule through elected representatives in a legislature. Sometimes called a "**republican**" form of government, or "**democracy in republic**," the United States is an example of this form of government.

Executive - A branch of the federal government. It consists of two office-holders, a President and a Vice-President, elected by indirect election for a period of four years. The President is responsible for carrying out the laws of Congress. The President may also propose new laws for Congressional consideration. (See: President and Vice-President)

Federal - The organization of the government of the United States. It consists of two parts that are the national government based in Washington D.C. and the various individual state governments.

House of Representatives - Part of the bicameral legislature of the United States chosen by direct election based on population for a period of two years. An individual must be twenty-five years old and a citizen of the United States for seven years in order to be eligible to be elected.

Legislative - The law-making branch of the government. In the United States, which is bicameral, it consists of the House of Representatives and the Senate.

Magna Carta - The document that guaranteed rights to English nobles, forced on the British King John in 1215. It is considered an important forerunner to the idea of government having a written limitation of its power.

Manifest Destiny - Belief of many Americans in the 1840s that the United States should own all the land between the Atlantic and Pacific oceans.

Monroe Doctrine - Policy statement made by President James Monroe in 1823 that warned the European powers that the United States considered the American continent and the western hemisphere as its special sphere of influence and that others should stay out of it.

Pocket Veto - When a President neither signs nor "officially" has vetoed a bill. If within ten days (not including Sundays) Congress adjourns, the bill is killed. If Congress is in session, the bill will automatically become a law at the end of the ten days if it has not been signed. (See: Veto)

Popular Sovereignty - In American history in the nineteenth century, it was the right of territorial inhabitants applying for statehood to determine whether or not their state would or would not permit slavery; rule by the people.

President - The Chief Executive of the United States, responsible for carrying out the laws passed by Congress, Commander-in-Chief of the armed forces, elected by indirect election for a period of four years. One must have been born a citizen and at least thirty-five years old in order to be eligible to be elected. (See: Executive)

Primary Election - Election in which candidates from a particular political party are chosen to run for office. As a rule, usually, only registered party members are allowed to vote in such elections.

Representative Government - Type of government in which voters elect representatives to make laws for them. (See: indirect democracy)

Senate - Part of the bicameral legislature of the United States government, consisting of two members from each state (one hundred members at present) chosen by direct election for a period of six years, called the "upper house". An individual must be thirty years old and a citizen of the United States for nine years in order to be eligible to be elected.

Separation of Powers - System of American government in which each branch of government has its own specifically designated powers and cannot interfere with the powers of another.

States' Rights - Idea that the individual states had the right to limit the power of the federal government, that the states' authority should be supreme within it, as opposed to guidance from the federal government. An important contributing factor to the American Civil War.

Supreme Court - The highest court in the land and the court of final appeal. Only court of law specifically established by the Constitution.

Unitary Government - A form of government in which power is held by the central government which may or may not choose to delegate power to lesser governmental units. Examples are Great Britain, France, and Israel. As opposed to *"Federal Government",* in which power is shared by national and state governments. (See: Federal)

Veto - To oppose a motion or enactment of a law from taking effect.

Vice-President - Assistant to the President, his immediate successor in case of disability or death. He also functions as the President of the Senate when it is in session. (See: Executive)

LEGAL TERMS

Bail - Money left with the court in order for an individual to be released from jail pending trial. When an individual appears for trial the money is returned. If one flees, the money is forfeited.

Civil - A lawsuit brought before a court, usually to recover monetary funds as opposed to a criminal action brought for a penal offense.

Criminal - A penal crime, one that normally results in an imposition of a term of imprisonment, or of a monetary fine imposed by the court or the state, or both.

Double Jeopardy - Subjecting an accused person to repeated trials for the same criminal offense. Forbidden by the Fifth Amendment to the Constitution.

Due Process - The right of a defendant to go through the established legal system before imprisonment, i.e., trial, have legal counsel, verdict rendered in a court of law; fairness of a procedure.

Equity - A branch of civil law that provides remedial justice when there is no remedy in common or prescribed law.

Grand Jury - As specified in the Constitution, it is a body of persons called to hear complaints of the commission of criminal offenses and to determine if enough evidence is available for a criminal indictment. It is normally composed of twelve to twenty-four individuals who hear the evidence and deliberate in private.

Habeas Corpus - The right to appear in court to determine if an imprisonment is lawful. Also known as a *"Writ of Habeas Corpus."*

Exclusionary Rule - As defined from the Fourth and Fifth Amendments, it is the inability of evidence seized unlawfully or statements gathered wrongly, to be brought into a court of law.

Ex Post Facto Law - A law created after an act to punish an act before the law was passed. Prohibited by the Constitution, i.e., you cannot prosecute someone for an act that was legal at the time of commission, even though a law was subsequently enacted to make the act a crime.

Impeach - To bring charges against an official in the government such as the President. In the case of the President, the House of Representatives is the only branch of government empowered to bring such charges. The impeached president or other official is then tried by the Senate.

Judicial Review - The right of the court to review laws and acts of the legislature and executive branches and to declare them unconstitutional. (Established by *Marbury* vs. *Madison* decision in 1803*)*.

Judiciary - The legal system, including but not limited to, courts of law and appeal.

Judiciary Act of 1789 - Law that organized the federal court system into Federal and Circuit Courts.

Jurisprudence - Relating to or pertaining to the law or the legal system and its practice or exercise thereof.

Miranda Rights - As defined in the case of *Miranda v. Arizona.* Flow from the Fifth and Sixth Amendments—the right to remain silent so one does not incriminate oneself and the right to legal counsel during questioning.

Penal - Having to do with punishment, most often in regards to imprisonment and incarceration by the state.

Tort - A private or civil action brought before a court of law i.e., a civil lawsuit.

Skill 15.2 Show knowledge of purposes of government and forms of governmental authority

Historically, the functions of government and people's concepts of government and its purpose and function have varied considerably. In the theory of political science, the function of government is to secure the common welfare of the members of the given society over which it exercises control. In different historical eras, governments have attempted to achieve the common welfare by various means in accordance with the traditions and ideology of the given society.

Among primitive peoples, systems of control were rudimentary at best. They arose directly from the ideas of right and wrong that had been established. Control was exercised most often by means of group pressure in the forms of taboos and superstitions and in many cases by ostracism or banishment from the group. Thus, because of the extreme tribal nature of society in those early times, this led to very unpleasant circumstances for the individual so treated. Without the protection of the group, a lone individual was most often in for a sad and short fate (No other group would accept such an individual into their midst and survival alone was extremely difficult if not impossible).

Among more civilized peoples, governments began to assume more institutional forms. They rested on a well-defined legal basis, imposed penalties on violators of the social order, and used force, which was supported and sanctioned by their people. The government was charged with establishing social order and was supposed to do so in order to be able to discharge its functions.

Eventually the ideas of government, who should govern, and how, came to be considered by various thinkers and philosophers. The most influential of these and those who had the most influence on our present society were the ancient Greek philosophers such as Plato and Aristotle.

Aristotle, the "father of political science", had a concept of government that was based on a simple idea: the function of government was to provide for the general welfare of its people. A good government, and one that should be supported, was one that did so in the best way possible with the least pressure on the people. Bad governments were those that subordinated the general welfare to that of the individuals who ruled. At no time should any function of any government be that of personal interest of any one individual, no matter who that individual was. This does not mean that Aristotle had no sympathy for the individual or individual happiness (as, at times, Plato has been accused by those who read his "*Republic*," which was the first important philosophical text to explore these issues). Rather, Aristotle believed that a society is greater than the sum of its parts, or that "the good of the many outweighs the good of the few and also of the one."

Yet, a good government and one that is carrying out its functions well will always weigh the relative merits of what is good for a given individual in society and what is good for the society as a whole. This basic concept has continued to our own time and has found its fullest expression in the idea of representative democracy and political and personal freedom. In addition, a government is one that maintains good social order, while allowing the greatest possible exercise of autonomy for individuals to achieve.

By the beginning of the nineteenth century, the **state** as we know it today had formed—a government claiming control over a specific area of land, uniting people of similar backgrounds and language, ruled either by some sort of monarch, or increasingly, by some sort of democratically elected government. The nineteenth century also saw the consolidation of several similar states into larger conglomerates, usually after some armed conflict such as the unification of the German States into one united nation in 1871 after the Franco-Prussian war.

By the twentieth century, in the aftermath of the Second World War, the breakdown of colonial empires and the force of nationalism had become the dominant factor in world affairs, a factor that continues to grow in present time at an ever-increasing rate, sometimes to the detriment of world peace and order.

Skill 15.3   Contrast the relationship between the evolution of political thought and the historical development of government

When looking at the modern major philosophies of the nature of government we will, by necessity, look at the works of men such as, **Niccolo Machiavelli, Thomas Hobbes, John Locke, Jean-Jacques Rousseau, and Karl Marx.** This list is by no means exhaustive. However, in distinguishing political science from political philosophy, and by using the term "modern" in a broad sense, we will examine those thinkers whose works have had an actual practical effect on society, as opposed to simply trying to interpret human events. In other words, we will examine those ideas that people at different times have tried to put into effect or have had, in the end, the longest lasting and widest influence.

Niccolo Machiavelli (1469–1527) was one of the most important thinkers on politics and the nature of political power. His most famous work is *The Prince* (1532). In it, Machiavelli describes the means of gaining and holding onto political power. He looked at his work as a simple recitation of obvious facts. All political leaders want to stay in power. In reality, he was merely describing the situation of his time. Nevertheless, his work has survived because it is a masterful piece that makes practical sense. It is a work that many leaders have since looked to as a guide for their own behavior. Throughout his career, Machiavelli sought to describe a state that would be capable of resisting foreign attack and in maintaining internal order and discipline. His writings are concerned with the principles upon which such a state could be founded and with the means on which they can be implemented and maintained.

In the *Prince*, he describes the method by which a "prince" (ruler) could acquire and maintain political power. This study has often been regarded as a defense of the despotism and tyranny of such rulers as Cesare Borgia (1476?–1507). However, it is in actuality based on Machiavelli's belief that a ruler is not bound by traditional ethical norms. In his view, a prince should be concerned only with power and should be bound only by rules that would lead to success in political actions. Machiavelli believed that these rules could be discovered by deduction from the political practices of the time as well as from those of earlier times. Specifically, he used examples from ancient Greece and Rome and later times, seeing what worked and what did not, then identified them in his theses in simple-to-understand ideas and explained how to follow them.

Skill 15.4 Be able to recognize and understand the characteristics of various forms of government

Parliamentary System - A system of government with a legislature, usually involving a multiplicity of political parties and often coalition politics. There is division between the head of state and head of government. The head of government is usually known as a Prime Minister who is also usually the head of the largest party. The head of government and cabinet usually both sit and vote in the parliament. Head of state is most often an elected president, (though in the case of a constitutional monarchy, like Great Britain, the sovereign may take the place of a president as head of state). A government may fall when a majority in parliament votes "no confidence" in the government.

Anarchism - Political movement believing in the elimination of all government and its replacement by a cooperative community of individuals. Sometimes it has involved political violence, such as assassinations of important political or governmental figures. The historical banner of the movement is a black flag.

Communism - A belief as well as a political system that is characterized by the ideology of class conflict and revolution, one party state and dictatorship, repressive police apparatus, and government ownership of the means of production and distribution of goods and services. It was a revolutionary ideology preaching the eventual overthrow of all other political orders and the establishment of one world Communist government. Same as Marxism. The historical banner of the movement is a red flag and variation of stars and/or hammer and sickles, representing the various types of workers.

Dictatorship - The rule by an individual or small group of individuals (**Oligarchy**) that centralizes all political control in itself and enforces its will with a terrorist police force.

Fascism - A belief as well as a political system, opposed ideologically to Communism, though similar in basic structure, with a one-party state, centralized political control and a repressive police system. It, however, tolerates private ownership of the means of production while maintaining tight overall control. Central to its belief is the idolization of the Leader, a "Cult of the Personality," and most often an expansionist ideology. Examples have been German Nazism and Italian Fascism.

Monarchy - The rule of a nation by a Monarch, (a non-elected, usually hereditary leader), most often a king or queen. It may or may not be accompanied by some measure of democratic open institutions and elections at various levels. A modern example is Great Britain, which is called a constitutional monarchy.

Socialism - Political belief and system in which the state takes a guiding role in the national economy and provides extensive social services to its population. It may or may not own outright means of production, but even where it does not, it exercises tight control. It usually promotes democracy, (Democratic Socialism), though the heavy state involvement produces excessive bureaucracy and usually inefficiency. Taken to an extreme it may lead to Communism as government control increases and democratic practices decrease. Ideologically the two movements are very similar in both belief and practice, as Socialists also preach the superiority of their system to all others and that it will become the eventual natural order. It is also considered for that reason a variant of Marxism. It also has used a red flag as a symbol.

Skill 15.5   Be able to compare historical and contemporary forms of government

In ancient times, early peoples developed primitive weapons and tools but were nomadic and mostly banded together in primitive hunting groups or "clans" in order to maximize their effectiveness in the hunt. The more people that went after the prey, the easier it would be to find it and kill it. In later times, when hunting grew scarce, people still banded together for protection from other clans in order to protect the diminishing available hunting grounds. Still later, when hunting no longer was able to sustain the clans they gradually turned to **hunting and gathering**—hunting when feasible, gathering fruits, vegetables, roots and berries and the like when there was no hunting available. These became known as **hunter-gatherer** societies and the first to begin to remain in one place for a time.

However, it was not until the invention of the **plow** and the fact that it made **farming** easier that people began to remain in one place for a long time. Increases in farming production supplied sufficient food to enable the first large organized **city-states** to emerge. This occurred on a large scale first in the ancient Mesopotamian region near the Tigris and Euphrates Rivers in what is now modern Iraq. The first large, organized city-states were those of the land known as **Sumer** or **Sumeria**, later known as the land of Babylonia.

In time, these early primitive city-states began to become united and to form bigger unions for greater protection and power, with each emerging new "nation" or "state" claiming control over a specific area of land and being willing to fight for it. Thus, with the emergence of the first large nations, the first large organized **armies** also came into being and regular warfare emerged as a universal and historical fact of human existence.

By the time known as the **classical period** of ancient history, that of ancient Egypt, Greece, and Rome, the city-state had emerged as the dominant political form. Uniting at times into larger entities for greater protection against outside enemies such as the **Delian League** of ancient Greece, a union of several Greek city-states united against the power of ancient Persia.

With the split, and then fall, of the Roman Empire in the fourth century, the growth of any further large political entities in Europe was temporarily halted. The breakup of the empire led to the establishment of very small units of political power, being the only ones surviving the interim period of chaos and confusion. However, also at this time the tribes that had originally fought the Romans now came to occupy the lands the Romans formerly controlled. Where the tribes had established themselves on the land, they became "united" out of sheer necessity against competing tribes. In many cases, this extended little farther than appeals to a common kinship, language, and customs. In some sense, this was a burgeoning nationalism and it began to be felt in the various interrelationships among themselves.

During the Middle Ages, **feudalism** was the dominant form of political organization in Europe. Feudalism was the organization of people based on the ownership of land by a **Lord** or other **Noble** who allowed individuals known as peasants or **serfs** to farm the land and to keep a portion of it. The lord or noble, in return for the serfs' loyalty, offered them his protection. In practical effect, the serf was considered owned by his lord with little or no rights at all. The lord's sole obligation to the serfs was to protect them so they could continue to work for him (most, though not all, lords were men). This system would last for many centuries. In Russia, it would last until the 1860s.

Warfare among the various tribes would continue until **Charlemagne the Great** in the year 800, united several of the larger tribes, such as the Germans and the Franks, into the political entity known as the **Holy Roman Empire**. This entity would last in some form until 1806, but by then it had been replaced by the smaller entities we know as modern states.

The final emergence of the nation-state is attributed to two principal causes. One major factor was the underlying fact of economic expansion that took place in the feudal system. This was mainly the result of a great expansion in trade and manufacturing, which the creation of the Holy Roman Empire had helped to facilitate. The feudal system had been dependent on small, isolated units and these were unable to cope with the great trade expansion that was occurring. This gave rise to the system known as **mercantilism**, a system in which certain lords started to take an interest in the growing merchant trade and used their power in order to facilitate it. This led to groups of powerful merchants gathering in the areas under the control of certain lords. The British also utilized the theory of mercantilism during the American colonial period to obtain a favorable balance of trade for England.

Thus, the various and independent feudal manors began to break up, leading to the growth of cities, expanded trade, and the growth of markets up through the period that came to be known as the **Renaissance**. At the same time, (the 1500s) the **Protestant Reformation** was beginning. This would lead to the waning influence of the massive power and control of Catholic Church and allow the growth of various independent and powerful lords. As they began to control greater and greater areas of land, they became known as **kings**. They involved themselves in and profited from the growth in trade that was taking place. This is in contrast to the earlier feudal lords who had opposed the rise in trade and manufacturing as undermining their authority and power.

The most familiar form of government throughout the history was the **monarchy**. We can include dictatorships or authoritarian governments in this description because the basic idea—that one person was in charge of the government—applies to all. In this kind of government, the head of state was responsible for governing his or her subjects. In earlier times, this meant laws that weren't exactly written down; written laws have increasingly been the standard as the centuries have progressed. Monarchies and one-person governments still exist today, although they are rare. In these states, the emphasis is on keeping the monarch in power, and many laws of the country have been written with that purpose in mind.

Authoritarian governments also still exist today, mostly in the form of communist societies, like China. In this form of government, all the members of the government belong to one political party; in China's case, it is the Communist Party. Not all members of the government agree on small issues, but significant issues require party unity. Organization of alternative political parties is widely and strongly discouraged. This was the case in the Soviet Union, the best-known communist state, which dissolved in 1991. Also, in many authoritarian governments, industries exist to produce revenues for the state. The flip side of this is that the government is responsible for the upkeep and outlays for these industries. This was much more the case in the Soviet Union than it is in China today, but certain elements of authoritarianism pervade Chinese society to this day.

The most familiar form of government to most Westerners is the **representative government**, commonly called a republic or democracy. The idea behind this form of government is that the people in a society are ultimately responsible for their government and the laws that it passes, enforces, and interprets in that they, the people, elect many of the members of that government. The members of a representative government are much more aware of public opinion than their authoritarian-government counterparts, although too much oppression can drive a desperate people to revolt, as has been done many times in the past, including in the U.S.

In Western tradition, the representative government began in Greece with democracy, then progressed to the republic in Rome, and continued into other democracies and republics, most famously the United States and many other countries around the world. These governments are termed **democracies** by many, but they are more properly called **republics**. A democracy involves *everyone* in a society having a say in who is elected to that society's government. This is certainly not the case in the U.S., where everyone does not vote nor can everyone vote. Another main difference between a true democracy and the kind of democracy that the U.S. and other countries are called these days is that in a true democracy, a vote on anything can be called at any time.

As the process continued, a split occurred in Europe at this time between those who still looked to the Catholic Church for guidance and the newly created and independent nation-states, which had by now had emerged and followed the new Protestant faith. This conflict would continue on and off, through many centuries and many wars, until the nineteenth century. Yet, even in those areas where the Catholic Church still had power and influence, a new sense of independence had emerged. The Church itself came to see the newly created states as a necessary factor in human affairs. Yet, ever since the **Pope** crowned Charlemagne as Emperor of the Holy Roman Empire, it has insisted (and has been granted in various ways) on its right to be considered above petty national considerations.

Prevalent during the Enlightenment was the idea of the **social contract**, the belief that government existed because people wanted it to, that the people had an agreement with the government that they would submit to it as long as it protected them and didn't encroach on their basic human rights. This idea was first made famous by the Frenchman Jean-Jacques Rousseau, but was also adopted by England's John Locke and America's Thomas Jefferson. **John Locke** was one of the most influential political writers of the seventeenth century because he put great emphasis on human rights and put forth the belief that when governments violate those rights, people should rebel. He wrote the book "*Two Treatises of Government*" in 1690, which had tremendous influence on political thought in the American colonies and helped to shape the U.S. Constitution and Declaration of Independence.

COMPETENCY 16.0 **THE PRINCIPLES OF THE FOUNDING DOCUMENTS OF U.S. GOVERNMENT AND THE STRUCTURE AND OPERATION OF THE U.S POLITICAL SYSTEM**

Skill 16.1 **Describe the origins and development of constitutional and democratic government**

Athenian democracy was a direct form of democracy, with every male citizen above the age of 20 able to vote in the legislative assembly. The assembly was made up of a minimum of 6,000 and voted on proposals made by a council of 500 citizens who were chosen by lot. Within the council of 500, one person was chosen each day to serve as the head of state. Trials were held by jury, without judges, with jurors being chosen from the pool of citizens. Athenian democracy differed from representative democracy in that each voter had the right to vote directly on public issues, and no formal leaders were elected.

The concept of a separation between political and religious aspects of society is ancient. Many old civilizations such as the ancient Hebrews had a religious hierarchy separate from the king and his advisors. In other civilizations, the head of state was also the head of the official state religion. In some cases, as in Rome, the head of state was proclaimed an actual divinity. The U.S. Constitution includes language that prevents the government from establishing an official religion and from impeding the free observance of any religion by U.S. citizens.

Witans were courts of prominent landholders, clergy, and titled men summoned by the Anglo-Saxon kings to advise on governmental affairs. These meetings had no regular time or location, but occurred at least annually. The witans had the power to approve the succession of the king, and even to depose sitting kings. Witans grew out of former tribal traditions around the 7th century, and operated until the Norman invasion of Britain in 1066.

The **Mayflower Compact** is considered the earliest American governmental document. Signed in 1620 by 41 passengers of the Mayflower, the compact pledged loyalty to King James and affirmed an agreement among the settlers at Plymouth to form a political body with the power to pass its own laws and ordinances. While simple in its structure, the Mayflower Compact expressed an ideal of self-government that was to flourish in America.

The Magna Carta has been considered the basis of English constitutional liberties. It was granted to a representative group of English barons and nobles on June 15, 1215, by the British King John after the nobility had forced it upon him. The English barons and nobles sought to limit what they had come to perceive as the overwhelming power of the monarchy in public affairs. The Magna Carta is considered to be the first modern document that sought to try to limit the powers of the given state's authority. It guaranteed feudal rights, regulated the justice system, and abolished many abuses of the King's power to tax and regulates trade. It provided that the king could not raise new taxes without first consulting a Great Council, made up of nobles, barons, and church leaders. Significantly, the Magna Carta only dealt with the rights of the upper classes of the nobility and all of its provisions excluded the rights of the common people. However, the rights won by the nobles were gradually given to other English people. The Great Council grew into a representative assembly called the Parliament.

By the 1600s, **Parliament** was divided into the House of Lords, made up of nobles, and the House of Commons. Members of the House of Commons were elected to office. In the beginning, only a few wealthy men could vote. Still, English people firmly believed that the ruler must consult Parliament on money matters and obey the law. Thus, it did set a precedent that there was a limit to the power of the state—precedent that would have no small effect on the history of political revolution, notably the American Revolution.

The Petition of Right was the title of a petition that was addressed to the King of England, **Charles I,** by the British parliament in **1628**. The Parliament demanded that the king stop proclaiming new taxes without its consent. Parliament demanded that he cease housing soldiers and sailors in the homes of private citizens, proclaiming martial law in times of peace, and imprisoning people without good cause being shown. After some attempts to circumvent these demands, King Charles finally agreed to them. They later had an important effect on the demands of the revolutionary colonists, as these were some of the rights that, as Englishmen, they felt were being denied to them. The Petition of Right was also the basis of specific protections that the designers of the U.S. Constitution made a point of inserting in the document.

The British Bill of Rights was known as the **Declaration of Rights**, and spelled out the rights that were considered to belong to Englishmen. It was granted by **King William III** in 1869. It had previously been passed by a convention of the Parliament and it came out of the struggle for power that took place in Great Britain and at that time and was known as **The Glorious Revolution**. It was known as a revolution that was accomplished with virtually no bloodshed and led to King William III and Queen Mary II becoming joint sovereigns.

The Declaration itself was very similar in style to the later American Bill of Rights. It protected the rights of individuals and gave anyone accused of a crime the right to trial by jury. It outlawed cruel punishments; also, it stated that a ruler could not raise taxes or an army without the consent of Parliament. As Englishmen, the colonists were protected by these provisions. The colonists considered that abridgments of these rights helped to contribute to the revolutionary spirit of the times.

All of these events and the principles that arose from them are of the utmost importance in understanding the process that eventually led to the ideals that are inherent in the Constitution of the United States. In addition, the fact is that all of these ideals are universal in nature and have become the basis for the idea of human freedoms throughout the world.

Skill 16.2   Know and understand the major principles of the Declaration of Independence, the U.S. Constitution, and The Federalist Papers

The **Declaration of Independence** is an outgrowth of both ancient Greek ideas of democracy and individual rights and the ideas of the European Enlightenment and the Renaissance, especially the ideology of the political thinker **John Locke**. Thomas Jefferson (1743–1826), the principle author of the Declaration of Independence, borrowed much from Locke's theories and writings.

Essentially, Jefferson applied Locke's principles to the contemporary American situation. Jefferson argued that the reigning King George III had repeatedly violated the rights of the colonists as subjects of the British Crown. Disdaining the colonial petition for redress of grievances (a right guaranteed by the Declaration of Rights of 1689), the King seemed bent upon establishing an "absolute tyranny" over the colonies. Such disgraceful behavior itself violated the reasons for which government had been instituted. The American colonists were left with no choice, *"It is their right, it is their duty, to throw off such a government, and to provide new guards for their future security,"* wrote Thomas Jefferson.

Yet, though his fundamental principles were derived from Locke's, Jefferson was bolder than his intellectual mentor was. His view of natural rights was much broader than Locke's and less tied to the idea of property rights.

Locke and Jefferson both stressed that the individual citizen's rights are prior to and more important than any obligation to the state. Government is the servant of the people. The officials of government hold their positions at the sufferance of the people. Their job is to ensure that the rights of the people are preserved and protected by that government. The citizen comes first, the government comes second. The Declaration that was produced turned out to be one of the most important and historic documents, expounding the inherent rights of all peoples— a document still looked up to as an ideal and an example.

The Declaration of Independence was the founding document of the United States of America. The Articles of Confederation were the first attempt of the newly independent states to reach a new understanding amongst themselves. The Declaration was intended to demonstrate the reasons that the colonies were seeking separation from Great Britain. Conceived by and written for the most part by Thomas Jefferson, it is important for what it says, and for how it says it. The Declaration is, in many respects, a poetic document. Instead of a simple recitation of the colonists' grievances, it set out clearly the reasons why the colonists were seeking their freedom from Great Britain, that they had tried all means to resolve the dispute peacefully, and that it was the right of a people, when all other methods of addressing their grievances have been tried and failed, to separate themselves from that power that was keeping them from fully expressing their rights to "**life, liberty, and the pursuit of happiness.**"

Within a few months from the adoption of the **Articles of Confederation**, it became apparent that there were serious defects in the system of government established for the new republic. There was a need for changes that led to the creation of a national government with adequate powers to replace the Articles of Confederation, which was actually only a league of sovereign states. In 1786, an effort to regulate interstate commerce ended in what is known as the **Annapolis Convention**. Because only five states were represented, this Convention was not able to accomplish definitive results. The debates, however, made it clear that foreign and interstate commerce could not be regulated by a government with as little authority as the government established by the Articles of Confederation. Congress was, therefore, asked to call a convention to provide changes that would address the emerging needs of the new nation.

The convention met in Philadelphia in 1787, with fifty-five of the sixty-five appointed members present. A constitution was written in four months. The **Constitution of the United States** is the fundamental law of the republic. It is a precise, formal, written document creating the organization of government for the United States. The founders of the Union established it as the highest governmental authority and the foundations were broadly laid so as to provide for the expansion of national life and to make it an instrument that could change with the changing needs of society. To maintain its stability, the framers created a difficult process for making any changes to it.

No amendment can become valid until it is ratified by three fourths of all of the states. The British system of government was part of the basis of the final document. But significant changes were necessary to meet the needs of a partnership of states that were tied together as a single federation, yet sovereign in their own local affairs. This constitution established a system of government that was unique and advanced far beyond other systems of its day.

The **Constitution** binds the states in a governmental unity in everything that affects the welfare of all. At the same time, it recognizes the right of the people of each state to independence of action in matters that relate only to them. Since the Constitution is the law of the land, all other laws must conform to it.

The debates conducted during the Constitutional Congress represent the issues and the arguments that led to the compromises in the final document. The debates also reflect the concerns of the Founding Fathers that the rights of the people be protected from abrogation by the government itself and the determination that no branch of government should have enough power to override the others. There is, therefore, a system of **checks and balances.**

The **Federalist Papers** were written to win popular support for the newly proposed Constitution. In these publications, the concerns of the founding fathers were made available to the people of the nation. In addition to providing an explanation of the underlying philosophies and concerns in drafting the Constitution and the compromises that were made, the Federalist Papers conducted what has frequently been called the most effective marketing and public relations campaign in human history.

Skill 16.3   Be able to show knowledge of the structure and functions of government at the local, state, and national levels

In the United States, the three branches of the federal government are the **Legislative**, the **Executive**, and the **Judicial**, and each branch has separate powers.

Legislative – Article I of the Constitution established the legislative, or law-making, branch of the government called the Congress. Congress is made up of two houses, the House of Representatives and the Senate. Voters in all states elect the members who serve in each respective house of Congress. The legislative branch is responsible for making laws, raising and printing money, regulating trade, establishing the postal service and federal courts, approving the President's appointments, declaring war, and supporting the armed forces. The Congress also has the power to change the Constitution itself, and to *impeach* (bring charges against) the President and other government officials. Charges for impeachment are brought by the House of Representatives and the impeached individuals are then tried by the Senate.

Executive – Article II of the Constitution created the executive branch of the government that is headed by the President, recommends new laws, and can veto bills passed by the legislative branch. As the chief of state, the President is responsible for carrying out the laws of the country and the treaties and declarations of war passed by and approved by the legislative branches. The President also appoints federal judges and is commander-in-chief of the military. Other members of the executive branch include the Vice-President, also elected, and various cabinet members as the President might appoint, ambassadors, presidential advisors, members of the armed forces, and other appointed and civil servants of government agencies, departments, and bureaus.

Although the President appoints many individuals to serve in the government, they must be approved by the Senate.

Judicial – Article III of the Constitution established the judicial branch of government headed by the Supreme Court. The Supreme Court has the power to rule that a law passed by the legislature or an act of the executive branch violates the Constitution and is, therefore, unconstitutional. Citizens, businesses, and government officials can also, in an appeal capacity, ask the Supreme Court to review a decision made in a lower court if someone believes that the ruling by the court is unconstitutional. The judicial branch also includes lower federal courts known as federal district courts that have been established by the Congress and federal courts of appeal. U.S. District Courts are the trial courts of the federal system and the U.S. Circuit Courts of Appeal are federal appellate courts.

The federal court system is provided for in the Constitution of the United States on the theory that the judicial power of the federal government could not be entrusted to the individual states, many of which had opposed the idea of a strong federal government in the first place. Thus, Article III, Section 1, of the Constitution states, *"The judicial power of the United States shall be vested in one Supreme Court, and in such inferior courts as the Congress may from time to time ordain and establish"*. In accordance with these provisions, Congress passed the Judiciary Act in 1789.

The **Judiciary Act** organized the Supreme Court of the United States and established a system of federal courts of inferior jurisdiction. The states were left to establish their own judicial systems subject to the exclusive overall jurisdiction of the federal courts and to Article VI of the Constitution declaring the judges of the state courts to be bound to the Constitution and to the laws and treaties of the United States. This Article developed a dual system of judicial power and authority in the United States.

The jurisdiction of the federal courts is further defined in Article III, Section 2 of the Constitution as extending in law and in equity to all cases arising under the Constitution and through federal legislation to controversies in which the United States is a party, including those arising from treaties with other governments, to maritime cases on the high seas in areas under American control, to disagreements between the states, between a citizen and a state, between citizens in different states, and between a citizen and a foreign nation. The federal courts were also originally empowered with jurisdiction over problems airing between citizens of one state and the government of another state.

The 11th Amendment to the Constitution (ratified 1795), however, removed from federal jurisdiction those cases in which citizens of one state were the plaintiffs and the government of another state was the defendant. The amendment, though, did not disturb the jurisdiction of the federal courts in cases in which a state government is a plaintiff and a citizen of another state the defendant. The federal courts also have exclusive jurisdiction in all patent and copyright cases and, by congressional law in 1898, the federal courts were empowered with original jurisdiction in all bankruptcy cases.

The courts established under the powers granted by Article III Sections 1 & 2 of the Constitution are known as Constitutional courts. Judges of the Constitutional courts are appointed for a term of good behavior, which is often for life, by the

President with the approval of the Senate. The "inferior" or lesser courts are the trial or U.S. District Courts and the U.S. Courts of Appeals, sometimes called the circuit courts of appeal, exercise appellate jurisdiction over the district court decisions and the **Supreme Court**. A district court functions in each of the more than ninety federal judicial districts and in the District of Columbia. Each state has at least one federal District Court.

There are currently 13 federal courts of appeal. The various appellate courts hear cases from the District Courts. For example, the Seventh Circuit hears cases from Indiana, Illinois, and Wisconsin.

The Supreme Court of the United States is the highest appellate court in the country and is a court of original jurisdiction according to the Constitution, *"in all cases affecting ambassadors, other public ministers and consuls, and those in which a state shall be a party".* By virtue of its power to declare legislation unconstitutional, the Supreme Court is also the final arbitrator of all Constitutional questions.

Other federal courts established by Congress under powers to be implied in other Articles of the Constitution, are called legislative courts. These courts are the **Court of Claims, the Court of Customs and Patent Appeals, the Customs Court,** and the territorial courts established in the federally administered territories of the United States.

The special jurisdictions of these courts are defined by the Congress of the United States. Except in the case of the territorial courts, which are courts of general jurisdiction, the specialized functions of these courts are suggested by their titles.

The state courts are part of each state's independent system of courts operating under the laws and constitution of that particular individual state. Broadly speaking, the state courts are based on the English judicial system as it existed in colonial times, but as modified by succeeding statues. The character and names of the various courts differ from state to state, but the state courts as a whole have general jurisdiction, except in cases in which exclusive jurisdiction has by law been vested in the federal courts. In cases involving the United States Constitution or federal laws or treaties and such, the state courts are governed by the decisions of the Supreme Court of the United States and their decisions are subject to review by it.

Cases involving the federal Constitution, federal laws, or treaties and the like, may be brought in either the state courts or the federal courts. Ordinary **civil suits** not involving any of the aforementioned elements can be brought only in the state courts, except in cases where there is different state citizenship between the parties. Where there is a diversity of citizenship, the suit may be filed in a federal court. By an act of Congress, however, suits involving federal questions, or different state citizenships, may be brought in a federal court only when it is a civil suit that involves $75,000 or more. All such cases that involve a smaller amount must be brought to a state court only. In accordance with a congressional law, a suit brought in a state court may be removed to a federal court at the option of the defendant if it involves a federal question.

County courts of general original jurisdiction exercise both criminal and civil jurisdictions in most states. A few states maintain separate courts of criminal and civil law inherited from the English judicial system. Between the lower courts and the supreme appellate courts of each state in a number of states, are intermediate appellate courts, which are similar to the federal courts of appeals. The highest appellate state court is generally called the state supreme court. This appellate court hears criminal and civil cases. It is from a state's highest appellate court that appeals are taken to the U.S. Supreme Court.

The state court system also includes the trial courts, from which appeals are taken, and a number of minor, local courts with limited jurisdictions. Local courts dispose of minor offenses and civil actions that involve small amounts of money. Included in this classification are police and municipal courts in various cities and towns, and the courts presided over by justices of the peace in rural areas.

Powers delegated to the federal government:

1. To tax.
2. To borrow and coin money
3. To establish postal service.
4. To grant patents and copyrights.
5. To regulate interstate and foreign commerce.
6. To establish courts.
7. To declare war.
8. To raise and support the armed forces.
9. To govern territories.
10. To define and punish felonies and piracy on the high seas.
11. To fix standards of weights and measures.
12. To conduct foreign affairs.

Powers reserved to the states:

1. To regulate intrastate trade.
2. To establish local governments.
3. To protect general welfare.
4. To protect life and property.
5. To ratify amendments.
6. To conduct elections.
7. To make state and local laws.

Concurrent powers of the federal government and states:

1. Both Congress and the states may tax.
2. Both may borrow money.
3. Both may charter banks and corporations.
4. Both may establish courts.
5. Both may make and enforce laws.
6. Both may take property for public purposes.

7. Both may spend money to provide for the public welfare.

Implied powers of the federal government:

1. To establish banks or other corporations, implied from delegated powers to tax, borrow, and to regulate commerce.
2. To spend money for roads, schools, health, insurance, etc. implied from powers to establish post roads, to tax to provide for general welfare and defense, and to regulate commerce.
3. To create military academies, implied from powers to raise and support an armed force.
4. To locate and generate sources of power and sell surplus, implied from powers to dispose of government property, commerce, and war powers.
5. To assist and regulate agriculture, implied from power to tax and spend for general welfare and regulate commerce.

Skill 16.4   The U.S. electoral system

The U.S. electoral process has many and varied elements, from simple voting to complex campaigning for office. Everything in between is complex and detailed.

First of all, American citizens **vote**. They vote for referendums and elected officials. They have to register in order to vote, and at that time they can declare their intended membership in a political party. America has a large list of political parties, which have varying numbers of membership. The Democratic and Republican parties are the two with the most money and power, but other political parties are involved in campaigning and elections.

In some cases, people who are registered members of a political party are allowed to vote for only members of that political party. This occurs in primary elections when, for example, a number of people are running to secure the nomination of one political party for a general election. If you are a registered Democrat, then in the primary election, you will be able to vote for only Democratic candidates if you reside in a state that does not have an open primary. In general elections you may vote for candidates from any party listed on the ballot.

Candidates affiliate themselves with political parties (or sometimes not—some candidates run unaffiliated, but often have trouble raising enough money to adequately campaign against their opponents). Candidates then go about the business of campaigning, which includes getting the word on out on their candidacy, what they believe in, and what they will do if elected. All of this costs money, of course, unless a candidate relies entirely on word-of-mouth or some sort of email campaign or finances the elections himself or herself. Candidates sometimes get together for **debates** to showcase their views on important issues of the day and how those views differ from those of their opponents. Candidates give public speeches, attend public functions, and explain their views to reporters to obtain coverage in newspapers and magazines and on radio, television, and the Internet.

The results of elections are made known very quickly, sometimes instantly, thanks to computerized vote tallying. Once results are finalized, winning candidates give victory speeches and losing candidates give concession speeches. Losing candidates go back to the lives they were leading, and winning candidates get ready to take their places in the local, state, or national government.

Elections take place regularly, so voters know just how long it will be before the next election. Some candidates begin planning their next campaign the day after their victory or loss. Voters have the option to **recall** elected candidates; such a measure, however, is drastic and requires a large number of signatures to get the motion on the ballot and then a large number of votes to have the measure approved. As such, recalls of elected candidates are relatively rare. One widely publicized recall in recent years was that of California Governor Gray Davis who was replaced by movie star Arnold Schwarzenegger who won the governorship in a special after Davis was recalled.

Another method of removing public officials from office is **impeachment**. This is also rare but still a possibility. Both chambers of Congress are involved in the impeachment process. The House of Representatives votes to impeach a federal official and the Senate votes to convict or acquit. Conviction means that the official must leave office immediately; acquittal results in no penalties or fines. If the President is being tried, the Chief Justice of the U.S. Supreme Court presides at the trial.

The College of Electors—or the **Electoral College** as it is more commonly known—has a long and distinguished history of mirroring the political will of the American voters. On some occasions, the results of the Electoral College vote may be different from the popular vote. In the 2000 election George Bush won the votes of the Electoral College while Al Gore won the popular vote. In the 2016 election, Hillary Clinton won the popular vote but Donald Trump won the electoral vote and became President.

Article II of the Constitution lists the specifics of the Electoral College. The Founding Fathers included the Electoral College as one of the famous "checks and balances" for two reasons: first, to give states with small populations more of an equal weight in the presidential election, and second, they did not trust the common man (women were unable to vote at that time) to be able to make an informed decision on which candidate would make the best president.

The same theory that created two Senators per state created the Electoral College. The large-population states had their populations reflected in the House of Representatives. New York and Pennsylvania, two of the states with the largest populations, had the highest number of members of the House of Representatives. But these two states still had only two senators, the exact same number that small-population states like Rhode Island and Delaware had. This was true as well in the Electoral College: Each state had just one vote, regardless of how many members of the House represented that state. So, the one vote that the state of New York cast would be decided by an initial vote of New York's electors. (If that initial vote was a tie, then that deadlock would have to be broken.)

In addition, when the Constitution was being written, not many people were involved in politics and knew little about government or presidential elections. A large number of people were farmers or lived in rural areas where they were far more concerned with making a living and providing for their families than they were with who was running for which office. Many of these "common people" could not read or write, either, and would not have been able to read a ballot. The Founding Fathers thought that even if these "common people" could vote, they wouldn't necessarily make the best decision for who would make the best president. So, the Electoral College was born.

Technically, the electors do not have to vote for anyone. The Constitution does not require them to do so. And throughout the history of presidential elections, some have voted for someone else other than the candidate who won their state. But tradition holds that the electors vote for the candidate chosen by their state, and so the vast majority of electors do just that. The Electoral College meets a few weeks after the presidential election, mostly as a formality. When all the electoral votes are counted, the president with the most votes wins. In most cases, the candidate who wins the popular vote also wins in the Electoral College. However, this has not always been the case.

Most recently, in 2000 in **Florida**, the outcome of the election was decided by the U.S. Supreme Court. The Democratic Party's nominee was Vice-President Al Gore. A presidential candidate himself back in 1988, Gore had served as vice-president for both of President Bill Clinton's terms. As such, he was both a champion of Clinton's successes and a reflection of his failures. The Republican Party's nominee was George W. Bush, governor of Texas and son of former President George H.W. Bush. He campaigned on a platform of a strong national defense and an end to questionable ethics in the White House. The election was hotly contested, and many states went down to the wire, being decided by only a handful of votes. The one state that seemed to be flip-flopping as Election Day turned into Election Night was Florida. In the end, Gore won the popular vote, by nearly 540,000 votes. But he didn't win the electoral vote. The vote was so close in Florida that a recount was necessary under federal law. Eventually, the Supreme Court weighed in and stopped all the recounts. The last count had Bush winning by less than a thousand votes. That gave him Florida and the White House.

Because of these irregularities, especially the last one, many have taken up the cry to eliminate the Electoral College, which they see as archaic and capable of distorting the will of the people. After all, they argue, elections these days come down to one or two key states, as if the votes of the people in all the other states don't matter. Proponents of the Electoral College point to the tradition of the entity and all of the other elections in which the electoral vote mirrored the popular vote.

Skill 16.5   Describe the role of political parties and interest groups

During the colonial period, political parties, as the term is now understood, did not exist. The issues which divided the people were centered on the relations of the colonies to the mother country. There was initially little difference of opinion on these issues. As the revolution drew near, the Tories, who favored English Rule, left the colonies and returned to England. Some moved to Canada. During the Constitutional convention and afterwards, when the drafters wanted ratification, those who were in favor of a strong central government expressed their views as Federalists. Those favoring states' rights were Anti-Federalists and later became known as Democratic-Republicans, one of the first political parties.

The most basic way for citizens to participate in the political process is to vote. Since the passing of the **26th Amendment** in 1971, U.S. citizens who are at least 18 years old are eligible to vote. Elections are held at regular intervals at all levels of government, allowing citizens to weigh in on local matters as well as those of national scope.

Citizens wishing to engage in the political process to a greater degree have several paths open, such as participating in local government. Counties, local governments, and sometimes even neighborhoods are governed by locally elected boards or councils that meet publicly. Citizens are usually able to address these boards, bringing their concerns and expressing their opinions on matters being considered. Citizens may even wish to stand for local election and join a governing board, or seek support for higher office.

Supporting a political party is another means by which citizens can participate in the political process. Political parties endorse certain platforms that express general social and political goals, and support member candidates in election campaigns. Political parties make use of much volunteer labor, with supporters making telephone calls, distributing printed material, and campaigning for the party's causes and candidates. Political parties solicit donations to support their efforts, as well. Contributing money to a political party is another form of participation citizens can undertake. Another form of political activity is to support an issue-related political group. Several political groups work actively to sway public opinion on various issues or on behalf of a segment of American society. These groups may have representatives who meet with state and federal legislators to "lobby" them, which means that they provide the legislators with information on an issue and attempt to persuade the legislators to take favorable action.

In regards to the American political system, it is important to realize that political parties are never mentioned in the United States Constitution. George Washington himself warned against the creation of "**factions**" in American politics that cause "jealousies and false alarms" and the damage they could cause to the body politic. Thomas Jefferson echoed this warning, yet he would come to lead a party.

Americans had good reason to fear the emergence of political parties. They had witnessed how parties worked in Great Britain. Parties, called "factions" in Britain, were made up of a few people who schemed to win favors from the government. They were more interested in their own personal profit and advantage than in the public good. Thus, the new American leaders were very interested in keeping factions from forming. It was, ironically, disagreements between two of Washington's chief advisors, Thomas Jefferson and Alexander Hamilton that spurred the formation of the first political parties in the newly formed United States of America.

By the time Washington retired from office in 1796, the new political parties would come to play an important role in choosing his successor. Each party would put up its own candidates for office. The **election of 1796** was the first one in which political parties played a role. A role that, for better or worse, parties have continued to play in various forms for all of American history. By the beginning of the 1800s, the Federalist Party, torn by internal divisions, began suffering a decline. Thomas Jefferson, a Democratic-Republican, was elected President in 1800. Alexander Hamilton, who was Jefferson's bitter rival and later, killed in 1804 in a duel with Aaron Burr. The Federalist Party began to collapse around that time. By 1816, after losing a string of important elections, (Jefferson was reelected in 1804, and James Madison, a Democratic-Republican was elected in 1808), the Federalist Party ceased to be an effective political force, and soon passed off the national stage.

(See also Skill 2.5)

By the late 1820s, new political parties had grown up. The **Democratic-Republican** Party, called the **Republican** Party, had been the major party for many years, but differences within it about the direction the country was headed caused a split after 1824. Those who favored strong national growth took the name **Whigs** after a similar party in Great Britain and united around then President John Quincy Adams. Many business people in the Northeast as well as some wealthy planters in the South supported it.

Those who favored slower growth and were more worker and small farmer oriented went on to form the new Democratic Party, with Andrew Jackson being its first leader as well as becoming the first President elected as a Democrat. It was the forerunner of today's present party of the same name.

The **Anti-Masonic Party** came into being to oppose the Freemasons whom they accused of being a secret society trying to take over the country. The Free Soil Party existed for the 1848 and 1852 elections only. They opposed slavery in the lands acquired from Mexico. The Liberty Party of this period was also abolitionist.

In the mid-1850s, the slavery issue was beginning to heat up and in 1854, those opposed to slavery, the Whigs, and some Northern Democrats opposed to slavery, united to form the Republican Party. The Whig Party was dying because of conflict among members about the Compromise of 1850. The Republicans were anti-slavery and adopted some of the policies of the Whigs. Before the Civil War, the Democratic Party was more heavily represented in the South and was pro-slavery for the most part. The American Party was called the "**Know Nothings**." They lasted from 1854 to 1858 and were opposed to Irish-Catholic immigration.

The **Constitution Union Party** was formed in 1860. It was made up of entities from other extinguished political powers. They claimed to support the Constitution above all and thought this would do away with the slavery issue. The **National Union Party** of 1864 was formed to re-elect Lincoln by gaining War Democrats who wanted to separate themselves from the Democratic party and the Copperheads who were anti-war Democrats.

Other political parties came and went in the post-Civil War era. The **Liberal Republican** Party formed in 1872 to oppose Ulysses S. Grant. They thought that Grant and his administration were corrupt and sought to displace them. The Anti-Monopoly Party of 1789 was more short-lived than the previous one. It billed itself as progressive and supported policies such as a graduated income tax system and the direct election of senators, etc. The **Greenback Party** was formed in 1878 and advocated the use of paper money. The Populist Party was a party consisting mostly of farmers who opposed the gold standard and favored the greenback.

The process of political parties with short life spans continued in the twentieth century. Most of this is due to the fact that these parties come into existence in opposition to some policy or politician. Once the "problem" was gone, so was the party that opposed it. The Farmer-Labor Party was a Minnesota-based political party that supported farmers, labor, and social security. It had moderate success in electing officials in Minnesota and merged with the Democratic Party in 1944. The Progressive Party was formed in 1912 due to a rift in the Republican Party that occurred when Theodore Roosevelt lost the nomination. This is not the same as the Progressive Party formed in 1924 to back LaFollette of Wisconsin. There have also been other parties that have had a short life in the years following the Great Depression. The **American Labor Party** was a socialist party that existed

in New York for a few years and the American Workers Party was another socialist party based on Marxism. Both parties were short-lived.
The **Progressive Party** came into being in 1948 to run candidates for President and Vice-President. The Dixiecrats, or States' Rights Democratic Party, also formed in 1948. They were a splinter group from the Democrats who supported Strom Thurmond. The party also supported Wallace in 1968. There have been various workers' parties that have come and gone. Most of these have had left-wing tendencies.

There are other political parties but they are not as strong as the Republicans and the Democrats. The **Libertarian** Party represents belief in the free rights of individuals to do as they wish without the interference of government. Libertarians favor a small government and propose a much lower level of government spending and services. The Libertarians are the third largest political party in America. The Socialist Party is also a political party that has candidates in the elections and favors the establishment of a radical democracy in which people control production and communities for all, not for the benefit of a few.

The **Communist Party** is a political party advocating very radical changes in American society. Communists are concerned with the revolutionary struggle and moving through Marx's stages of history. There are many other parties. The American First Party is conservative as is the American Party. The American Nazi Party was formed in 1959 and gained momentum in the 1970s. The Constitution Party is also representative of conservative views. The **Reform Party** was founded by Ross Perot in 1995, after his bid for President as an Independent in 1992. Many of these parties are regional and small and do not select candidates to run for election on the national scene. Many of the smaller third-parties form for a purpose, such as an election, and then dwindle in size and strength.

A **special interest** is nothing more than a subject that a person or people who pursue above all others. As more and more people gained more and more money, they began to pressure their lawmakers to pass laws that favored their interests. Exporters of goods from U.S. ports to destinations overseas that would not want to see heavy taxes on such exports constitute a special interest group. People who own large amounts of land and do not want to see a sharp increase in property taxes provide another example of a special interest. Today's special interest groups focus on ways to influence legislatures and spend great amounts of money to present their interests.

Special interest groups are not necessarily economic powers but rather groups whose people want to effect political change (or make sure that such change doesn't take place, depending on the status of the laws at the time). A good example of a special interest group is an anti-abortion group or a pro-choice group. The abortion issue is still a divisive one in American politics, and many groups will want to protect or defend or ban—depending on which side they're on—certain rights and practices. An anti-abortion group, for example, might pay big money to candidates who pledge to work against laws that protect the right for women to have abortions.

As long as these candidates continue to assure their supporters that they will keep on fighting the fight, the money will continue to flow. This kind of social group usually has a large number of dedicated individuals who do much more than vote: They organize themselves into political action committees, attend meetings and rallies, and work to make sure that their message gets out to a wide audience. Methods of spreading the word often include media advertising on behalf of their chosen candidates. This kind of expenditure is welcomed by the candidates, who benefit from the exposure but don't have to spend money, as someone else is paying for the advertisements.

Skill 16.6   Recognize the rights and responsibilities of U.S. citizenship

A citizen of the United States may either be native-born or a **naturalized** citizen. **Naturalization** is the process by which one acquires citizenship. Upon a specialized occasion, one may also have **dual-citizenship**, that is citizenship in the United States as well as in another country.

In order to become a citizen several requirements must be met. **Seven specific steps** to gaining citizenship are as follows:

1. An individual applying for citizenship must be at least 18 years old.
2. The individual must have been lawfully admitted into the United States for permanent residence.
3. The individual must have lived in the United States on a continual basis for at least five years, not counting short trips outside the United States. In addition, one must have resided for at least six months in the state where one is going to file a petition for citizenship (There are some important exceptions to this residency requirement. One exception is marriage to a spouse who is a citizen, which can shorten the residency requirement to three years. Other exceptions are made for certain spouses of citizens employed overseas and for alien members of the United States armed forces. Still other exceptions to the five-year residency requirement apply to certain refugee groups under various specific federal laws on a case-by-case basis).
4. The individual must show a good moral character and believe in the principles of the Constitution of the United States of America.
5. The individual must have not broken any immigration laws or have been ordered to leave the United States.
6. The individual must be able to speak, understand, read, and write simple English and must pass an examination about the history and government of the United States.

7. The individual must take an oath promising to give up foreign allegiance, to obey the Constitution and laws of the United States, and to fight for the United States of America or do work of importance to the nation if asked lawfully to do so.

The naturalization process is accomplished in three separate steps. The first is to file an application for naturalization. The "**Application to File Petition for Naturalization,**" Form N-400, is used if an individual is applying for his/her own naturalization. The Immigration and Naturalization Service revises this form periodically, and while they will accept the "older" application forms, it is important for applicants to obtain the latest form. The form itself consists of three parts, the application, Form N-400, a fingerprint chart, and Form G-325, entitled *"**Biographic Information.**"* All applications must be properly filled out in order to be accepted. Once this part of the process is completed and filed with the Immigration and Naturalization Service, it is reviewed, and if accepted, the applicant will be so informed. The applicant must then go to an appointed court to be officially sworn in by a judge or magistrate as a new citizen.

Once this is done, the individual is considered a citizen of the United States of America with all the privileges, rights, and responsibilities that citizenship entails. In addition to those rights that have previously been enumerated, the responsibilities include voting, jury duty, and the proper observance of the laws of the United States.

It is presumed that citizens of the United States would recognize their responsibilities to the country and that the surest way of protecting their rights is by exercising those rights, which also entails a responsibility. Some examples include the right to vote and the responsibility to be well informed on various issues, the right to a trial by jury and the responsibility to ensure the proper working of the justice system by serving on a jury (rather than avoiding doing so). In the end, it is only by the mutual recognition of the fact that an individual has both rights and responsibilities in society that enables the society to function in order to protect those very rights.

COMPETENCY 17.0   FUNDAMENTAL ECONOMIC CONCEPTS AND THEORIES, CHARACTERISTICS OF MAJOR ECONOMIC SYSTEMS, AND THE ORGANIZATION AND OPERATION OF THE U.S. ECONOMIC SYSTEM

Skill 17.1   Describe basic economic concepts

Economics is the study of how a society allocates its resources to satisfy what are basically unlimited and competing wants. Economics can also be defined as a study of the production, consumption, and distribution of goods and services. Both of these definitions are the same. A fundamental fact of economics is that resources are scarce and that wants are infinite. The fact that scarce resources have to satisfy unlimited wants means that choices have to be made. If society uses its resources to produce Good, A then it doesn't have those resources to produce Good B. More of Good A means less of Good B. This trade-off is referred to as the **opportunity cost**, or the value of the sacrificed alternative.

On the consumption side of the market, consumers buy the goods and services that give them satisfaction, or **utility**. They want to obtain the most utility they can for their dollar. The quantity of goods and services that consumers are willing and able to purchase at different prices during a given period of time is referred to as **demand**. Since consumers buy the goods and services that give them satisfaction, this means that, for the most part, they don't buy the goods and services that they don't want that don't give them satisfaction.

Consumers are, in effect, voting for the goods and services that they want with their dollars, called **dollar voting**. Consumers are basically signaling firms as to how they want society's scarce resources used with their dollar votes. A good that society wants acquires enough dollar votes for the producer to experience profits—a situation where the firm's revenues exceed the firm's costs. The existence of profits indicates to the firm that it is producing the goods and services that consumers want and that society's scarce resources are being used in accordance with consumer preferences.

This process where consumers vote with their dollars is called **consumer sovereignty**. Consumers are basically directing the allocation of scarce resources in the economy with their dollar spending. Firms, who are in business to earn profit, then hire resources, or inputs, in accordance with consumer preferences. This is the way in which resources are allocated in a market economy.

Price plays an important role in a market economy. **Demand** is the amount of any good that is desired by society. **Supply** is based on production costs. The supply of a good or service is defined as the quantities of a good or service that a producer is willing and able to sell at different prices during a given period of time. **Market equilibrium** occurs where the buying decisions of buyers are equal to the selling decision of seller, or where the demand and supply curves intersect. At this point the quantity that sellers want to sell at a price is equal to the quantity the buyers want to buy at that same price. This is the market equilibrium price.

The price of an input or output allocates that input or output to those who are willing and able to transact at the market price. Those who can transact at the market price or better are included in the market; those that can't or won't transact at the market price are excluded.

Skill 17.2   Be knowledgeable about major economic theorists and theories

Laissez-faire economics, or pure capitalism, is based on free markets without government interference in the market place. The role for government is to establish the framework for the functioning of the economy, determine things like standards of weights and measures, providing public goods, etc. **Adam Smith**, author of *The Wealth of Nations*, believed that free markets should exist without government interference because any interference interfered with the rights and liberties of the market participants even though laissez-faire economics results in an unequal distribution of income. The economy, if left alone, would function as if an invisible hand guided it to an efficient allocation of resources.

Parson Malthus was an economist whose theories led to economics being called the dismal science. His theory can best be summed as saying that the population growth would exceed the growth of the food supply. This would result in the lower classes experiencing increased poverty.

Karl Marx viewed economics in a different perspective. He felt that labor was the value-determining factor and that workers and owners were in continual conflict. Since it was labor that gave a commodity value, labor was entitled to the value of what it produced, or the **surplus**. The capitalist didn't do anything to earn the surplus. He appropriated it from labor and, therefore, exploited labor. This is the basis for Marxian economics. Marx goes on to apply the doctrine of historical necessity and the Hegelian triad to history and predicts a revolution based on the exploitation of labor. Marxian theories were the basis for the former Soviet and Eastern-bloc economies.

The theories of **John Maynard Keynes** are the basis for modern macroeconomics. **Keynesian theory** is demand-side theory. Keynes felt that the level of economic activity in an economy is determined by the level of aggregate spending. If there is excess aggregate demand, or spending, then the economy can't produce enough output to satisfy that demand, and the result is rising prices, or **inflation**. The way to cure the inflation is for government to implement contractionary fiscal policy; raise taxes or lower government spending. This will slow down an economy that is expanding too quickly. If there is a deficiency in aggregate demand, then there is not enough spending in the economy to cause suppliers to produce enough output to employ the labor force. The Keynesian solution is to stimulate the economy with expansionary fiscal policy, to lower taxes and/or increase spending. In the Keynesian framework, government policy action is required to rid the economy of inflation and unemployment. Keynesians believe the economy will not self-correct.

Milton Friedman disagrees with Keynes on the role of fiscal policy. Friedman and the **Monetarists** believe that money supply is the most important variable affecting the level of economic activity. The equation describing the economy is $MV=PQ$, where M = money supply, V = velocity, P = price level and Q equals the number of transactions in the economy. Increasing the money supply directly leads to a higher level of economic activity; decreasing the money supply directly causes a lower level of economic activity. Monetarists do not advocate the use of fiscal or monetary policy. Fiscal policy can be negated by the crowding out effect, a situation where an increase in government spending to stimulate the economy is offset by a decrease in private sector spending. Monetary policy can result in an overcorrection because of time lags. The expansionary monetary policy the government implements in the current time period to counter unemployment results in inflation in a later time period. Monetarists and Keynesians differ in their beliefs concerning the effectiveness of monetary and fiscal policy.

Skill 17.3 Be able to discuss the characteristics of historical and contemporary economic systems

Economic systems refer to the arrangements a society has devised to answer what are known as the **Three Questions**: What goods to produce? How to produce the goods? For Whom are the goods being produced? It can also be stated as how the allocation of the output is determined. Different economic systems answer these questions in different ways. The different "isms" that exist define the method of resource and output allocation. Feudalism was a form of slavery, with a feudal lord functioning as a local government. The serfs worked for the feudal lord on very unfavorable terms and had to pay taxes to the lord. The economy was pretty much contained on the lord's estate. The three questions were addressed by the policies of the feudal lord.

A **market economy** answers these questions in terms of demand and supply and the use of markets. Consumers vote for the products they want with their dollar spending. Goods acquiring enough dollar votes are profitable, signaling to the producers that society wants their scarce resources used in this way. This is how the "**What**" question is answered. The producer then hires inputs in accordance with the goods consumers want, looking for the most efficient or lowest cost method of production. The lower the firm's costs for any given level of revenue, the higher the firm's profits. This is the way in which the "**How**" question is answered in a market economy. The "**For Whom**" question is answered in the marketplace by the determination of the equilibrium price. Price serves to ration the good to those who can and will transact at the market price or better. Those who can't or won't are excluded from the market. The United States has a market economy.

The opposite of the market economy is called the **centrally planned economy**. This used to be called Communism, even though the term is not correct in a strict Marxian sense. In a planned economy, the means of production are publicly owned with little, if any, public ownership. Instead of the Three Questions being solved by markets, the government has a **planning authority** that makes the decisions in place of markets. The planning authority decides what will be produced and how. Since most planned economies direct resources into the production of capital and military goods, there is little remaining for consumer goods and the result is chronic shortages. Price functions as an accounting measure and does not reflect scarcity. The former Soviet Union and most of the Eastern Bloc countries were planned economies.

In between the two extremes is **market socialism**. This is a mixed economic system that uses both markets and planning. Planning is usually used to direct resources at the upper levels of the economy, with markets being used to determine prices of consumer goods and wages. This kind of economic system answers the three questions with planning and markets. The former Yugoslavia was a market socialist economy.

Skill 17.4   Components of the U.S. economic system; the role of government in the U.S. economy; and factors influencing the activities of American producers and consumers in the global economy

The U.S. economy consists of the household or **consumer** sector, the **business** sector, and the **government** sector. Households earn their incomes by selling their factors of production in the input market. Businesses hire their inputs in the factor market and use them to produce outputs. Households use their incomes earned in the factor market to purchase the output of businesses. Both households and businesses are active participants in both the input and output market. Households do not spend all of their income; they save some of it in banks. A well-organized smoothly functioning banking system is required for the operation of the economy.

The function of organized labor is to help obtain a higher factor income for workers. They negotiate the work agreement, or contract, for their union members. This **collective bargaining** agreement states the terms and conditions of employment for the length of the contract and is a contract between the worker and the employers.

Even in a capitalist economy, there is a role for government. **Government** is required to provide the framework for the functioning of the economy. This requires a legal system, a monetary system, and a watchdog authority to protect consumers from bad or dangerous products and practices. We need a government to correct for the misallocation of resources when the market doesn't function properly, as in the case of externalities, like pollution. Government functions to provide public goods, such as national defense, and to correct for macro instability like inflation and unemployment through the use of monetary and fiscal policy. These are the more important roles that we define for government in our economy.

In today's world, markets are international. U.S. consumers and producers are affected by events on world markets. Our domestic prices, employment, and income levels are affected by **exchange rate changes**. If the dollar depreciates in value, the cheaper dollar makes U.S. exports more attractive to foreigners who buy the relatively cheaper U.S. exports instead of the now relatively higher priced domestic goods. The increased demand for U.S. exports leads to higher employment levels in the export industries in the U.S. The lower demand for domestic products in the foreign country leads to unemployment in their domestic industries.

Trade barriers function in the same way. Suppose the domestic government is confronted with rising unemployment in the domestic industry due to cheaper foreign imports. Consumers are buying the cheaper foreign import instead of the higher priced domestic good.

In order to protect domestic labor, government imposes a **tariff,** thus raising the price of the more efficiently produced foreign good. The result of the tariff is that consumers buy more of the domestic good and less of the foreign. This leads to higher levels of income and employment in the domestic country.

Trade pacts can be any kind of agreement between countries regarding any aspect of trade. They will affect U.S. consumers and producers in that they affect the price of imports and exports. This will cause effects in income and employment levels. Depending on the trade pact, this may help or hurt U.S. consumers and producers.

Bibliography

Adams, James Truslow. (2006). "The March of Democracy," Vol 1. "The Rise of the Union". New York: Charles Scribner's Sons, Publisher.

Barbini, John & Warshaw, Steven. (2006). "The World Past and Present." New York: Harcourt, Brace, Jovanovich, Publishers.

Berthon, Simon & Robinson, Andrew. (2006. "The Shape of the World." Chicago: Rand McNally, Publisher.

Bice, David A. (2006). "A Panorama of Florida II". (Second Edition). Marceline, Missouri: Walsworth Publishing Co., Inc.

Bram, Leon (Vice-President and Editorial Director). (2006). "Funk and Wagnalls New Encyclopedia." United States of America.

Burns, Edward McNall & Ralph, Philip Lee. (2006. "World Civilizations Their History and Culture" (5th ed.). New York: W.W. Norton & Company, Inc., Publishers.

Dauben, Joseph W. (2006). "The World Book Encyclopedia." Chicago: World Book Inc. A Scott Fetzer Company, Publisher.

De Blij, H.J. & Muller, Peter O. (2006). "Geography Regions and Concepts" (Sixth Edition). New York: John Wiley & Sons, Inc., Publisher.

Encyclopedia Americana. (2006). Danbury, Connecticut: Grolier Inc, Publisher.

Heigh, Christopher (Editor).   (2006). "The Cambridge Historical Encyclopedia of Great Britain and Ireland." Cambridge: Cambridge University Press, Publisher.

Hunkins, Francis P. & Armstrong, David G. (2006). "World Geography People and Places." Columbus, Ohio: Charles E. Merrill Publishing Co. A Bell & Howell Company, Publishers.

Jarolimek, John; Anderson, J. Hubert & Durand, Loyal, Jr. (2006). "World Neighbors." New York: Macmillan Publishing Company. London: Collier Macmillan Publishers.

McConnell, Campbell R. (2006). "Economics-Principles, Problems, and Policies" (Tenth Edition). New York: McGraw-Hill Book Company, Publisher.

Millard, Dr. Anne & Vanags, Patricia. (2006). "The Usborne Book of World History." London: Usborne Publishing Ltd., Publisher.

Novosad, Charles (Executive Editor). (2006). "The Nystrom Desk Atlas."
Chicago:
Nystrom Division of Herff Jones, Inc., Publisher.

Patton, Clyde P.; Rengert, Arlene C.; Saveland, Robert N.; Cooper, Kenneth S. & Cam, Patricia T. (2006). "A World View." Morristown, N.J.: Silver Burdette Companion, Publisher.

Schwartz, Melvin & O'Connor, John R. (2006). "Exploring A Changing World." New York: Globe Book Company, Publisher.

"The Annals of America: Selected Readings on Great Issues in American History 1620-1968." (2006). United States of America: William Benton, Publisher.

Tindall, George Brown & Shi, David E. (2006). "America-A Narrative History" (Fourth Edition). New York: W.W. Norton & Company, Publisher.

Todd, Lewis Paul & Curti, Merle. (2006). "Rise of the American Nation" (Third Edition). New York: Harcourt, Brace, Jovanovich, Inc., Publishers.

Tyler, Jenny; Watts, Lisa; Bowyer, Carol; Trundle, Roma & Warrender, Annabelle (2006) 'The Usbome Book of World Geography." London: Usbome Publishing Ltd., Publisher.

Willson, David H. (2006). "A History of England." Hinsdale, Illinois: The Dryder Press, inc., Publisher

SAMPLE TEST

1. Which of the following is not a native North American tribe?
    (Average) (Skill 1.1)

    A. Algonquian
    B. Inca
    C. Iroquois
    D. Pueblo

2. Which one of the following is not a reason why Europeans came to the New World?
    (Average) (Skill 1.2)

    A. To find resources in order to increase wealth
    B. To establish trade
    C. To increase a ruler's power and importance
    D. To spread Christianity

3. The only colony not founded and settled for religious, political or business reasons was:
    (Easy) (Skill 1.2)

    A. Delaware
    B. Virginia
    C. Georgia
    D. New York

4. What country did not have a colonial stake in America?
    (Easy) (Skills 1.2)

    A. France
    B. Spain
    C. Mexico
    D. China

5. The year 1619 was a memorable or the colony of Virginia. Three important events occurred resulting in lasting effects on U.S. history. Which one of the following is not one of the events?
    (Rigorous) (Skill 1.2)

    A. Twenty African slaves arrived.
    B. The London Company granted the colony a charter, making it independent.
    C. The colonists were given the right by the London Company to govern themselves through representative government in the Virginia House of Burgesses
    D. The London Company sent to the colony 60 women who were quickly married, establishing families and stability in the colony.

6. After 1783, the largest "land owner" in the Americas was:
    (Rigorous) (Skill 1.2)

    A. Britain
    B. Spain
    C. France
    D. United States

7. **What was not one of the Acts leading to the Revolutionary War?**
(Average) (Skill 1.6)

A. Stamp Act
B. Quartering Act
C. Sugar Act
D. Monroe Doctrine

8. **France decided in 1777 to help the American colonies in their war against Britain. This decision was based on:**
(Rigorous) (Skill 2.2)

A. The naval victory of John Paul Jones over the British ship "Serapis"
B. The survival of the terrible winter at Valley Forge
C. The success of colonial guerilla fighters in the South
D. The defeat of the British at Saratoga

9. **Under the brand-new Constitution, the most urgent of the many problems facing the new federal government was that of:**
(Average) (Skill 2.5)

A. Maintaining a strong army and navy
B. Establishing a strong foreign policy
C. Raising money to pay salaries and war debts
D. Setting up courts, passing federal laws, and providing for law enforcement officers

10. **There is no doubt of the vast improvement of the U.S. Constitution over the weak Articles of Confederation. Which one of the four accurate statements below is a unique yet eloquent description of the document?**
(Rigorous) (Skill 2.3)

A. The establishment of a strong central government in no way lessened or weakened the individual states.
B. Individual rights were protected and secured.
C. The Constitution is the best representation of the results of the American genius for compromise.
D. Its flexibility and adaptation to change gives it a sense of timelessness.

11. **The Federalists:**
(Rigorous) (Skill 2.4)

A. Favored state's rights
B. Favored a weak central government
C. Favored a strong federal government
D. Supported the British

12. **Which one of the following was not a reason why the United States went to war with Great Britain in 1812?**
(Rigorous) (Skill 2.5)

A. Resentment by Spain over the sale exploration, and settlement of the Louisiana Territory
B. The U.S. merchant fleet was a threat to the British
C. Americans wanted to trade with the French
D. Britain continued to seize American ships on the high seas and force American seamen to serve aboard British ships

13. **After the War of 1812, Henry Clay and others proposed economic measures, including raising tariffs to protect American farmers and manufacturers from foreign competition. These measures were proposed in the:**
(Average) (Skill 2.6)

A. Era of Nationalism
B. American Expansion era
C. Era of Good Feeling
D. American System

14. **From about 1870 to 1900 the settlement of the West, America's "last frontier," was completed. One attraction for settlers was free land but it would have been to no avail without:**
(Easy) (Skill 2.7)

A. Better farming methods and technology
B. Surveying to set boundaries
C. Immigrants and others seeking new land
D. The railroad to get them there

15. **The American labor union movement started gaining new momentum:**
(Average) (Skill 2.7)

A. During the building of the railroads
B. After 1865 with the growth of cities
C. With the rise of industrial giants such as Carnegie and Vanderbilt
D. During the war years of 1861–1865

16. **The belief that the United States should control all of North America was called:**
(Easy) (Skill 3.1)

A. Westward Expansion
B. Pan Americanism
C. Manifest Destiny
D. Nationalism

17. **Which one of the following events did not occur during the period known as the "Era of Good Feeling?"**
(Average) (Skill 3.3)

   A. President Monroe issued the Monroe Doctrine
   B. Spain ceded Florida to the United States
   C. The building of the National Road
   D. The charter of the Second Bank of the United States

18. **As a result of the Missouri Compromise:**
(Average) (Skill 3.3)

   A. Slavery was not allowed in the Louisiana Purchase
   B. The Louisiana Purchase was nullified
   C. Louisiana separated from the Union
   D. The Embargo Act was repealed

19. **The term Sectionalism refers to:**
(Easy) (Skill 3.3)

   A. Different regions of the continent
   B. The issues between the North and South
   C. Different regions of the country
   D. Different groups of countries

20. **The principle of "popular sovereignty", allowing people in any territory to make their own decision concerning slavery, was stated by;**
(Average) (Skill 3.4)

   A. Henry Clay
   B. Daniel Webster
   C. John C. Calhoun
   D. Stephen A. Douglas

21. **The Radical Republicans who pushed the harsh Reconstruction measures through Congress after Lincoln's death lost public and moderate Republican support when they went too far:**
(Rigorous) (Skill 3.5)

   A. In their efforts to impeach the President
   B. By dividing ten southern states into military-controlled districts
   C. By making the ten southern states give freed African Americans the right to vote
   D. Sending carpetbaggers into the South to build up support for Congressional legislation

22. **The Union had many strengths over the Confederacy. Which was not a strength?**
(Easy) (Skill 3.5)

   A. Railroads
   B. Industry
   C. Slaves
   D. Manpower

23. The post-Civil War years were a time of low public morality, a time of greed, graft, and dishonesty. Which one of the reasons listed would not be accurate?
(Rigorous) (Skill 3.5)

A. The war itself because of the money and materials needed to carry on the War
B. The very rapid growth of industry and big business after the War
C. The personal example set by President Grant
D. Unscrupulous heads of large impersonal corporations

24. The three-day Battle of Gettysburg was the turning point of the Civil War for the North leading to ultimate victory. The battle in the West reinforcing the North's victory and sealing the South's defeat was the day after Gettysburg at:
(Average) (Skill 3.5)

A. Perryville
B. Vicksburg
C. Stones River
D. Shiloh

25. What event sparked a great migration of people from all over the world to California?
(Easy) (Skill 4.1)

A. The birth of Labor Unions
B. California statehood
C. The invention of the automobile
D. The gold rush

26. In the 1800s, the era of industrialization and growth was characterized by:
(Average) (Skill 4.3)

A. Small firms
B. Public ownership
C. Worker-owned enterprises
D. Monopolies and trusts

27. **Historians state that the West helped to speed up the Industrial Revolution. Which one of the following statements was not a reason for this?**
(Rigorous) (Skill 4.4)

A. Food supplies for the ever increasing urban populations came from farms in the West
B. A tremendous supply of gold and silver from western mines provided the capital needed to built industries
C. Descendants of western settlers, educated as engineers, geologists, and metallurgists in the East, returned to the West to mine the mineral resources needed for industry

D. Iron, copper, and other minerals from western mines were important resources in manufacturing products

28. **In the United States, federal investigations into business activities are handled by the:**
(Easy) (Skill 4.5)

A. Department of Treasury
B. Security & Exchange Commission
C. Government Accounting Office
D. Federal Trade Commission

29. **Jim Crow refers to:**
(Easy) (Skill 4.6)

A. Equality
B. Labor Movements
C. Racism
D. Free trade

30. **What Supreme Court ruling dealt with the issue of civil rights?**
(Average) (Skill 3.4)

A. Jefferson v. Madison
B. Lincoln v. Douglas
C. Dred Scott v. Sanford
D. Marbury vs Madison

31. **After the Civil War, the U.S. adapted an attitude of isolation from foreign affairs. But the turning point marking the beginning of the U.S. becoming a world power was:**
(Rigorous) (Skill 5.1)

A. World War I
B. Expansion of business and trade overseas
C. The Spanish-American War
D. The building and financial of the Panama Canal

32. **What event triggered World War I?**
(Average) (Skill 5.2)

A. The fall of the Weimar Republic
B. The resignation of the Czar
C. The assassination of Austrian Archduke Ferdinand
D. The assassination of the Czar

33. **Which country was not a part of the Axis in World War II?**
(Easy) (Skill 5.3)

A. Germany
B. Italy
C. Japan
D. United States

34. **Which country was a Cold War foe?**
(Easy) (Skill 5.6)

A. Russia
B. Brazil
C. Canada
D. Argentina

35. **Which one of the following was not a post-World War II organization?**
(Average) (Skill 5.4, 14.5)

A. Monroe Doctrine
B. Marshall Plan
C. Warsaw Pact
D. North Atlantic Treaty Organization

36. **What conflict brought the United States and the Soviet Union to the brink of war in 1962?**
(Average)(Skill 5.5)

A. Cuban Missile Crisis
B. Viet Nam war
C. Crisis in Brazil
D. Crisis in India

37. **After World War II, the United States:**
(Average) (Skill 6.4)

A. Limited its involvement in European affairs
B. Shifted foreign policy emphasis from Europe to Asia
C. Passed significant legislation pertaining to aid to farmers and tariffs on imports
D. Entered the greatest period of economic growth in its history

38. **It can be reasonably stated that the change in the United States from primarily an agricultural country into an industrial power was due to all of the following except:**
(Rigorous) (Skill 6.1)

A. Tariffs on foreign imports
B. Millions of hardworking immigrants
C. An increase in technological developments
D. The change from steam to electricity for powering industrial machinery

39. A political philosophy favoring or supporting rapid social changes in order to correct social and economic inequalities is called: *(Rigorous) (Skill 6.2)*

   A. Nationalism
   B. Liberalism
   C. Conservatism
   D. Federalism

40. The New Deal was: *(Average) (Skill 6.2)*

   A. A trade deal with England
   B. A series of programs to provide relief during the Great Depression
   C. A new exchange rate regime
   D. A plan for tax relief

41. McCarthyism refers to: *(Average) (Skill 6.4)*

   A. Pacifism
   B. Racism
   C. Anti-Communism
   D. Fascism

42. What Supreme Court ruling overturned the concept of "separate but equal" on schools? *(Rigorous) (Skill 6.5)*

   A. Jefferson v. Madison
   B. Plessy v. Ferguson
   C. Brown v. Board of Education
   D. Dred Scot

43. Which of the following is not a name associated with the Civil Rights movement? *(Average) (Skill 6.5)*

   A. Rosa Parks
   B. Emmett Till
   C. Tom Dewey
   D. Martin Luther King, Jr.

44. Which of the following women was not part of the women's rights movement? *(Easy) (Skill 6.6)*

   A. Elizabeth Cady Stanton
   B. Lucretia Borgia
   C. Lucretia Mott
   D. Susan B. Anthony

45. On the spectrum of American politics, the label that most accurately describes voters to the "right of center" is: *(Rigorous) (Skill 6.8)*

   A. Moderates
   B. Liberals
   C. Conservatives
   D. Socialists

46. The Fertile Crescent was not bounded by the: *(Rigorous) (Skill 7.1)*

   A. Mediterranean Sea
   B. Arabian Desert
   C. Taurus Mountains
   D. Ural Mountains

47. The study of past human cultures based on physical artifacts is:
(Average) (Skill 7.1)

A. History
B. Anthropology
C. Cultural Geography
D. Archaeology

48. The chemical process of radiocarbon dating would be most useful and beneficial in the field of:
(Average) (Skill 7.1)

A. Archaeology
B. Geography
C. Sociology
D. Anthropology

49. The end to hunting, gathering, and fishing of prehistoric people was due to:
(Average) (Skill 7.1)

A. Domestication of animals
B. Building crude huts and houses
C. Development of agriculture
D. Organized government

50. "Participant observation" is a method of study most closely associated with and used in:
(Average) (Skill 7.1)

A. Anthropology
B. Archaeology
C. Sociology
D. Political Science

51. The study of human culture and man's relationship to that culture is:
(Average) (Skill 7.1)

A. Sociology
B. Psychology
C. Anthropology
D. Cultural Geography

52. Bathtubs, hot and cold running water, and sewage systems with flush toilets were developed by the:
(Rigorous) (Skill 7.2)

A. Minoans
B. Mycenaeans
C. Phoenicians
D. Greeks

53. The principle of zero in mathematics is the discovery of the ancient civilization found in:
(Rigorous) (Skill 7.2)

A. Egypt
B. Persia
C. India
D. Babylon

54. Which ancient civilization is credited with being the first to develop irrigation techniques through the use of canals, dikes, and devices for raising water?
(Rigorous) (Skill 7.2)

A. The Sumerians
B. The Egyptians
C. The Babylonians
D. The Akkadians

55. An early cultural group was so skillful in navigating on the seas that they were able to sail at night guided by stars. They were the:
(Rigorous) (Skill 7.2)

A. Greeks
B. Persians
C. Minoans
D. Phoenicians

56. Development of a solar calendar, invention of the decimal system, and contributions to the development of geometry and astronomy are all the legacy of:
(Rigorous) (Skill 7.2)

A. The Babylonians
B. The Persians
C. The Sumerians
D. The Egyptians

57. The first ancient civilization to introduce and practice monotheism was the:
(Rigorous) (Skill 7.4)

A. Sumerians
B. Minoans
C. Phoenicians
D. Hebrews

58. The world religion which includes a caste system is:
(Average) (Skill 7.4)

A. Buddhism
B. Hinduism
C. Confucianism
D. Jainism

59. The Roman Empire gave so much to the world, especially the Western world. Of the legacies below, the most influential, effective, and lasting is:
(Average) (Skill 7.7)

A. The language of Latin
B. Roman law, justice, and political system
C. Engineering and building
D. The writings of its poets an historians

60. What was the major factor in the establishment and existence of feudalism?
(Rigorous) (Skill 7.8)

A. The Church
B. The king
C. The nobility
D. The serfs

61. Which one of the following did not contribute to the early medieval European civilization?
(Rigorous) (Skill 7.9)

A. The heritage from the classical cultures
B. The Christian religion
C. The influence of the German Barbarians
D. The spread of ideas through trade and commerce

62. Which one of the following is not an important legacy of the Byzantine Empire?
(Rigorous) (Skill 7.10)

A. It protected Western Europe from various attacks from the East by such groups as the Persians, Ottoman Turks, and Barbarians
B. It played a part in preserving the literature, philosophy, and language of ancient Greece
C. Its military organization was the foundation for modern armies
D. It kept the legal traditions of Roman government, collecting and organizing many ancient Roman laws

63. Which of the following is an example of a direct democracy?
(Easy) (Skill 7.11)

A. Elected representatives
B. Greek city-states
C. The United States Senate
D. The United States House of Representative

64. The holy book of Islam is:
(Easy) (Skill 8.2)

A. The Bible
B. The Kaaba
C. The Koran
D. The Torah

65. The difference between manorialism and feudalism was:
(Rigorous) (Skill 8.4)

A. Land was owned by the noblemen in manorialism
B. Land was owned by noblemen in both feudalism and manorialism
C. Land was owned by the noblemen in feudalism
D. The king owned all the land in both.

66. Native North and South American tribes included all of the following except:
(Easy) (Skill 8.8)

A. Aztec
B. Inca
C. Minoans
D. Maya

67. India's greatest ruler is considered to be:
(Rigorous) (Skill 8.8)

A. Akbar
B. Asoka
C. Babur
D. Jahan

68. The pyramids in Central America were built by:
(Average) (Skill 8.8)

A. The Incas
B. The Atacamas
C. The Mayas
D. The Tarapacas

69. In Western Europe, the achievements of the Renaissance were unsurpassed and made these countries outstanding cultural centers on the continent. All of the following were accomplishments except: *(Rigorous) (Skill 9.1)*

   A. Investment of the printing press
   B. A rekindling of interest in the learning of classical Greece and Rome
   C. Growth in literature, philosophy and art
   D. Better military tactics

70. The "father of anatomy" is considered to be: *(Rigorous) (Skill 9.1)*

   A. Vesalius
   B. Servetus
   C. Galen
   D. Harvey

71. The ideas and innovations of the period of the Renaissance were spread throughout Europe mainly because of: *(Average) (Skill 9.1)*

   A. Extensive exploration
   B. Craft workers and their guilds
   C. The invention of the printing press
   D. Increased travel and trade

72. Who is considered to be the most important figure in the spread of Protestantism across Switzerland? *(Average) (Skill 9.2)*

   A. Calvin
   B. Zwingli
   C. Munzer
   D. Leyden

73. The English explorer who gave England its claim to North American was: *(Average) (Skill 9.3)*

   A. Raleigh
   B. Hawkins
   C. Drake
   D. Cabot

74. Studies in astronomy, skills in mapping, and other contributions to geographic knowledge came from: *(Average) (Skill 9.3 & 14.2)*

   A. Galileo
   B. Columbus
   C. Eratosthenes
   D. Ptolemy

75. The Age of Exploration begun in the 1400s was led by: *(Easy) (Skill 9.3)*

   A. The Portuguese
   B. The Spanish
   C. The English
   D. The Dutch

76. **Which of the following does not pertain to the Ottoman Empire?**
(Average) (Skill 9.5)

A. Victorious in World War I
B. Adopted policy of modernization based on European standards
C. Sided with Germany in World War I
D. Overthrown in 1922

77. **Karl Marx believed in:**
(Easy) (Skill 10.2)

A. Free enterprise
B. Utopian Socialism
C. Absolute Monarchy
D. Scientific Socialism

78. **Which of the following took a scientific view of the world:**
(Average) (Skill 10.2)

A. Rousseau
B. Immanuel Kant
C. Montesquieu
D. John Locke

79. **The concepts of social contract and natural law were espoused by:**
(Rigorous) (Skill 10.2)

A. Locke
B. Rousseau
C. Aristotle
D. Montesquieu

80. **One South American country quickly and easily gained independence in the 19th century from European control and was noted for the uniqueness of its political stability and gradual orderly changes. This most unusual Latin American country is:**
(Rigorous) (Skill 10.4)

A. Chile
B. Argentina
C. Venezuela
D. Brazil

81. **Colonial expansion by Western European powers in the 18th and 19th centuries was due primarily to:**
(Average) (Skill 10.5)

A. Building and opening the Suez Canal
B. The Industrial Revolution
C. Marked improvements in transportation
D. Complete independence of all the Americas and loss of European domination and influence

82. Nineteenth century imperialism by Western European nations had important and far-reaching effects on the colonial peoples they ruled. All four of the following are the result of this. Which one was most important and had lasting effects on key 20th century events?
(Average) (Skill 10.7)

A. Local wars were ended
B. Living standards were raised
C. Demands for self government and feelings of nationalism surfaced
D. Economic developments occurred

83. Of all the major causes of both World Wars I and II, the most significant one is considered to be:
(Easy) (Skill 11.1)

A. Extreme nationalism
B. Military buildup and aggression
C. Political unrest
D. Agreements and alliances

84. Which did not contribute to the 1917 Revolution in Russia?
(Easy) (Skill 11.2)

A. World War I
B. Worker Strikes
C. Starving Peasants
D. Promise of aid from Germany

85. In the United States government, power or control over public education, marriage, and divorce is:
(Average) (Skill 16.3)

A. Implied or suggested
B. Concurrent or shared
C. Delegated or expressed
D. Reserved

86. A well-known World War II figure who was the leader of Italy:
(Easy) (Skill 11.5)

A. Hitler
B. Stalin
C. Tojo
D. Mussolini

87. Which one of the following would not be considered a result of World War II?
(Rigorous) (Skill 11.6)

A. Economic depressions and slow resumption of trade and financial aid
B. Western Europe was no longer the center of world power
C. The beginnings of new power struggles not only in Europe but in Asia as well
D. Territorial and boundary changes for many nations, especially in Europe

88. Which of the following is an organization or alliance for defense purposes?
(Average) (Skill 12.1)

A. North Atlantic Treaty Organization
B. The Common Market
C. The European Union
D. North American Free Trade Association

89. The international organization established to work for world peace at the end of the Second World War is the:
(Average) (Skill 12.6)

A. League of Nations
B. United Federation of Nations
C. United Nations
D. United World League

90. Which contributed to the writings of the Renaissance?
(Rigorous) (Skill 13.3)

A. Francois Rabelais
B. Desiderius Erasmus
C. Michel de Montaigne
D. Sir Francis Bacon

91. The Yangtze is an example of:
(Easy) (Skill 14.1)

A. Plains
B. Canal
C. River
D. Ocean

92. A famous canal is the:
(Easy) (Skill 14.1)

A. Pacific Canal
B. Arctic Canal
C. Panama Canal
D. Atlantic Canal

93. Which one of the following does not affect climate?
(Average) (Skill 14.1)

A. Elevation or altitude
B. Ocean currents
C. Latitude
D. Longitude

94. The study of a people's culture would be part of all of the following except:
(Average) (Skill 7.1)

A. Science
B. Archaeology
C. History
D. Anthropology

95. In which of the following disciplines would the study of physical mapping, modern or ancient, and the plotting of points and boundaries be least useful?
(Average) (Skill 14.2)

A. Sociology
B. Geography
C. Archaeology
D. History

96. The circumference of the earth, which greatly contributed to geographic knowledge, was calculated by:
(Rigorous) (Skills 14.2, 14.3)

A. Ptolemy
B. Eratosthenes
C. Galileo
D. Strabo

97. The study of "spatial relationships and interaction" would be done by people in the field of:
(Average) (Skill 14.2)

A. Political Science
B. Anthropology
C. Geography
D. Sociology

98. Meridians, or lines of longitude, not only help in pinpointing locations but are also used for:
(Average) (Skill 14.4)

A. Measuring distance from the Poles
B. Determining direction of ocean currents
C. Determining the time around the world
D. Measuring distance on the equator

99. The early ancient civilizations developed systems of government:
(Rigorous) (Skill 14.5)

A. To provide for defense against attack
B. To regulate trade
C. To regulate and direct the economic activities of the people as they worked together in groups
D. To decide on the boundaries of the different fields during planting seasons

100. The study of the ways in which different societies around the world deal with the problems of limited resources and unlimited needs and wants is in the area of:
(Average) (Skill 14.5)

A. Economics
B. Sociology
C. Anthropology
D. Political Science

101. Another name for pure capitalism is:
(Average) (Skill 17.2)

A. Macro-economy
B. Micro-economy
C. Laissez-faire
D. Free enterprise

102. The idea that continued population growth would, in future years, seriously affect a nation's productive capabilities was stated by:
(Rigorous) (Skill14.5 & 17.2)

A. Keynes
B. Mill
C. Malthus
D. Friedman

103. The United States legislature is bi-cameral, which means:
(Easy) (Skill 15.1)

A. It consists of several houses
B. It consists of two houses
C. The Vice-President is in charge of the legislature when in session
D. It has a single house

104. Which of the following is not a part of the Bill of Rights?
(Easy) (Skill 15.1)

A. Freedom of speech
B. Right against self-incrimination
C. Right to violate and abuse others
D. Right to trial by jury

105. The study of the exercise of power and political behavior in human society today would be conducted by experts in:
(Average) (Skill 15.1)

A. History
B. Sociology
C. Political Science
D. Anthropology

106. *Marbury vs Madison* (1803) was an important Supreme Court case which set the precedent for:
(Rigorous) (Skill 15.1)

A. The elastic clause
B. Judicial review
C. The supreme law of the land
D. Popular sovereignty in the territories

107. The term that best describes how the Supreme Court can block laws that may be unconstitutional from being enacted is:
(Rigorous) (Skill 15.1)

A. Jurisprudence
B. Judicial Review
C. Exclusionary Rule
D. Right of Petition

108. The "father of political science" is considered to be:
(Average) (Skill 15.2)

A. Aristotle
B. John Locke
C. Plato
D. Thomas Hobbes

109. A political system in which there is a one-party state, centralized control, and a repressive police system with private ownership is called:
(Rigorous) (Skill 15.4)

A. Communism
B. Fascism
C. Socialism
D. Constitutional Monarchy

110. Government regulation of economic activities for favorable balance of trade was the first major economic theory. It was called:
(Rigorous) (Skill 15.5)

A. Laissez-faire
B. Globalism
C. Mercantilism
D. Syndicalism

111. Charlemagne's most important influence on Western civilization is seen today in:
(Rigorous) (Skill 15.5)

A. Relationship of church and state
B. Strong military for defense
C. The criminal justice system
D. Education of women

112. The Constitution can:
(Average) (Skill 16.2)

A. Never be changed
B. Be rewritten
C. Be discarded
D. Be amended

113. Which is not a branch of the federal government?
(Average) (Skill 16.3)

A. Popular
B. Legislative
C. Executive
D. Judicial

114. The Electoral College:
(Rigorous) (Skill 16.4)

A. Elects the Senate but not the House
B. Elects the House but not the Senate
C. Elects both the House and Senate
D. Elects the President

115. In the U.S. government, the power of coining money is:
(Rigorous) (Skill 16.3)

A. Implied or suggested
B. Concurrent or shared
C. Delegated or expressed
D. Reserved

116. In the United States government, the power of taxation and borrowing is:
(Rigorous) (Skill 16.3)

A. Implied or suggested
B. Concurrent or shared
C. Delegated or expressed
D. Reserved

117. The regulation of intrastate
      commerce is the
      responsibility of:
      (Rigorous) (Skill 16.3)

      A. Federal government
      B. Local government
      C. State government
      D. Communal government

118. The source of authority for
      national, state, and local
      governments in the U.S. is:
      (Average) (Skill 16.4)

      A. The will of the people
      B. The U.S. Constitution
      C. Written laws
      D. The Bill of Rights

119. Which one of the following
      is not a function or
      responsibility of the U.S.
      political parties?
      (Rigorous) (Skill 16.5)

      A. Conducting elections or the
          voting process
      B. Obtaining funds needed for
          election campaigns
      C. Choosing candidates to run
          for public office
      D. Making voters aware of
          issues and other public
          affairs information

120. In a market economy,
      markets function on the
      basis of:
      (Rigorous) (Skill 17.1)

      A. Government control
      B. Manipulation
      C. Demand and Supply
      D. Planning

121. Potential customers for any
      product or service are not
      only called consumers but
      can also be called a:
      (Average) (Skill 17.1)

      A. Resource
      B. Base
      C. Commodity
      D. Market

122. The economist who
      disagreed with the idea that
      free markets lead to full
      employment and prosperity
      and suggested that
      increasing government
      spending would end
      depressions was:
      (Rigorous) (Skill 17.2)

      A. Keynes
      B. Malthus
      C. Smith
      D. Friedman

123. Who promoted laissez-faire
      economics:
      (Rigorous) (Skill 17.2)

      A. Thomas Robert Malthus
      B. John Stuart Mill
      C. Adam Smith
      D. John Maynard Keynes

124. Marxism believes which two
      groups are in continual
      conflict?
      (Rigorous) (Skill 17.2)

      A. Farmers and landowners
      B. Kings and the nobility
      C. Workers and owners
      D. Structure and
          superstructure

125. **Who controls production in a planned economy?**
(Rigorous) (Skill 17.3)

A. Government
B. Private individuals
C. Stockholders
D. The public

SAMPLE ESSAY QUESTION #1: Social Studies

For example: **Discuss the emergence, expansion, and evolution of Islam**

Islam is a monotheistic faith that traces its traditions to Abraham and considers the Jewish patriarchs and prophets, especially Moses, King Solomon, and Jesus Christ as earlier "Prophets of God".

Mohammed was born in 570 CE in a small Arabian town. Around 610, **Mohammed** came to some prominence through a new religion called **Islam** or submission to the will of God and his followers were called **Muslims.** His first converts were members of his family and his friends. As the new faith began to grow, it remained a secret society. But when they began to make their faith public, they met with opposition and persecution from the pagan Arabians who feared the loss of profitable trade with the pilgrims who came to the Kaaba every year. In 622, Mohammed and his close followers fled persecution in Mecca and found refuge in **Medina.** His flight is called the **Hegira.** Mohammed took advantage of feuds between Jews and Arabs and became the ruler, making it the capital of a rapidly growing state.

Islam changed significantly. It became a fighting religion and Mohammed became a political leader. The group survived by raiding caravans on the road to Mecca and plundering nearby Jewish tribes. It attracted many converts from Bedouin tribes. By 630, Mohammed conquered Mecca and made it the religious center of Islam, toward which all Moslems turned to pray. By taking over the sacred city, Mohammed made it easier for converts to join the religion. By the time of his death in 632, most of the people of Arabia had become adherents of Islam.

Mohammed left behind a collection of revelations (**surahs**) he believed were delivered by the angel Gabriel. The **Quran** was reputedly dictated to Mohammed as the Word of God and published in a book called the **Koran.** The revelations were never dated or kept in any kind of order. After Mohammed's death, they were organized by length in diminishing order. The Koran contains Mohammed's teachings on moral and theological questions, his legislation on political matters, and his comments on current events. Five basic principles of Islam are: Allah, pray five times a day facing Mecca, charity, fasting during Ramadan, and pilgrimage to Mecca.

The Islamic armies spread their faith by conquering the Arabian Peninsula, Mesopotamia, Egypt, Syria, and Persia by 650 CE and expanding to North Africa and most of the Iberian Peninsula by 750 CE. During this period of expansion, the Muslim conquerors established great centers of learning in the Middle East.

ANSWER KEY

1.	B	41.	C	81.	B	121.	D
2.	B	42.	C	82.	C	122.	A
3.	C	43.	C	83.	A	123.	C
4.	D	44.	B	84.	D	124.	C
5.	B	45.	C	85.	D	125.	A
6.	B	46.	D	86.	D		
7.	D	47.	D	87.	A		
8.	D	48.	A	88.	A		
9.	C	49.	C	89.	C		
10.	C	50.	A	90.	C		
11.	C	51.	C	91.	C		
12.	A	52.	A	92.	C		
13.	D	53.	C	93.	D		
14.	D	54.	A	94.	A		
15.	B	55.	D	95.	A		
16.	C	56.	D	96.	B		
17.	C	57.	D	97.	C		
18.	A	58.	B	98.	C		
19.	B	59.	B	99.	C		
20.	D	60.	A	100.	A		
21.	A	61.	D	101.	C		
22.	C	62.	C	102.	C		
23.	C	63.	B	103.	B		
24.	B	64.	C	104.	C		
25.	D	65.	A	105.	C		
26.	D	66.	C	106.	B		
27.	C	67.	A	107.	B		
28.	D	68.	C	108.	A		
29.	C	69.	D	109.	B		
30.	C	70.	A	110.	C		
31.	C	71.	C	111.	A		
32.	C	72.	A	112.	D		
33.	D	73.	D	113.	A		
34.	A	74.	D	114.	D		
35.	A	75.	A	115.	C		
36.	A	76.	A	116.	B		
37.	D	77.	D	117.	C		
38.	A	78.	B	118.	A		
39.	B	79.	D	119.	A		
40.	B	80.	D	120.	C		

RIGOR TABLE

	Easy %20	Average Rigor %40	Rigorous %40
Question #	3,4, 14, 16, 19, 22, 25, 28, 29, 33, 34, 44, 45, 63, 64, 66, 75, 77, 83, 84, 86, 91, 92, 103, 104	1, 2, 7, 9, 13, 15, 17, 18, 20, 24, 26, 30, 32, 35, 36, 37, 40, 41 ,43, 47, 48, 49, 50, 51, 58, 59 ,68, 71, 72, 73, 74, 76, 78, 81, 82, 85, 88, 89, 93, 94, 95, 97, 98, 100, 101, 105, 108, 112, 113, 118, 121	5, 6, 8,10, 11, 12, 21, 23, 23, 27, 31, 38, 39, 42, 46, 52, 53, 54, 55, 56, 57, 60, 61, 62, 65, 67, 69, 70, 79, 80, 87, 90, 96, 99, 102, 106, 107, 109, 110, 111, 114 115, 116, 117, 119, 120, 122, 123, 124, 125

RATIONALES

1. **Which of the following is not a native North American tribe?** *(Average) (Skill 1.1)*

    A. Algonquian
    B. Inca
    C. Iroquois
    D. Pueblo

The correct answer is B. Inca
The (A) Algonquian and (C) Iroquois are teams native to the American Northeast. The (D) Hopi are a Native American Southwestern tribe. The (B) Incas are native to Peru.

2. **Which one of the following is not a reason why Europeans came to the New World?** *(Average) (Skill 1.2)*

    A. To find resources in order to increase wealth
    B. To establish trade
    C. To increase a ruler's power and importance
    D. To spread Christianity

The correct answer is B. To establish trade
The Europeans came to the New World for a number of reasons; often they came to find new natural resources to extract for manufacturing. The Portuguese, Spanish, and English were sent over to increase the monarch's power and spread influences such as religion (Christianity) and culture. Therefore, the only reason given that Europeans didn't come to the New World was to establish trade.

3. **The only colony not founded and settled for religious, political, or business reasons was:** *(Easy) (Skill 1.2)*

    A. Delaware
    B. Virginia
    C. Georgia
    D. New York

The correct answer is C. Georgia
The Swedish and the Dutch established Delaware and New York as Middle Colonies. They were established with the intention of growth by economic prosperity from farming across the countryside. The English, with the intention of generating a strong farming economy settled Virginia, a Southern Colony. Georgia was the only one of these colonies not settled for religious, political, or business reasons as it was started as a place for debtors from English prisons.

4.   **What country did not have a colonial stake in America?**
       (Easy) (Skills 1.2)

       A. France
       B. Spain
       C. Mexico
       D. China

The correct answer is D. China
(A) France, (B) Spain and (C) Mexico all had colonies in America. The country that didn't was (D) China. There were Chinese immigrants but no Chinese colonies.

5.   **The year 1619 was a memorable year for the colony of Virginia. Three important events occurred resulting in lasting effects on U.S. history. Which one of the following was not one of the events?**
       (Rigorous) (Skill 1.2)

       A. Twenty African slaves arrived.
       B. The London Company granted the colony a charter making it independent.
       C. The colonists were given the right by the London Company to govern themselves through representative government in the Virginia House of Burgesses.
       D. The London Company sent to the colony 60 women who were quickly married, establishing families and stability in the colony.

The correct answer is B. The London Company granted the colony a charter making it independent.
In the year 1619, the Southern colony of Virginia had an eventful year including the first arrival of twenty African slaves, the right to self-governance through representative government in the Virginia House of Burgesses (their own legislative body), and the arrival of sixty women sent to marry and establish families in the colony. The London Company did not, however, grant the colony a charter in 1619.

6. **After 1783, the largest "land owner" in the Americas was:**
(Rigorous) (Skill 1.2)

   A. Britain
   B. Spain
   C. France
   D. United States

The correct answer is B. Spain
Despite the emergence of the United States as an independent nation in control of the colonies over the British, and the French control of Canada, Spain remained the largest "land owner" in the Americas, controlling much of the southwest as well as much of Central and South America.

7. **What was not one of the Acts leading to the Revolutionary War?**
(Average) (Skill 1.6)

   A. Stamp Act
   B. Quartering Act
   C. Sugar Act
   D. Monroe Doctrine

The correct answer is D. Monroe Doctrine
The (A) Stamp Act placed a tax on newspapers and other items. The (B) Quartering Act required the colonists to house British troops in their homes. The (C) Sugar Act placed a tax on molasses. The (D) Monroe Doctrine did not occur until 1823 when the President declared that any attempts at other countries trying to establish colonies in the Americas would be seen as a threat.

8. **France decided in 1777 to help the American colonies in their war against Britain. This decision was based on:**
(Rigorous) (Skill 2.2)

   A. The naval victory of John Paul Jones over the British ship "Serapis"
   B. The survival of the terrible winter at Valley Forge
   C. The success of colonial guerilla fighters in the South
   D. The defeat of the British at Saratoga

The correct answer is D. The defeat of the British at Saratoga
The defeat of the British at Saratoga was the overwhelming factor in the Franco-American alliance of 1777 that helped the American colonies defeat the British. Some historians believe that without the Franco-American alliance, the American Colonies would not have been able to defeat the British and American would have remained a British colony.

9.   **Under the brand-new Constitution, the most urgent of the many problems facing the new federal government was that of:**
     (Average) (Skill 2.5)

   A. Maintaining a strong army and navy
   B. Establishing a strong foreign policy
   C. Raising money to pay salaries and war debts
   D. Setting up courts, passing federal laws, and providing for law enforcement officers

The correct answer is C. Raising money to pay salaries and war debts
Maintaining strong military forces, establishment of a strong foreign policy, and setting up a justice system were important problems facing the United States under the newly ratified Constitution. However, the most important and pressing issue was how to raise money to pay salaries and war debts from the Revolutionary War. Alexander Hamilton then Secretary of the Treasury proposed increased tariffs and taxes on products such as liquor. This money would be used to pay off war debts and to pay for internal programs. Hamilton also proposed the idea of a National Bank.

10. There is no doubt of the vast improvement of the U.S. Constitution over the weak Articles of Confederation. Which one of the four statements below is not a description of the document?
(Rigorous) (Skill 2.3)

   A. The establishment of a strong central government in no way lessened or weakened the individual states
   B. Individual rights were protected and secured
   C. The Constitution demands unquestioned respect and subservience to the federal government by all states and citizens
   D. Its flexibility and adaptation to change gives it a sense of timelessness

The correct answer is C. The Constitution demands unquestioned respect and subservience to the federal government by all states and citizens.
The U.S. Constitution was indeed a vast improvement over the Articles of Confederation and the authors of the document took great care to assure longevity. It clearly stated that the establishment of a strong central government in no way lessened or weakened the individual states. In the Bill of Rights, citizens were assured that individual rights were protected and secured. Possibly the most important feature of the new Constitution was its flexibility and adaptation to change which assured longevity.

Therefore, the only statement made that doesn't describe some facet of the Constitution is "The Constitution demands unquestioned respect and subservience to the federal government by all states and citizens". On the contrary, the Constitution made sure that citizens could critique and make changes to their government and encourages such critiques and changes as necessary for the preservation of democracy.

11. The Federalists:
(Rigorous) (Skill 2.4)

   A. Favored state's rights
   B. Favored a weak central government
   C. Favored a strong federal government
   D. Supported the British

The correct answer is C. Favored a strong federal government
The Federalists were opposed to (A) state's rights and a (B) weak federal government. (D) Most of them opposed the British. (C) The Federalists favored a strong federal government.

12. **Which one of the following was not a reason why the United States went to war with Great Britain in 1812?**
(Rigorous) (Skill 2.5)

A. Resentment by Spain over the sale, exploration, and settlement of the Louisiana Territory
B. The U.S. merchant fleet was a threat to the British
C. The Americans wanted to trade with the French
D. Britain continued to seize American ships on the high seas and force American seamen to serve aboard British ships

The correct answer is A. Resentment by Spain over the sale, exploration, and settlement of the Louisiana Territory

The United States went to war with Great Britain in 1812 for a number of reasons. Britain and France were fighting for dominance over the sea and trade. The Americans wanted to trade with the French, and the American merchant fleet was a threat to the British. The continued seizures of American ships by the British on the high seas outraged the Americans. Therefore, the only statement given that was not a reason for the War of 1812 was the resentment by Spain over the sale, exploration and settlement of the Louisiana Territory. In fact, the Spanish continually held more hostility towards the British than toward the United States.

13. **After the War of 1812, Henry Clay and others proposed economic measures, including raising tariffs to protect American farmers and manufacturers from foreign competition. These measures were proposed in the:**
(Average) (Skill 2.6)

A. Era of Nationalism
B. American Expansion era
C. Era of Good Feeling
D. American System

The correct answer is D. American System

Although there is no official (A) "Era of Nationalism," it could be used to describe the time leading up to and including the First and Second World Wars, as nationalism was on the rise. (B) American Expansion era describes the movement of American settlers across the frontier toward the West. The so-called (C) "Era of Good Feeling" is the period after the War of 1812 but doesn't describe the policies proposed by Clay. The economic measures, including raising tariffs to protect American farmers and manufacturers from foreign competition, was known as the (D) American System.

14. **From about 1870 to 1900, the last settlement of America's "last frontier", the West, was completed. One attraction for settlers was free land but it would have been to no avail without:**
    (Easy) (Skill 2.7)

    A. Better farming methods and technology
    B. Surveying to set boundaries
    C. Immigrants and others to see new lands
    D. The railroad to get them there

The correct answer is D. The railroad to get them there
From about 1870 to 1900, the settlement for America's "last frontier" in the West was made possible by the building of the railroad. Without the railroad, the settlers never could have traveled such distances in an efficient manner.

15. **The American labor union movement started gaining new momentum:**
    (Average) (Skill 2.7)

    A. During the building of the railroads
    B. After 1865 with the growth of cities
    C. With the rise of industrial giants such as Carnegie and Vanderbilt
    D. During the war years of 1861–1865

The correct answer is B. After 1865 with the growth of cities
The American Labor Union movement had been around since the late eighteenth and early nineteenth centuries. The Labor movement began to first experience persecution by employers in the early 1800s. The American Labor Movement remained relatively ineffective until after the Civil War. In 1866, the National Labor Union was formed, pushing such issues as the eight-hour workday and new policies of immigration. This gave rise to the Knights of Labor and eventually the American Federation of Labor (AFL) in the 1890s and the Industrial Workers of the World (1905). Therefore, it was the period following the Civil War that empowered the labor movement in terms of numbers, militancy, and effectiveness.

16. **The belief that the United States should control all of North America was called:**
    (Easy) (Skill 3.1)

    A. Westward Expansion
    B. Pan Americanism
    C. Manifest Destiny
    D. Nationalism

The correct answer is C. Manifest Destiny
The belief that the United States should control all of North America was called (B) Manifest Destiny. This idea fueled much of the violence and aggression toward those already occupying the lands, such as the Native Americans. Manifest Destiny was certainly driven by sentiments of (D) nationalism and gave rise to (A) westward expansion.

17. **Which one of the following events did not occur during the period known as the "Era of Good Feeling"?**
    (Average) (Skill 3.3)

    A. President Monroe issued the Monroe Doctrine
    B. Spain ceded Florida to the United States
    C. The building of the National Road
    D. The charter of the Second Bank of the United States

The correct answer is C. The building of the National Road
The so-called "Era of Good Feeling" describes the period following the War of 1812, from about 1815 to 1825. This was the period during and the nation focused on internal national improvements such as the building of the Second National Bank and construction of new roads, as well as the Treaty of Ghent, ending the War of 1812, and forcing Spain to cede Florida to the United States. The Monroe Doctrine (1823), which called for an end to any European occupation and colonization in the Americas, came near the end of the "Era of Good Feeling." Although the nation focused on internal improvements during time, the building of the National Road had started before the War of 1812. Funding was approved during President Jefferson's tenure in office and construction of the road began in 1811.

18. **As a result of the Missouri Compromise:**
    (Average) (Skill 3.3)

    A. Slavery was not allowed in the Louisiana Purchase
    B. The Louisiana Purchase was nullified
    C. Louisiana separated from the Union
    D. The Embargo Act was repealed

The correct answer is A. Slavery was not allowed in the Louisiana Purchase
The Missouri Compromise was the agreement that eventually allowed Missouri to enter the Union. It did not nullify (B) the Louisiana Purchase and (D) the Embargo Act and did not (C) separate Louisiana from the Union. (A) As a result of the Missouri Compromise, slavery was specifically banned north of the boundary 36° 30'.

19. **The term Sectionalism refers to:**
    (Easy) (Skill 3.3)

    A. Different regions of the continent
    B. The issues between the North and South
    C. Different regions of the country
    D. Different groups of countries

The correct answer is B. The issues between the North and South
The terms Sectionalism referred to the slavery issue before the Civil War. The southern economy was agricultural and used slave labor. The North was anti-slavery and industrial.

20. **The principle of "popular sovereignty," allowing people in any territory to make their own decision concerning slavery was stated by:**
    (Average) (Skill 3.4)

    A. Henry Clay
    B. Daniel Webster
    C. John C. Calhoun
    D. Stephen A. Douglas

The correct answer is D. Stephen A. Douglas
(A) Henry Clay and (B) Daniel Webster were prominent Whigs whose main concern was keeping the United States one nation and were in favor of promoting what Clay called "the American System." (C) John C. Calhoun was very pro-slavery and a champion of states' rights. The principle of "popular sovereignty", in which people in each territory could make their own decisions concerning slavery, was the doctrine of (D) Stephen A. Douglas.

21. **The Radical Republicans who pushed the harsh Reconstruction measures through Congress after Lincoln's death lost public and moderate Republican support when they went too far:**
(Rigorous) (Skill 3.5)

A. In their efforts to impeach the President
B. By dividing ten southern states into military-controlled districts
C. By making the ten southern states give freed African-Americans the right to vote
D. Sending carpetbaggers into the South to build up support for Congressional legislation

The correct answer is A. In their efforts to impeach the President
The moderate Republicans were actually being drawn toward the more radical end of the Republican spectrum during Reconstruction because many felt Andrew Johnson's policies toward the South were too soft and ran the risk of rebuilding the old system of white power and slavery. However, the radical Republicans were so frustrated that the President would make concessions to the old Southerners that they attempted to impeach him. This turned back the support that they had received from the public and from moderates.

22. **The Union had many strengths over the Confederacy. Which was not a strength?**
(Easy) (Skill 3.5)

A. Railroads
B. Industry
C. Slaves
D. Manpower

The correct answer is C. Slaves
At the time of the Civil War, the South was mostly a plantation economy based on using slaves. The industry, railroads, and manpower were located in the North, which made transportation and weapons easy for the North to obtain and use than the South.

23. **The post-Civil War years were a time of low public morality, a time of greed, graft, and dishonesty. Which one of the reasons listed would not be accurate?**
(Rigorous) (Skill 3.5)

    A. The war itself because of the money and materials needed to carry on war
    B. The very rapid growth of industry and big business after the war
    C. The personal example set by President Grant
    D. Unscrupulous heads of large impersonal corporations

The correct answer is C. The personal example set by President Grant
The Civil War had plunged the country into debt and ultimately into a recession by the 1890s. The rapid growth of industry and big business caused a polarization of rich and poor, workers and owners. The heads of large impersonal corporations were arrogant in treating their workers inhumanely and letting morale drop to a record low. Despite accusations against his Presidency, however, Grant was an honest man who would have been a positive example.

24. **The three-day Battle of Gettysburg was the turning point of the Civil War for the North leading to ultimate victory. The battle in the West reinforcing the North's victory and sealing the South's defeat was the day after Gettysburg at:**
(Average) (Skill 3.5)

    A. Perryville
    B. Vicksburg
    C. Stones River
    D. Shiloh

The correct answer is B. Vicksburg
The Battle of Vicksburg was crucial in reinforcing the North's victory and sealing the South's defeat for a couple of reasons. First, the Battle of Vicksburg potentially gave the Union full control of the Mississippi River. More importantly, the battle split the Confederate Army and allowed General Grant to reach his goal of restoring commerce to the important northwest area.

25. **What event sparked a great migration of people from all over the world to California?**
   (Easy) (Skill 4.1)

   A. The birth of Labor Unions
   B. California statehood
   C. The invention of the automobile
   D. The gold rush

The correct answer is D. The gold rush
The discovery of gold in California created a lust for gold that quickly brought immigrants from the eastern United States and many parts of the world. To be sure, there were struggles and conflicts, as well as the rise of nativism. Yet this vast migration of people from all parts of the world began the process that has created California's uniquely diverse culture.

26. **In the 1800s, the era of industrialization and growth were characterized by:**
   (Average) (Skill 4.3)

   A. Small firms
   B. Public ownership
   C. Worker owned enterprises
   D. Monopolies and trusts

The correct answer is D. Monopolies and trusts
Industrialization and business expansion were characterized by big businesses and monopolies that merged into trusts. There were few (A) small firms and there was no (B) public ownership or (C) worker-owned enterprises.

27.   **Historians state that the West helped to speed up the Industrial Revolution. Which one of the following statements was not a reason for this?**
   (Rigorous) (Skill 4.4)

   A.   Food supplies for the ever-increasing urban populations came from farms in the West.
   B.   A tremendous supply of gold and silver from western mines provided the capital needed to build industries.
   C.   Descendants of western settlers, educated as engineers, geologists, and metallurgists in the East, returned to the West to mine the mineral resources needed for industry.
   D.   Iron, copper, and other minerals from western mines were important resources in manufacturing products.

The correct answer is C. Descendants of western settlers, educated as engineers, geologists, and metallurgists in the East, returned to the West to mine the mineral resources needed for industry.
The West helped to speed up the Industrial Revolution in a number of important and significant ways, including providing food, gold and silver, and natural resources for mining. The miners themselves, however, were typically working class and not the educated descendants of western settlers.

28.   **In the United States, federal investigations into business activities are handled by the:**
   (Easy) (Skill 4.5)

   A. Department of Treasury
   B. Security and Exchange Commission
   C. Government Accounting Office
   D. Federal Trade Commission

The correct answer is D. Federal Trade Commission
The Department of Treasury (A), established in 1789, is an executive government agency that is responsible for advising the president on fiscal policy. The Government Accounting Office is an independent, nonpartisan agency that is an investigative arm of Congress that makes government accountable to the citizens. In the United States, Federal Trade Commission or FTC handles federal investigations into business activities. The establishment of the FTC in 1915 as an independent government agency was done so as to assure fair and free competition among businesses.

29. **Jim Crow refers to:**
    (Easy) (Skill 4.6)

    A. Equality
    B. Labor Movement
    C. Racism
    D. Free trade

The correct answer is C. Racism
(C) Jim Crow is a term used to describe the policies of racism and discrimination. It has nothing to do with the (B) labor movement or (D) free trade and is the opposite of (A) the concept of equality.

30. **What Supreme Court ruling dealt with the issue of civil rights?**
    (Average) (Skill 3.4)

    A. Jefferson v. Madison
    B. Lincoln v. Douglas
    C. Dred Scott v. Sanford
    D. Marbury v. Madison

The correct answer is C. Dred Scott v. Sanford
Marbury v. Madison established the principal of judicial review. The Supreme Court ruled that it held no authority in making the decision (regarding Marbury's commission as Justice of the Peace in District of Columbia) as the Supreme Court's jurisdiction (or lack thereof) in the case, was conflicted with Article III of the Constitution. (D) The Dred Scot case is the well-known civil rights case that had to do with the rights of the slave.

31. After the Civil War, the United States adapted an attitude of isolation from foreign affairs. But the turning point marking the beginning of the U.S. becoming a world power was:
(Rigorous) (Skill 5.1)

A. World War I
B. Expansion of business and trade overseas
C. The Spanish-American War
D. The building and financing of the Panama Canal

The correct answer is C. The Spanish-American War
The United States' relatively easy defeat of Spain in the Spanish-American War marked the beginning of a continuing era of dominance for the United States. In the post-Civil War era, Spain was the largest landowner in the Americas. Their easy defeat at the hands of the United States in Cuba, the Philippines, and elsewhere showed the strength of the United States across the globe. This was seen as an extension of the Monroe doctrine, calling for United States dominance in the Western Hemisphere and removal of European powers in the region.

32. What event triggered World War I?
(Average) (Skill 5.2)

A. The fall of the Weimar Republic
B. The resignation of the Czar
C. The assassination of Austrian Archduke Ferdinand
D. The assassination of the Czar

The correct answer is C. The assassination of Austrian Archduke Ferdinand
There were regional conflicts and feeling of intense nationalism prior to the outbreak of World War I. The precipitating factor was the assassination of Austrian Archduke Ferdinand and his wife while they were in Sarajevo.

33. Which country was not a part of the Axis in World War II?
(Easy) (Skill 5.3)

A. Germany
B. Italy
C. Japan
D. United States

The correct answer is D. United States
(A) Germany, (B) Italy, and (C) Japan were the members of the Axis in World War II. (D) The United States was a member of the Allies which opposed the Axis.

HISTORY 261

34. **Which country was a Cold War foe?**
     (Easy) (Skill 5.6)

     A. Russia
     B. Brazil
     C. Canada
     D. Argentina

The correct answer is A. Russia
(B) Brazil and (D) Argentina are in South America and (C) Canada is in North America. (A) Russia is the country that was a Cold War superpower and foe of the United States.

35. **Which one of the following was not a post-World War II organization?**
     (Average) (Skill 5.4, 14.5)

     A. Monroe Doctrine
     B. Marshall Plan
     C. Warsaw Pact
     D. North Atlantic Treaty Organization

The correct answer is A. Monroe Doctrine
(B) The Marshall Plan provided funds for the reconstruction of Europe after World War II. (C) The Warsaw Pact and (D) NATO were both organizations that came into being for defense purpose. The Warsaw Pact was for the defense of Eastern Europe and NATO was for the defense of Western Europe. (A) The Monroe Doctrine was a nineteenth century policy in which the United States was committed to defend all countries in the hemisphere.

36. **What conflict brought the United States and the Soviet Union to the brink of war in 1962?**
     (Average) (Skill 5.5)

     A. Cuban Missile Crisis
     B. Viet Nam war
     C. Crisis in Brazil
     D. Crisis in India

The correct answer is A. Cuban Missile Crisis
In 1962, the Russian were installing nuclear missiles in Cuba to prevent another U.S. invasion. The missiles were detected by U.S. reconnaissance flights and the U.S. quarantined Russian ships to prevent them from reaching Cuba. The Russian ships turned back and averted further conflict.

37.   **After World War II, the United States:**
       (Average) (Skill 6.4)

       A. Limited its involvement in European affairs
       B. Shifted foreign policy emphasis from Europe to Asia
       C. Passed significant legislation pertaining to aid to farmers and tariffs on imports
       D. Entered the greatest period of economic growth in its history

The correct answer is D. Entered the greatest period of economic growth in its history
After World War II, the United States entered into the Cold War with the Soviet Union at a swift pace and attempted to contain Communism to prevent its spread across Europe. There was no significant legislation pertaining to aid to farmers and tariffs on imports. In fact, since World War II, trade has become more liberal than ever. Free trade has become the economic policy of the United States. Due to this, the United States after World War II entered the greatest period of economic growth in its history and remains a world superpower.

38.   **It can be reasonably stated that the change in the United States from primarily an agricultural country into an industrial power was due to all of the following except:**
       (Rigorous) (Skill 6.1)

       A. Tariffs on foreign imports
       B. Millions of hardworking immigrants
       C. An increase in technological developments
       D. The change from steam to electricity for powering industrial machinery

The correct answer is A. Tariffs on foreign imports
Change in the United States from a primarily agricultural country into an industrial power was due to a great degree to a combination of millions of hard-working immigrants, an increase in technological developments, and the change from steam to electricity for powering industrial machinery. The only reason given that really had little effect was the tariffs on foreign imports.

39. **A political philosophy favoring or supporting rapid social changes in order to correct social and economic inequalities is called:**
(Rigorous) (Skill 6.2)

A. Nationalism
B. Liberalism
C. Conservatism
D. Federalism

The correct answer is B. Liberalism
A political philosophy favoring rapid social changes in order to correct social and economic inequalities are called Liberalism. Liberalism was a theory that could be said to have started with the great French philosophers Montesquieu and Rousseau. It should be noted that political, economic, and social liberalism, are different and they sometimes contrast one another in the modern world.

40. **The New Deal was:**
(Average) (Skill 6.2)

A. A trade deal with England
B. A series of programs to provide relief during the Great Depression
C. A new exchange rate regime
D. A plan for tax relief

The correct answer is B. A series of programs to provide relief during the Great Depression
The New Deal consisted of a myriad of different programs aimed at providing relief during the Great Depression. Many of the programs were public works programs building bridge and roads.

41. **McCarthyism refers to:**
(Average) (Skill 6.4)

A. Pacifism
B. Racism
C. Anti-Communism
D. Fascism

The correct answer is C. Anti-Communism
McCarthyism refers to the investigations of Senator Joe McCarthy of Wisconsin in the 1940s and 1950s. Many people were blacklisted and smeared due to these Congressional hearings and charges of being Communist sympathizers. McCarthy was eventually censured.

42. **What Supreme Court ruling overturned the concept of "separate but equal" on schools?**
    (Rigorous) (Skill 6.5)

    A. Jefferson v. Madison
    B. Plessy v. Ferguson
    C. Brown v. Board of Education
    D. Dred Scot

The correct answer is C. Brown v. Board of Education
Brown v. Board of Education, 1954, was the court case in which the Supreme Court declared that Plessy v. Ferguson was unconstitutional, insofar as schools were concerned. Plessy was the ruling that had established "Separate but Equal" as the basis for segregation. With this decision, the Court ordered immediate desegregation.

43. **Which of the following is not a name associated with the Civil Rights movement?**
    (Average) (Skill 6.5)

    A. Rosa Parks
    B. Emmett Till
    C. Tom Dewey
    D. Martin Luther King, Jr.

The correct answer is C. Tom Dewey
(A) Rosa Parks was the black lady who wouldn't move to the back of the bus. (B) Emmett Till was the civil rights worked who was killed. (C) Martin Luther King, Jr. was a Civil Rights leader. (C) Tom Dewey was never involved in the Civil Rights movement but was a presidential candidate.

44. **Which of the following women was not a part of the women's rights movement?**
    (Easy) (Skill 6.6)

    A. Elizabeth Cady Stanton
    B. Lucretia Borgia
    C. Lucretia Mott
    D. Susan B. Anthony

The correct answer is B. Lucretia Borgia
Although many women worked hard in the early nineteenth century to make gains in medicine, writing, and temperance movements, the names associated with the women's rights movement are (A) Elizabeth Cady Stanton, (C) Lucretia Mott, and (D) Susan B. Anthony. (B) Lucretia Borgia is not a name associated

with women's rights. She was a daughter of an important person who lived during the Renaissance.

45. **On the spectrum of American politics, the label that most accurately describes voters to the "right of center" is:**
   (Easy) (Skill 6.8)

   A. Moderates
   B. Liberals
   C. Conservatives
   D. Socialists

The correct answer is C. Conservatives
(A) Moderates are considered voters who teeter on the line of political centrality or drift slightly to the left or right. (B) Liberals are voters who stand on the left of center. (C) Conservative voters are those who are "right of center." (D) Socialists would land far to the left on the political spectrum of America.

46. **The Fertile Crescent was not bounded by:**
   (Rigorous) (Skill 7.1)

   A. Mediterranean Sea
   B. Arabian Desert
   C. Taurus Mountains
   D. Ural Mountains

The correct answer is D. Ural Mountains
(A) The Mediterranean Sea forms the western border of the Fertile Crescent, (B) the Arabian Desert is the southern boundary and (C) the Taurus Mountains form the northern boundary. (D) The Ural Mountains are further north in Russia and form the border between Russia and Europe.

47. **The study of past human cultures based on physical artifacts is:**
   (Average) (Skill 7.1)

   A. History
   B. Anthropology
   C. Cultural Geography
   D. Archaeology

The correct answer is D. Archaeology
Archaeology is the study of past human cultures based on physical artifacts such as fossils, carvings, paintings, and engraved writings.

48. **The chemical process of radiocarbon dating would be most useful and beneficial in the field of:**
     (Average) (Skill 7.1)

     A. Archaeology
     B. Geography
     C. Sociology
     D. Anthropology

The correct answer is A. Archaeology
Radiocarbon dating is a chemical process that helps generate a more absolute method for dating artifacts and remains by measuring the radioactive materials present in them today and calculating how long it takes for certain materials to decay. Since geographers mainly study locations and special properties of earth's living things and physical features, sociologists mostly study human society and social conditions and anthropologists generally study human culture and humanity, the answer is archaeology because archeologists study past human cultures by studying their remains.

49. **The end to hunting, gathering, and fishing of prehistoric people was due to:**
     (Average) (Skill 7.1)

     A. Domestication of animals
     B. Building crude huts and houses
     C. Development of agriculture
     D. Organized government in villages

The correct answer is C. Development of agriculture
Although the domestication of animals, the building of huts and houses and the first organized governments were all very important steps made by early civilizations, it was the development of agriculture that ended the once dominant practices of hunting, gathering, and fishing among prehistoric people. The development of agriculture provided a more efficient use of time and for the first time a surplus of food. This greatly improved the quality of life and contributed to early population growth.

50.   "Participant observation" is a method of study most closely
        associated with and used in:
        (Average) (Skill 7.1)

        A. Anthropology
        B. Archaeology
        C. Sociology
        D. Political science

The correct answer is A. Anthropology
"Participant observation" is a method of study most closely associated with and used in (A) anthropology or the study of current human cultures. (B) Archaeologists typically study the remains of people, animals, or other physical things. (C) Sociology is the study of human society and usually consists of surveys, controlled experiments, and field studies. (D) Political science is the study of political life including justice, freedom, power, and equality in a variety of methods.

51.   The study of human culture and man's relationship to that culture is:
        (Average) (Skill 7.1)

        A. Sociology
        B. Psychology
        C. Anthropology
        D. Cultural Geography

The correct answer is C. Anthropology
Anthropology is the scientific study of human culture and humanity and the relationship between man and his culture. It looks at groups and how they relate to the culture and what their patterns of behavior are.

52.   Bathtubs, hot and cold running water, and sewage systems with flush toilets were developed by the:
      (Average) (Skill 7.2)

      A. Minoans
      B. Mycenaeans
      C. Phoenicians
      D. Greeks

The correct answer is A. Minoans
Both the (A) Minoans on Crete and the (B) Mycenaeans on the mainland of Greece flourished from about 1600 BCE to about 1400 BCE. However, it was the Minoans on Crete that are best known for their advanced ancient civilization in which such advances as bathtubs, hot and cold running water, sewage systems, and flush toilets were developed. The (C) Phoenicians created an alphabet that has still considerable influence in the world today. The great developments of the (D) Greeks were primarily in the fields of philosophy, political science, and early ideas of democracy.

53.   The principle of zero in mathematics is the discovery of the ancient civilization found in:
      (Rigorous) (Skill 7.2)

      A. Egypt
      B. Persia
      C. India
      D. Babylon

The correct answer is C. India
Although the Egyptians practiced algebra and geometry, the Persians developed an alphabet, and the Babylonians developed Hammurabi's Code, which would come to be considered among the most important contributions of the Mesopotamian civilization, it was the Indians that created the idea of zero in mathematics, changing drastically our ideas about numbers.

54. **Which ancient civilization is credited with being the first to develop irrigation techniques through the use of canals, dikes, and devices for raising water?** *(Rigorous) (Skill 7.2)*

    A. The Sumerians
    B. The Egyptians
    C. The Babylonians
    D. The Akkadians

The correct answer is A. The Sumerians
The ancient (A) Sumerians of the Fertile Crescent of Mesopotamia are credited with being the first to develop irrigation techniques through the use of canals, dikes, and devices for raising water. The (B) Egyptians also practiced controlled irrigation but that was primarily through the use of the Nile's predictable flooding schedule. The (C) Babylonians were more noted for their revolutionary systems of law than their irrigation systems. The Akkadians were the first world's empire and lived in Mesopotamia from about 2700 BCE to 2154 BCE.

55. **An early cultural group was so skillful in navigating on the sea that they were able to sail at night guided by stars. They were the:** *(Rigorous) (Skill 7.2)*

    A. Greeks
    B. Persians
    C. Minoans
    D. Phoenicians

The correct answer is D. Phoenicians
Although the Greeks were quite able sailors and developed a strong navy in their defeat of the Persians at sea in the Battle of Marathon, it was the Eastern Mediterranean culture of the Phoenicians that had first developed the astronomical skill of sailing at night with the stars as their guide. The Minoans were an advanced early civilization off the Greek coast on Crete and were more noted for their innovations in terms of sewage systems, toilets, and running water.

56. **Development of a solar calendar, invention of the decimal system, and contributions to the development of geometry and astronomy are all the legacy of:** *(Rigorous) (Skill 7.2)*

   A. The Babylonians
   B. The Persians
   C. The Sumerians
   D. The Egyptians

The correct answer is D. The Egyptians
The (A) Babylonians of ancient Mesopotamia flourished for a time under their great contribution of organized law and code, called Hammurabi's Code (1750 BCE), after the ruler Hammurabi. The fall of the Babylonians to the Persians in 539 BCE made way for the warrior-driver Persian Empire that expanded from Pakistan to the Mediterranean Sea until the conquest of Alexander the Great in 331 BCE. The Sumerians of ancient Mesopotamia were most noted for their early advancements as one of the first civilizations and their contributions toward written language known as cuneiform. It was the (D) Egyptians who were the first true developers of a solar calendar, the decimal system, and made significant contributions to the development of geometry and astronomy.

57. **The first ancient civilization to introduce and practice monotheism was the:** *(Rigorous) (Skill 7.4)*

   A. Sumerians
   B. Minoans
   C. Phoenicians
   D. Hebrews

The correct answer is D. Hebrews
The (A) Sumerians and (C) Phoenicians both practiced religions in which many gods and goddesses were worshipped. The (B) Minoan culture shared many religious practices with the ancient Egyptians. It seems that the king was somewhat of a god figure and the queen, a goddess. Much of the Minoan art points to worship of multiple gods. Therefore, only the (D) Hebrews introduced and fully practiced monotheism, or the belief in one God.

58.   The world religion which includes a caste system, is:
        (Average) (Skill 7.4)

        A. Buddhism
        B. Hinduism
        C. Confucianism
        D. Jainism

The correct answer is B. Hinduism
Buddhism and Jainism all rose out of protest against Hinduism and its practices of sacrifice and the caste system. The caste system, in which people were born into castes, would determine their class for life including who they could marry, what jobs they could perform, and their overall quality of life. Confucianism is an ethical and philosophical system that is also a religion.

59.   The Roman Empire gave so much to the world, especially the Western world. Of the legacies below, the most influential, effective and lasting is:
        (Average) (Skill 7.7)

        A. The language of Latin
        B. Roman law, justice, and political system
        C. Engineering and building
        D. The writings of its poets and historians

The correct answer is B. Roman law, justice, and political system
It is the law, justice, and political systems of the Roman Empire that have been the most effective and influential on our Western world today. The idea of a Senate and different houses came from Rome, and their legal justice system is also the foundation of our own. Although, the Roman language was the basis for many modern languages, Latin itself has died out. Roman engineering and building, their writings and poetry have also been influential but not nearly to the degree that their government and justice systems have been.

60.   What was the major factor in the establishment and existence of feudalism?
        (Rigorous) (Skill 7.8)

        A. The Church
        B. The king
        C. The nobility
        D. The serfs

The correct answer is A. The Church
The reason for the existence of feudalism was mainly due to the Church. Feudalism was a way of controlling the population. It kept people in their places.

This benefited the upper classes who were friends of the clergy. Europe remained united through Christianity and the Church did not want this to change.

61. **Which one of the following did not contribute to the early medieval European civilization?**
(Rigorous) (Skill 7.9)

    A. The heritage from the classical cultures
    B. The Christian religion
    C. The influence of the German Barbarians
    D. The spread of ideas through trade and commerce

The correct answer is D. The spread of ideas through trade and commerce
The heritage of the classical cultures such as Greece, the Christian religion which became dominant, and the influence of the Germanic Barbarians (Visigoths, Saxons, Ostrogoths, Vandals and Franks) were all contributions to early medieval Europe and its plunge into feudalism. During this period, lives were often difficult and lived out on one single manor, with very little travel or spread of ideas through trade or commerce. Civilization seems to have halted progress during these years.

62. **Which one of the following is not an important legacy of the Byzantine Empire?**
(Rigorous) (Skill 7.10)

    A. It protected Western Europe from various attacks from the East by such groups as the Persians, Ottoman Turks, and Barbarians
    B. It played a part in preserving the literature, philosophy, and language of ancient Greece
    C. Its military organization was the foundation for modern armies
    D. It kept the legal traditions of Roman government and collecting and organizing many ancient Roman laws.

The correct answer is C. Its military organization was the foundation for modern armies
The Byzantine Empire (1353–1453) protected Western Europe from invaders such as the Persians and Ottomans. It was a Christian incorporation of Greek philosophy, language, and literature along with Roman government and law. Therefore, although regarded as having a strong military, the Byzantine Empire is not particularly considered a foundation for modern armies.

63. **Which of the following is an example of a direct democracy?**
   (Easy) (Skill 7.11)

   A. Elected representatives
   B. Greek city-states
   C. The Constitution
   D. The Confederate States

The correct answer is B. Greek city-states
The Greek city-states are an example of a direct democracy as their leaders were elected directly by the citizens and the citizens themselves were given voice in government. (A) Elected representatives in the United States as in the case of the presidential elections are actually elected by an electoral college that is supposed to be representative of the citizens. The United States Congress, the Senate, and the House of Representatives are also examples of indirect democracy as they represent the citizens in the legislature as opposed to having citizens represent themselves.

64. **The holy book of Islam is:**
   (Easy) (Skill 8.2)

   A. The Bible
   B. The Kaaba
   C. The Koran
   D. The Torah

The correct answer is C. The Koran
The (A) Bible is the holy book of Christianity; the (D) Torah is the holy book of Judaism. The (B) Kaaba means the Circle and is in Mecca. The holy book of Islam is (C) the Koran.

65. **The difference between manorialism and feudalism was:**
   (Rigorous) (Skill 8.4)

   A. Land was owned by the noblemen in manorialism
   B. Land was owned by noblemen in both feudalism and manorialism
   C. Land was owned by the noblemen in feudalism
   D. The king owned all the land in both.

The correct answer is A. Land was owned by the noblemen in manorialism
The difference between feudalism and manorialism lay in who owned the land. In feudalism the land was owned by the king. In manorialism the land is owned by the noblemen.

66. **Native North and South American tribes included all of the following except:**
(Easy) (Skill 8.8)

   A. Aztec
   B. Inca
   C. Minoans
   D. Maya

The correct answer is C. Minoans
The (A) Aztec were a tribe in Mexico and Central America. (B) The Inca and (D) the Maya were South American tribes. The Minoans were an early civilization but not from the Americas.

67. **India's greatest ruler is considered to be:**
(Rigorous) (Skill 8.8)

   A. Akbar
   B. Asoka
   C. Babur
   D. Jahan

The correct answer is A. Akbar
Akbar is considered to be India's greatest ruler. He combined a drive for conquest with a magnetic personality and went so far as to invent his own religion, Dinillahi, a combination of Islam, Christianity, Zoroastrianism, and Hinduism. Asoka was also an important ruler as he was the first to bring together a fully united India. Babur was considered to be a failure as he struggled to maintain any power early in his reign, but later to be somewhat successful in his quest to reunite Northern India. Jahan's rule of India is considered to be the golden age of art and literature in the region.

68. **The pyramids in Central America were built by:**
(Average) (Skill 8.8)

   A. The Incas
   B. The Atacamas
   C. The Mayas
   D. The Tarapacas

The correct answer is C. The Mayas
The Incas (A) lived in South America. The Atacamas (B) lived in northern Chile in the Atacama Desert. Tarapaca is an area in northern Chile in the Atacama Desert. The Mayas lived in Central America and built pyramids.

69. In Western Europe, the achievements of the Renaissance were unsurpassed and made these countries outstanding cultural centers on the continent. All of the following were accomplishments except: (Rigorous) (Skill 9.1)

    A. Invention of the printing press
    B. A rekindling of interest in the learning of classical Greece and Rome
    C. Growth in literature, philosophy, and art
    D. Better military tactics

The correct answer is D. Better military tactics
Some of the most important developments during the Renaissance were Gutenberg's invention of the printing press and a reexamination of the ideas and philosophies of classical Greece and Rome. Also, important during the Renaissance was the growth in literature, philosophy, and art. Therefore, improved military tactics is the only possible answer as it was clearly not a characteristic of the Renaissance in Western Europe.

70. The "father of anatomy" is considered to be: (Rigorous) (Skill 9.1)

    A. Vesalius
    B. Servetus
    C. Galen
    D. Harvey

The correct answer is A. Vesalius
Andreas Vesalius is considered to be the "father of anatomy" as a result of his revolutionary work on the human anatomy based on dissections of human cadavers. Prior to Vesalius, men such as Galen had done work in the field of anatomy but they had based the majority of their work on animal studies.

71. The ideas and innovations of the period of the Renaissance were spread throughout Europe mainly because of: (Average) (Skill 9.1)

    A. Extensive exploration
    B. Craft workers and their guilds
    C. The invention of the printing press
    D. Increased travel and trade

The correct answer is C. The invention of the printing press
The ideas and innovations of the Renaissance were spread throughout Europe for a number of reasons. While exploration, increased travel, and spread of craft may have aided the spread of the Renaissance to small degrees, nothing was as

important to the spread of ideas as Gutenberg's invention of the printing press in Germany.

72.   **Who is considered to be the most important figure in the spread of Protestantism across Switzerland?**
(Average) (Skill 9.2)

    A. Calvin
    B. Zwingli
    C. Munzer
    D. Leyden

The correct answer is A. Calvin
While Huldreich Zwingli was the first to spread the Protestant Reformation in Switzerland around 1519, it was John Calvin, whose less radical approach to Protestantism, who really made the most impact in Switzerland. Calvin's ideas separated from the Lutherans over the "Lord's Supper" debate over the sacrament, and his branch of Protestants became known as Calvinism. Thomas Munzer was a German Protestant reformer whose radical and revolutionary ideas about God's will to overthrow the ruling classes and his siding with the peasantry got him beheaded. Leyden (or Leiden) was a founder of the University of Leyden, a Protestant place for study in the Netherlands.

73.   **The English explorer who gave England its claim to North America was:**
(Average) (Skill 9.3)

    A. Raleigh
    B. Hawkins
    C. Drake
    D. Cabot

The correct answer is D. Cabot
Sir Walter Raleigh was an English explorer and navigator who was sent to the New World in search of riches. He founded the lost colony at Roanoke, Virginia, and was later imprisoned for a supposed plot to kill the King for which he was later released. Sir John Hawkins and Sir Francis Drake were both navigators who worked in the slave trade, made some voyages to the New World, and commanded ships against and defeated the Spanish Armada in 1588. John Cabot was the English explorer who gave England claim to North America.

74. **Studies in astronomy, skills in mapping, and other contributions to geographic knowledge came from:**
   (Average) (Skill 9.3 & 14.2)

   A. Galileo
   B. Columbus
   C. Eratosthenes
   D. Ptolemy

The correct answer is D. Ptolemy
Ptolemy was active in the field of astronomy, but was also important for his contributions to the fields of mapping, mathematics, and geography. Galileo was also important in the field of astronomy but did not make the mapping and geographic contributions of Ptolemy.

75. **The Age of Exploration begun in the 1400s was led by:**
   (Easy) (Skill 9.3)

   A. The Portuguese
   B. The Spanish
   C. The English
   D. The Dutch

The correct answer is A. The Portuguese
Although the Age of Exploration had many important players among them, the Dutch, Spanish, and English, it was the Portuguese who sent the first explorers to the New World.

76. **Which of the following does not pertain to the Ottoman Empire?**
   (Average) (Skill 9.5)

   A. Victorious in World War I
   B. Adopted policy of modernization based on European standards
   C. Sided with Germany in World War I
   D. Overthrown in 1922

The correct answer is A. Victorious in World War I
The Ottoman Empire was not victorious in World War I. They had sided with Germans and were defeated and were overthrown by Turkish revolutionaries in 1922.

77.   **Karl Marx believed in:**
       (Easy) (Skill 10.2)

       A. Free Enterprise
       B. Utopian Socialism
       C. Absolute Monarchy
       D. Scientific Socialism

The correct answer is D. Scientific Socialism
Marx did not believe in (A) Free Enterprise, (B) Utopian Socialism, or (C) Absolute Monarchy. He believed that he applied a scientific process in his analysis and he named this Scientific Socialism.

78.   **Which of the following took a scientific view of the world:**
       (Average) (Skill 10.2)

       A. Rousseau
       B. Immanuel Kant
       C. Montesquieu
       D. John Locke

The correct answer is B. Immanuel Kant
Immanuel Kant (1724–1804) was the German metaphysician and philosopher who was a founding proponent of the idea that world organization was the means for achieving universal peace. Kant's ideas helped to found such world peace organizations as the League of Nations in the wake of World War I. He also took a scientific view of the world.

79.   **The concepts of social contract and natural law were espoused by:**
       (Rigorous) (Skill 10.2)

       A. Locke
       B. Rousseau
       C. Aristotle
       D. Montesquieu

The correct answer is D. Montesquieu
The principle that "men entrusted with power tend to abuse it" is attributed to Montesquieu, the great French philosopher whose ideas based much on Locke's ideas, along with Rousseau, had a strong influence on the French Revolution of 1789. Although it would be reasonable to assume that Locke, Rousseau, and Aristotle would probably agree with the statement, all four of these men had profound impacts on the ideas of the Enlightenment, from humanism to constitutionals.

80. One South American country quickly and easily gained independence in the 19th century from European control and was noted for the uniqueness of its political stability and gradual orderly changes. This most unusual Latin American country is:
(Rigorous) (Skill 10.4)

A. Chile
B. Argentina
C. Venezuela
D. Brazil

The correct answer is D. Brazil
While Chile, Argentina, and Venezuela all have had histories marred by civil wars, dictatorships, and numerous violent coups during their quests for independence, Brazil experienced a more rapid independence. Independence was gained quickly and more easily than the other countries due to a bloodless revolution in 1889 that officially made Brazil a republic. The country also had economic stability because they had a strong coffee- and rubber-based economy.

81. Colonial expansion by Western European powers in the 18th and 19th centuries was due primarily to:
(Average) (Skill 10.5)

A. Building and opening the Suez Canal
B. The Industrial Revolution
C. Marked improvements in transportation
D. Complete independence of all the Americas and loss of European domination and influence

The correct answer is B. The Industrial Revolution
Colonial expansion by Western European powers in the late eighteenth and nineteenth centuries was due primarily to the Industrial Revolution in Great Britain that spread across Europe and needed new natural resources and, therefore, new locations from which to extract the raw materials needed to feed the new industries.

82. **Nineteenth century imperialism by Western Europe nations had important and far-reaching effects on the colonial peoples they ruled. All four of the following are the results of this. Which one was the most important and had lasting effects on key 20th century events?**
(Average) (Skill 10.7)

    A. Local wars were ended
    B. Living standards were raised
    C. Demands for self-government and feelings of nationalism surfaced
    D. Economic developments occurred

The correct answer is C. Demands for self-government and feelings of nationalism surfaced
The nineteenth century imperialism by Western European nations had some very serious and far-reaching effects. However, both World War I and World War II were caused to a large degree by the rise of nationalist sentiment across Europe and Asia. Nationalism has also fueled numerous liberation movements and revolutionary movements across the globe from Central and South America to the South Pacific to Africa and Asia.

83. **Of all the major causes of both World Wars I and II, the most significant one is considered to be:**
(Easy) (Skill 11.1)

    A. Extreme nationalism
    B. Military buildup and aggression
    C. Political unrest
    D. Agreements and alliances

The correct answer is A. Extreme nationalism
Although military buildup and aggression, political unrest, and agreements and alliances were all characteristic of the world climate before and during World War I and World War II, the most significant cause of both wars was extreme nationalism. Nationalism is the idea that the interests and needs of a particular nation are of the utmost and primary importance above all else. The nationalism that sparked WWI included a rejection of German, Austro-Hungarian, and Ottoman imperialism by Serbs, Slavs, and others culminating in the assassination of Archduke Ferdinand by a Serb nationalist in 1914. Following WWI and the Treaty of Versailles, many Germans and others in the Central Alliance Nations, malcontent at the concessions and reparations of the treaty, started a new form of nationalism. Adolf Hitler and the Nazi regime led this extreme nationalism. Hitler's ideas were an example of extreme, oppressive nationalism combined with political, social and economic scapegoating and were the primary cause of WWII.

84. **Which did not contribute to the 1917 Revolution in Russia?**
(Easy) (Skill 11.2)

A. World War I
B. Worker Strikes
C. Starving Peasants
D. Promise of aid from Germany

The correct answer is D. Promise of aid from Germany
At the time of the 1917 Revolution, (A) World War I was in progress taking a heavy toll of the Russians. The (C) peasants were starving and there were (B) many worker strikes. There was no (D) promise of aid from Germany.

85. **In the United States government, power or control over public education, marriage, and divorce is:**
(Average) (Skill 16.3)

A. Implied or suggested
B. Concurrent or shared
C. Delegated or expressed
D. Reserved

The correct answer is D. Reserved
In the United States government, power or control over public education, marriage, and divorce is reserved for the states. This is to say that these powers are reserved for the people of the states to decide for themselves.

86. **A well-known World War II figure who was the leader of Italy was:**
(Easy) (Skill 11.5)

A. Hitler
B. Stalin
C. Tojo
D. Mussolini

The correct answer is D. Mussolini
(A) Adolf Hitler, the Nazi leader of Germany, and (C) Hideki Tojo, the Japanese General and Prime Minister, were well known World War II figures who led Axis forces into war on a quest of spreading fascism. (B) Joseph Stalin was the Communist Russian head of state during World War II. Although all three were repressive in their actions, it was (D) Benito Mussolini, the Fascist and widely-considered incompetent leader of Italy during World War II, who once said "democracy was like a rotting corpse that had to be replaced by a superior way of life and more efficient government".

87. **Which one of the following would not be considered a result of World War II?**
     (Rigorous) (Skill 11.6)

     A. Economic depressions and slow resumption of trade and financial aid
     B. Western Europe was no longer the center of world power
     C. The beginnings of new power struggles not only in Europe but in Asia, as well
     D. Territorial and boundary changes for many nations, especially in Europe

The correct answer is A. Economic depressions and slow resumption of trade and financial aid
Following World War II, the economy was vibrant and flourished from the stimulant of war and an increased dependence of the world on United States industries. Therefore, World War II didn't result in economic depressions and slow resumption of trade and financial aid. Western Europe was no longer the center of world power. New power struggles arose in Europe and Asia and many European nations underwent changing territories and boundaries.

88. **Which of the following is an organization or alliance for defense purposes?**
     (Average) (Skill 12.1)

     A. North Atlantic Treaty Organization
     B. The Common Market
     C. The European Union
     D. North American Free Trade Association

The correct answer is A. North Atlantic Treaty Organization
(B) The Common Market, (C) The European Union, and (D) the North American Free Trade Organization are all forms of economic integration and are in place to promote free trade and factor mobility. (D) The North Atlantic Treaty Organization, NATO, is the organization that provides for the defense of Europe.

89. The international organization established to work for world peace at the end of the Second World War is the:
     (Average) (Skill 12.6)

     A. League of Nations
     B. United Federation of Nations
     C. United Nations
     D. United World League

The correct answer is C. United Nations
The international organization established to work for world peace at the end of the Second World War was the United Nations. From the ashes of the failed League of Nations, established following World War I, the United Nations continues to be a major player in world affairs today.

90. Which contributed to the writings of the Renaissance?
     (Rigorous) (Skill 13.3)

     A. Francois Rabelais
     B. Desiderius Erasmus
     C. Michel de Montaigne
     D. Sir Francis Bacon

The correct answer is C. Michel de Montaigne
(A) Francois Rabelais was a French writer and physician who was both a practicing monk and a respected humanist thinker of the Renaissance. (B) Desiderius Erasmus was a Dutch humanist who was very critical of the Catholic Church but was equally conflicted with Luther's Protestant Reformation. (D) Sir Francis Bacon was an English philosopher and writer who pushed the idea that knowledge must come from thorough scientific knowledge and experiment, and insufficient data must not be used in reaching conclusions. (C) Michel de Montaigne, a French essayist from a mixed background, half Catholic and half Jewish, did write some about the dangers of absolute powers, primarily monarchs but also of the Church. His attitude changed as his examination of his own life developed into a study of mankind and nature.

91.   **The Yangtze is an example of:**
      (Easy) (Skill 14.1)

      A. Plains
      B. Canal
      C. River
      D. Ocean

The correct answer is C. River
  The Yangtze River runs from Tibet through China and flows eastward to the Pacific Ocean. The Yangtze River is an important travel and trade route through China and meets the Pacific at Shanghai.

92.   **A famous canal is the:**
      (Easy) (Skill 14.1)

      A. Pacific Canal
      B. Arctic Canal
      C. Panama Canal
      D. Atlantic Canal

The correct answer is C. Panama Canal
The only canal is the selection of answers is the Panama Canal. The Pacific, Artic and Atlantic are oceans, not canals.

93.   **Which one of the following does not affect climate?**
      (Average) (Skill 14.1)

      A. Elevation and altitude
      B. Ocean currents
      C. Latitude
      D. Longitude

The correct answer is D. Longitude
Latitude is the primary influence of earth's climate as it determines the climatic region in which an area lies. Elevation or altitude and ocean currents are considered to be secondary influences on climate. Longitude is considered to have no important influence over climate.

94. **The study of a people's culture would be part of all of the following except:**
(Average) (Skill 7.1)

   A. Science
   B. Archaeology
   C. History
   D. Anthropology

The correct answer is A. Science
The study of a people's culture would be a part of studies in the disciplines of archaeology, (study of ancient artifacts including written works), and history (the study of the past) and anthropology, the study of the relationship between man and his culture. Culture would be less important in science that is based on hard facts.

95. **In which of the following disciplines would the study of physical mapping, modern or ancient, and the plotting of points and boundaries be least useful?**
(Average) (Skills 14.2, 14.3)

   A. Sociology
   B. Geography
   C. Archaeology
   D. History

The correct answer is A. Sociology
In geography, archaeology, and history, the study of maps and plotting of points and boundaries is very important as all three of these disciplines hold value in understanding the spatial relations and regional characteristics of people and places. Sociology, however, mostly focuses on the social interactions of people and while location is important, the physical location is not as important as the social location, such as the differences between studying people in groups or as individuals.

96.   The circumference of the earth, which greatly contributed to geographic knowledge, was calculated by:
      (Rigorous) (Skill 14.2)

      A. Ptolemy
      B. Eratosthenes
      C. Galileo
      D. Strabo

The correct answer is B. Eratosthenes
There is no doubt to Ptolemy and Galileo's influence as astronomers. (A) Ptolemy was an earlier theorist and (C) Galileo was a founder of modern scientific knowledge of astronomy and our place in the galaxy. However, it was (B) Eratosthenes, the Greek writer, philosopher, and astronomer, who is credited with measuring the earth's circumference as well as the distances between Earth, sun, and moon. (D) Strabo was more concerned with geography and history than astronomy.

97.   The Study of "spatial relationships and interaction" would be done by people in the field of:
      (Average) (Skill 14.2)

      A. Political Science
      B. Anthropology
      C. Geography
      D. Sociology

The correct answer is C. Geography
Geography is the discipline within social science that most concerns itself with the study of "spatial relationships and interaction".

98.   Meridians, or lines of longitude, not only help in pinpointing locations, but are also used for:
      (Average) (Skill 14.4)

      A. Measuring distance from the Poles
      B. Determining direction of ocean currents
      C. Determining the time around the world
      D. Measuring distance on the Equator

The correct answer is C. Determining the time around the world
Meridians, or lines of longitude, are the determining factor in separating time zones and determining time around the world.

99. **The early ancient civilizations developed systems of government:**
(Rigorous) (Skill 14.5)

   A. To provide for defense against attack
   B. To regulate trade
   C. To regulate and direct the economic activities of the people as they worked together in groups
   D. To decide on the boundaries of the different fields during planting seasons

The correct answer is C. To regulate and direct the economic activities of the people as they worked together in groups
Although ancient civilizations were concerned with defense, trade regulation, and the maintenance of boundaries in their fields, they could not have been any of them without first regulating and directing the economic activities of the people as they worked in groups. This provided for a stable economic base from which they could trade and actually had something worth providing defense for.

100. **The study of ways in which different societies around the world deal with the problems of limited resources and unlimited needs and wants is in the area of:**
(Average) (Skill 14.5)

   A. Economics
   B. Sociology
   C. Anthropology
   D. Political Science

The correct answer is A. Economics
The study of the ways in which different societies around the world deal with the problems of limited resources and unlimited needs and wants is a study of Economics. Economists consider the law of supply and demand as fundamental to the study of the economy. However, Sociology and Political Science also consider the study of economics and its importance in understanding social and political systems.

101. **Another name for pure capitalism is:**
(Average) (Skill 17.2)

A. Macro-economy
B. Micro-economy
C. Laissez-faire
D. Free enterprise

The correct answer is C.Laissez-faire
(D) Free enterprise or capitalism is the economic system that promotes private ownership of land, capital, and business with minimal government interference. (A) Macro-economy has to do with the large economy, and (B) Micro-economy has to do with small segments of the economy.

102. **The idea that continued population growth would, in future years, seriously affect a nation's productive capabilities was stated by:**
(Rigorous) (Skill 14.5 & 17.2)

A. Keynes
B. Mill
C. Malthus
D. Friedman

The correct answer is C. Malthus
(A) John Maynard Keynes advocated an economic system in which government regulations and spending on public works would stimulate the economy and lead to full employment. (C) Thomas Malthus was the English economist who had the idea that population growth would seriously affect a nation's productive capabilities. Malthus's ideas also included predictions about running out of food and a natural selection-like process brought about by population that would maintain balance. His theory was proven wrong long ago. (B) Mill, an English economist and (D) Friedman, an American economist, contrasted one another greatly. Mill was almost a Socialist and wrote early works about political economy while Friedman was a financial advisor in the archconservative government of President Ronald Reagan.

103. **The United States legislature is bi-cameral, which means:**
(Easy) (Skill 15.1)

   A. It consists of several houses
   B. It consists of two houses
   C. The Vice-President is in charge of the legislature when in session
   D. It has a single house

The correct answer is B. It consists of two houses
The bi-cameral nature of the United States legislature means that it has two houses, the Senate and the House of Representatives that make up the Congress. The Vice-President is part of the executive branch of government but presides over the Senate and may act as a tiebreaker. An upper and lower house would be parts of a parliamentary system of government such as the governments of Great Britain and Israel. A single-house legislature is a unicameral legislature.

104. **Which of the following is not a part of the Bill of Rights?**
(Easy) (Skill 15.1)

   A. Freedom of speech
   B. Right against self-incrimination
   C. Right to violate and abuse others
   D. Right to trial by jury

The correct answer is C. Right to violate and abuse others
(C) The Bill of Rights does not give people the right to do literally anything that they want. There are constraints. The Bill of Rights does not give anyone the rights to violate and abuse others.

105. **The study of the exercise of power and political behavior in human society today would be conducted by experts in:**
(Average) (Skill 15.1)

   A. History
   B. Sociology
   C. Political Science
   D. Anthropology

The correct answer is C. Political Science
Experts in the field of political science today would likely conduct the study of exercise of power and political behavior in human society. However, it is also reasonable to suggest that such studies would be important to historians (study of the past, often in an effort to understand the present), sociologists (often concerned with power structure in the social and political worlds), and even some anthropologists (study of culture and their behaviors).

106. *Marbury v. Madison* (1803) was an important Supreme Court case which set the precedent for:
(Rigorous) (Skill 15.1)

    A. The elastic clause
    B. Judicial review
    C. The supreme law of the land
    D. Popular sovereignty in the territories

The correct answer is B. Judicial review
Madison v. Marbury (1803) was an important case for the Supreme Court as it established judicial review (B). In that case, the Supreme Court set precedent to declare laws passed by Congress as unconstitutional. Popular sovereignty (D) in the territories was a failed plan pushed to allow states to decide the slavery question for themselves. The supreme law of the land (C) is the Constitution, the highest law that rules. (A) The elastic clause refers to the Necessary and Proper Clause that permits Congress to make law that is implied from the enumerated powers and law that is necessary and proper for the nation.

107. The term that best describes how the Supreme Court can block laws that may be unconstitutional from being enacted is:
(Rigorous) (Skill 15.1)

    A. Jurisprudence
    B. Judicial Review
    C. Exclusionary Rule
    D. Right of Petition

The correct answer is B. Judicial Review
(A) Jurisprudence is the study of the development and origin of law. (B) Judicial review is the term that best describes how the Supreme Court can block laws that they deem as unconstitutional as set forth in *Marbury v. Madison*. The (C) "exclusionary rule" is a reference to the Fourth Amendment of the Constitution and says that evidence gathered in an illegal manner or search must be thrown out and excluded from evidence. (D), the Right of Petition refers to the right to petition redress of grievances, a right listed in the First Amendment to the Constitution.

108. The "father of political science" is considered to be:
(Average) (Skill 15.2)

A. Aristotle
B. John Locke
C. Plato
D. Thomas Hobbes

The correct answer is A. Aristotle
(D) Thomas Hobbes wrote the important work *Leviathan* in which he argued for the need for a strong state. (B) John Locke's book *Two Treatises of Government* has long been considered a founding document on the rights of people to rebel against an unjust government. (C) Plato and (D) Aristotle both contributed to the field of political science. Both believed that political order would result in the greatest stability. In fact, Aristotle studied under Plato. Aristotle, however, is considered to be "the father of political science" because of his development of systems of political order the true development, a scientific system to study justice and political order.

109. A political system in which there is a one-party state, centralized control, and a repressive police system with private ownership is called:
(Rigorous) (Skill 15.4)

A. Communism
B. Fascism
C. Socialism
D. Constitutional Monarchy

The correct answer is B. Fascism
(A) Communism and (C) Socialism both are based on the public ownership of the means of production. (D) A constitutional monarchy would have private ownership. (B) Fascism is the only form of government that has all of the characteristics mentioned in the statement.

110. Government regulation of economic activities for favorable balance of trade was the first major economic theory. It was called:
(Rigorous) (Skill 15.5)

A. Laissez-faire
B. Globalism
C. Mercantilism
D. Syndicalism

The correct answer is C. Mercantilism
(A) Laissez-faire is the doctrine that calls for no government interference in economic and political policy. (B) Globalism is not an economic or political theory. Globalization is the idea that we are all increasingly connected in a worldwide system. (D) Syndicalism is similar to anarchism claiming that workers should control and govern economic policies and regulations as opposed to state control. Therefore, (C) mercantilism is the best regulation of economic activities for a favorable balance of trade.

111. Charlemagne's most important influence on Western civilization is seen today in:
(Rigorous) (Skill 15.5)

A. Relationship of church and state
B. Strong military for defense
C. The criminal justice system
D. Education of women

The correct answer is A. Relationship of church and state
Charlemagne was responsible for the promotion of the Holy Roman Empire across Europe. Although he unified governments and aided the Pope, he re-crowned himself in 802 CE to demonstrate that his power and right to rule was not a grant from the Pope, but rather a secular achievement. This redefined the role of the church in regard to the state and had a lasting influence on Western Civilization since.

112. The Constitution can:
(Average) (Skill 16.2)

A. Never be changed
B. Be rewritten
C. Be discarded
D. Be amended

The correct answer is D. Be amended
The Constitution is the law of the land. As such, it cannot be discarded. It can be changed officially through the amendment process.

113. **Which is not a branch of the federal government?**
(Average) (Skill 16.3)

   A. Popular
   B. Legislative
   C. Executive
   D. Judicial

The correct answer is A. Popular
The three branches of government are the (B) legislative, (C) executive and (D) judicial branches. Each has its own distinct functions and duties. There is not such branch as the (A) popular.

114. **The Electoral College:**
(Rigorous) (Skill 16.4)

   A. Elects the Senate but not the House
   B. Elects the House but not the Senate
   C. Elects both the House and Senate
   D. Elects the President

The correct answer is D. Elects the President
The Electoral College only exists to casts its votes for the President of the United States. Both Senators and Representatives are elected by majority vote of the voters.

115. **In the United States government, the power of coining money is:**
(Rigorous) (Skill 16.3)

   A. Implied or suggested
   B. Concurrent or shared
   C. Delegated or expressed
   D. Reserved

The correct answer is C. Delegated or expressed
In the United States government, the power of coining money is delegated or expressed. Therefore, only the United States government may coin money. The states may not coin money for themselves.

116. **In the United States government, the power of taxation and borrowing is:**
(Rigorous) (Skill 16.3)

   A. Implied or suggested
   B. Concurrent or shared
   C. Delegated or expressed
   D. Reserved

The correct answer is B. Concurrent or shared
In the United States government, the power of taxation is concurrent or shared with the states. An example of this is the separation of state and federal income tax and the separate filings of tax returns for each.

117. **The regulation of intrastate commerce is the responsibility of:**
(Rigorous) (Skill 16.3)

   A. Federal Government
   B. Local Government
   C. State Government
   D. Communal Government

The correct answer is C. State Government
Intra means "within." State government has the responsibility of regulating trade within the state.

118. **The source of authority for national, state, and local governments in the United States is:**
(Average) (Skill 16.4)

   A. The will of the people
   B. The United States Constitution
   C. Written laws
   D. The Bill of Rights

The correct answer is A. The will of the people
The source of authority for national, state, and local governments in the United States is the will of the people. Although the United States Constitution, the Bill of Rights, and the other written laws of the land are important guidelines for authority, they may ultimately be altered or changed by the will of the people.

119. **Which one of the following is not a function or responsibility of the U.S. political parties?**
(Rigorous) (Skill 16.5)

A. Conducting elections or the voting process
B. Obtaining funds needed for election campaigns
C. Choosing candidates to run for public office
D. Making voters aware of issues and other public affairs information

The correct answer is A. Conducting elections or the voting process
The U.S. political parties have numerous functions and responsibilities. Among them are obtaining funds needed for election campaigns, choosing the candidates to run for office, and making voters aware of the issues. The political parties, however, do not conduct elections or the voting process, as that would be an obvious conflict of interest.

120. **In a market economy, markets function on the basis of:**
(Rigorous) (Skill 17.1)

A. Government control
B. Manipulation
C. Demand and Supply
D. Planning

The correct answer is C. Demand and Supply
(A) Government control is not a manifestation of the functioning of free markets since government interferes with the operating mechanism of the market. (C) Manipulation refers to the interfering with the price-quantity adjustment mechanism that prevents markets from operating efficiently. (D) Planning is a mechanism that replaces the market. (C) Demand and supply describes the basis for the adjustment mechanism, which is how free markets function.

121. **Potential customers for any product or service are not only called consumers but can also be called a:**
(Average) (Skill 17.1)

A. Resource
B. Base
C. Commodity
D. Market

The correct answer is D. Market
Potential customers for any product or service are not only customers but can also be called a market. A resource is a source of wealth; natural resources are the basis for manufacturing goods and services. A commodity is anything that is bought or sold, any product.

122. **The economist who disagreed with the idea that free markets lead to full employment and prosperity and suggested that increasing government spending would end depressions was:**
(Rigorous) (Skill 17.2)

    A. Keynes
    B. Malthus
    C. Smith
    D. Friedman

The correct answer is A. Keynes
John Maynard Keynes advocated an economic system in which government regulations and spending on public works would stimulate the economy and lead to full employment. This broke from the classical idea that free markets would lead to full employment and prosperity. In contrast, Adam Smith's *Wealth of Nations* advocated for little or no government interference in the economy. Smith claimed that an individual's self-interest would bring about the public's welfare.

123. **Who promoted laissez-faire economics?**
(Rigorous) (Skill 17.2)

    A. Thomas Robert Malthus
    B. John Stuart Mill
    C. Adam Smith
    D. John Maynard Keynes

The correct answer is C. Adam Smith
Adam Smith is considered by many to be the "father" of modern economics. In the *Wealth of Nations,* Smith advocated for little or no government interference in the economy. Smith claimed that individuals' self-interest would bring about the public's welfare. It is important to note that Smith was firmly against the free market systems of monopoly power and warned that the private sector, particularly large manufacturers, if left unregulated could potentially stand in opposition to the public welfare. John Maynard Keynes advocated an economic system in which government regulations and spending on public works would stimulate the economy and lead to full employment. John Stuart Mill was a progressive British philosopher and economist, whose ideas came closer to socialism than to the classical capitalist ideas of Adam Smith. Mill constantly advocated for political and social reforms, including emancipation for women, labor organizations, and farming cooperatives. Thomas Malthus was a British economist who introduced the study of population and early on considered famine, war, and disease to be the primary checks on world population. He later modified his views and shifted his focus to the causes of unemployment.

124. **Marxism believes which two groups are in continual conflict:**
(Rigorous) (Skill 17.2)

   A. Farmers and landowners
   B. Kings and the nobility
   C. Workers and owners
   D. Structure and superstructure

The correct answer is C. Workers and owners
Marxism believes that the workers and owners are in continual conflict. Marxists refer to these two groups as the proletariat and the bourgeoisie. The proletariat is exploited by the bourgeoisie and will, according to Marxism, rise up over the bourgeoisie in class warfare in an effort to end private control over the means of production.

125. **Who controls production in a planned economy?**
(Rigorous) (Skill 17.3)

   A. Government
   B. Private individuals
   C. Stockholders
   D. The public

The correct answer is A. Government
(B) Private owner ship is a facet of capitalism and (C) stockholder control and (D) elected management board are parts of private ownership. (A) The government has a role in a planned economy.

CPSIA information can be obtained
at www.ICGtesting.com
Printed in the USA
LVOW09s2134180418
573964LV00009B/369/P

9 781607 874690